Microelectronics

Microelectronics

A practical introduction

R. A. Sparkes

Hutchinson

London   Melbourne   Sydney   Auckland   Johannesburg

The programs listed in this book have been checked carefully. In the hands of a competent user, all programs listed should perform their intended function satisfactorily. But no program can ever be entirely free from error, even when copied exactly from an accurate print-out. Therefore the publishers do not guarantee the programs and take no responsibility for any errors in or omissions from them. No liability is assumed for any damage, either physical or psychological, that ensues from the use of any information contained in this book. Neither is there is any guarantee that the equipment described in this book will not change, thus rendering all programs unworkable.

PET is a registered trademark of Commodore Business Machines Ltd.
Apple is a registered trademark of Apple Computer Inc.
ZX 81 and ZX Spectrum are registered trademarks of Sinclair Research Ltd.

Hutchinson & Co. (Publishers) Ltd

An imprint of the Hutchinson Publishing Group

17-21 Conway Street, London W1P 6JD

Hutchinson Group (Australia) Pty Ltd
30-32 Cremorne Street, Richmond South, Victoria 3121
PO Box 151, Broadway, New South Wales 2007

Hutchinson Group (NZ) Ltd
32-34 View Road, PO Box 40-086, Glenfield, Auckland 10

Hutchinson Group (SA)(Pty) Ltd
PO Box 337, Bergvlei 2012, South Africa

First published 1984

© R.A.Sparkes 1984

Printed and bound in Great Britain by Anchor Brendon Ltd, Tiptree, Essex

British Library Cataloguing in Publication Data
Sparkes, R.A.
  Microelectronics.
  1. Microelectronics — Study and teaching — Great Britain
  I. Title
  621.381'7'0710141   TK7874

ISBN 0 09 154581 1

Dedicated to the memory of
Ann and Joanna

Acknowledgements

Special thanks are due to St Andrew's College of Education for the use of their PET computer in writing this book and the programs in it, also to the Scottish Microelectronics Development Programme for the loan of the Apple II on which programs were also written. The BBC microcomputer belongs to my wife and I am especially grateful for the use of it (not to mention the television set too). I am pleased to acknowledge Griffin and George Ltd, who supplied the ZX 81 and the ZX Spectrum microcomputers in addition to the interfaces used to connect these machines to the outside world. Thanks too are due to those students and teachers who attended courses at St Andrew's College and provided useful comments on the notes and programs and on the teaching of microelectronics in general. Once again I am grateful to Annie Hynes for producing the art work and not protesting at the number of times I changed my mind. Bill Docherty must also be remembered for converting my crude diagrams into reliable circuits, so that teachers could try out my ideas. Bob Osborne of Hutchinson Education has helped tremendously in the development of this book and all praise is due to Sue Walton for maintaining some semblance of order in the finished product. However, none of the above can share any blame for the errors and omissions that occur in this book, and I take full responsibility for them. I look forward to receiving comments from readers on how this book and the teaching of microelectronics might be improved.

But again most thanks are due to my wife, Margaret, for her encouragements and criticisms and for her patience and understanding. The development of this book and the ideas in it has been at the expense of both Margaret and the children. I can only hope and trust that their sacrifice is found to be worthwhile.

The University of Stirling, 1984

The photographs in this book have all been donated or loaned by equipment manufacturers and I am most grateful to them for all their assistance. The origin of each photograph is acknowledged as follows:

Plate 1 El-socket breadboard B. Hepworth & Co. Ltd, Plate 2 Pulse unit Unilab Ltd, Plate 3 Pulse unit Griffin & George Ltd, Plate 4 Four-switch unit Griffin & George Ltd, Plate 5 NAND gate unit Unilab Ltd, Plate 6 NAND gate unit Griffin & George Ltd, Plate 7 Binary counter Griffin & George Ltd, Plate 8 Transistor unit Unilab Ltd, Plate 9 Additional units Griffin & George Ltd, Plate 10 Op.amp. unit Unilab Ltd, Plate 11 5 V power supply unit (PSU) Griffin & George Ltd, Plate

12 Extension units Griffin & George Ltd, Plate 13 16-bit memory unit Unilab Ltd, Plate 14 Seven-segment display unit Griffin & George Ltd, Plate 15 ADC – DAC unit Unilab Ltd, Plate 16 Relay unit Griffin & George Ltd, Plate 17 Apple connector card Verospeed Components Ltd, Plate 18 Interspec (Griffin I-pack) DCP Microdevelopments Ltd, Plate 19 P-pack for ZX 81 Griffin & George Ltd, Plate 20 Blank IC unit Griffin & George Ltd, Plate 21 The tutorkit range Tutorkit Products Plate 22 Nuffield electronic units Unilab Ltd, Plate 23 Nuffield extension units Unilab Ltd, Plate 24 Adventures with electronics Unilab Ltd, Plate 25 Digi designer B. Hepworth & Co. Ltd, Plate 26 Harris electronic units Philip Harris Ltd, Plate 27 Microprofessor Philip Harris Ltd, Plate 28 Microprocessor tutor/ demonstrator Philip Harris Ltd, Plate 29 One-bit microprocessor Unilab Ltd, Plate 30 One-bit microprocessor link units etc. Unilab Ltd, Plate 31 Mini-microprocessor Griffin & George Ltd.

Contents

Introduction

'How am I to get in?' asked Alice again in a louder tone.
'*Are* you to get in at all?' said the Footman.
'That's the first question you know.'
(Lewis Carroll, *Alice's Adventures in Wonderland*)

A few thousand years ago information was passed from one person to another by word of mouth. The amount of information that a man could have was limited by his memory. So in one day a man could achieve very little to satisfy his needs and most people had to work very hard just to feed, clothe and house themselves. With the invention of writing and printing people were able to learn new ideas more quickly. They learned better ways of growing crops and making tools. They eventually learned how to make machines which worked faster that humans. So fewer people were needed to produce more food and life became a little easier.

Today we have computers to run the machines for us. They also have large memories to store vast amounts of information and more and more people have access to this information. Microelectronics holds the promise of a better life for everyone, but we need to learn quickly how to control microelectronics before it controls us. The more we understand about what microelectronics can and cannot do, the more we shall be able to use this gift properly. This is just one of the arguments for giving microelectronics a place in everyone's education.

But do we really need to teach microelectronics in schools? After all, inventions like the motor car and the aeroplane have had far reaching effects on our everyday lives, but they do not feature in the school curriculum. Won't pupils learn about microelectronics outside school? I think the answer to this is 'yes', but such learning is incomplete and often confused. In any case the reasons for including microelectronics in the school curriculum are not solely based on this 'need to know' at all. More important is the contribution that microelectronics can make to general education.

Other arguments are based on the future economic prosperity of the country. It is claimed that students need to be encouraged to take up a career in the new technologies, while they are still at school, through the provision of electronics courses. Some students have broadly decided on their future careers before leaving school and they can begin to specialize. Provided that such courses do not become too narrow, I can accept this argument. Dr Gomersall (*Phys. Bull.* 34, 3, Mar 1983) saw this as the main reason for introducing electronics, '...it would clearly be a very useful preparation for a wide range of courses in further and higher education.' However I do think that caution is needed. Teachers are very familiar with students whose career choice is restricted because of an unwise early choice of subjects. Most teachers would want students to keep their options open for as long as possible.

For this reason I argue for the inclusion of microlectronics within physics, so that other subjects are not displaced. The biggest difficulty is to persuade physicists to make room for microelectronics. There are those who claim that engineering has no place in school physics, which is purely a study of fundamentals. This view is peculiar to schools and universities, most practising physicists are employed in the technological applications of their subject. It is also a very modern view. Lord Kelvin, for one, saw no division between his researches into the properties of electricity and the development of the transatlantic cable telegraph. There is, and always has been, a continual interplay between science and technology, with advances in the one leading to new tools or discoveries for the other. School physics does a disservice to this truth by relegating 'applications' to a mere subsidiary role.

This situation has come about over the last twenty years through efforts to revitalize school physics. Previously the emphasis was upon remembering facts, definitions and standard experiments and solving contrived problems. The reforms of the sixties tried to introduce more scientific method. Mechanics, for example, was seen as a medium for observing, making predictions, devising tests, experimenting and drawing conclusions. With so much emphasis on experiment there was little time to consider the applications of mechanics to things like railway trains and motor cars. The technological element disappeared to make way for better science. Looking at the present situation in many schools, where mechanics is treated as a branch of applied mathematics, we have to question what went wrong.

There is no doubt in my mind that the real culprit is the examination. This tests mainly that which can be measured objectively and largely ignores higher abilities and practical skills. Some examinations do set project work, but hard-pressed teachers are given little credit for the resulting increase in their workload, so it is easy to see why projects are not popular. Similarly, overcrowded syllabuses leave little time for open-ended experiment and discovery. Given the need to produce 'results', the pressures on teachers to revert to rote memorization techniques are enormous.

Protagonists for a separate subject of electronics should be aware of these problems. School electronics would not be immune from the same pressures. However enlightened initially, it could soon revert to an arid diet of reciting truth tables, applying Boolean algebra to improvised problems, learning standard jargon (RAM, EAROM, etc.) and regurgitating the minutae of long-tailed pairs, fan-outs and op. codes. It would become solely a preparation for the same diet at university. What would be the point?

Education is 'learning how to learn'. What is learned is largely irrelevant. An emphasis on the skills of learning means that topics for study can be chosen without an eye on what a higher stage of education 'needs'. School physics should be free to pick topics that fulfil proper educational criteria instead. Microelectronics meets certain of these criteria very well.

The present curriculum only pays lip-service to problem solving. In one form or another this features as an objective in many school subjects, but pupils are rarely given learning experiences to achieve it. Too often learning in school is closed and pupils are only required to provide standard responses to standard problems. If I build a circuit to a standard pattern and it works, I have learned very little. I am merely confirming existing knowledge. But if my circuit fails, I have to discover the reason. I hypothesize, devise tests, make guesses and eventually identify and solve the problem. At school students are rarely given such opportunities. Mistakes are regarded as wrong and are discouraged, even punished. Electronics, particularly when programming a microprocessor, is ideally suited to fulfilling the problem-solving role. Mistakes become steps on the road to solving the problem, and students can be taught how to discover and rectify them. Above all, they can be taught not to fear mistakes, because they are essential to the learning process.

Secondly, the school curriculum lacks a practical dimension. Students do experiments, but these are usually to reinforce some aspect of theory. There is generally little emphasis on the practical skills themselves. The ability to write an essay on 'Flowers' is more highly regarded than the ability to grow them. The traditional craft subjects, even when made 'respectable' as CDT, are not included in everyone's education, they are not considered suitable for academics! Microelectronics is generally free from this tarnished image. It is clearly linked to the academic world of science and mathematics and it is generally regarded as both useful and exciting. It does not carry the same sexist image as traditional crafts either, girls find the subject as fascinating as boys. Electronics and microelectronics is comparatively cheap and does not need expensive workshop facilities. It is also far safer than other crafts. Above all it is supremely practical.

Thirdly, electronic projects allow pupils to make a contribution to society. When studying most subjects, pupils know that they are treading a well-worn path, and that the problems they encounter have already been solved by others. The world of microelectronics contains real problems, which need a real solution. For example, the difficulties of many handicapped people are specific and it is rarely economic for a commercial company to devise ways of helping them. Students looking for projects can discover ideas in plenty by visiting a local special school and talking to the teachers and pupils. By tackling such real and urgent problems, even if they don't actually solve them, students are not just pretending to solve problems.

The biggest difficulty, of how to assess students, remains. I am sufficient of a realist to see that examinations cannot be abolished, but do we need to examine everything? What I should like to see is a compulsory part of the physics syllabus free from the pressures of external examinations. This would be assessed in a different way, internally by teachers, looking at perseverance, dedication, motivation, problem-solving ability and, above all, enthusiasm. Within the overall physics syllabus students would still need to learn some basic facts, some fundamental concepts and some standard skills in physics, but far fewer than at present. I would hope that time could also be found to let students design solutions to problems, build and test apparatus, evaluate a product and find out what engineering is really about. Physics and electronics could be taught as a single subject. Why do we want to force students to choose between physics and electronics, or even between chemistry and electronics as Dr Gomersall proposed? Why can't we offer a balanced education instead?

If it is accepted that microelectronics should be included in the curriculum for all children, how should we teach it? In an earlier book, *Electronics,* I tried to present electronics differently, putting the emphasis on what transistors do, rather than on their physical properties. In that book the transistor was introduced at a very early stage as a switching device and it was soon being put to practical use in burglar alarms and thermostats. Characteristic curves, load lines and hybrid parameters were totally ignored.

At that time this approach was not popular with most teachers, it was generally believed that a study of *fundamentals* was essential for understanding electronics. There was, however, no way that more than a few secondary pupils would have the ability or the time to devote to such a study. The 'systems approach' to electronics seemed to offer the only solution to this problem. Significantly this method was developed independently by several different authors around the same time. Most notable of these developments is the 'Electronics and Reactive Circuits' unit of *Nuffield Advanced Physics,* devised by G.E. Foxcroft. We can now see that this approach has turned out to be a most useful way of getting to the heart of electronics, without having to wade through difficult abstract ideas first. Practically all CSE and GCE courses now take a systems approach.

This present book takes the view, that microelectronics is relatively easy to understand, provided one knows the right way to begin. Most of us find abstract ideas difficult, we need to see real cases of the things we are talking about, before we can grasp the theoretical, underlying ideas. I therefore believe that the systems approach must be extended to microelectronics too, but this creates a real difficulty.

In learning by the systems approach, practical work is essential. This has resulted in considerable development of electronic kits, from simple switching circuits to complete analogue computers. How is this to be extended to microelectronics? Although microprocessors themselves are not expensive, it is difficult to make them do anything without a large number of other 'chips' too. Microprocessors only 'talk' in digital code and this is difficult for beginners to use. So there has to be some way of telling the microprocessor what to do in a simpler language, which requires a relatively large and expensive program. There must also be ways of getting information into and out of the microprocessor and memory in which to keep it. This all increases the cost of microelectronic systems.

A popular non-solution to these difficulties is the practice of teaching about integrated circuits and calling that 'microelectronics'. There is no objection to integrated circuits as such, a large portion of this book is devoted to them, but the microprocessor is very much more than an integrated circuit. Pupils must grasp the essential concept of 'programming' a microprocessor to carry out different tasks. Anything less is not microelectronics.

The approach taken by this book is to use a microcomputer, which contains a microprocessor. This can be programmed in the relatively simple, BASIC language and provides a good basis for understanding all programmable devices. Cheap microcomputers are fast becoming available in all schools. Although each type of microcomputer behaves slightly differently, the basic principles are the same for them all. I have specifically written for the PET, the Apple, the ZX 81, ZX Spectrum and the

BBC microcomputers, but the ideas are readily adapatable to other microcomputers also.

There is clearly a limit to what can be achieved by this general approach. This book is therefore incomplete and is intended to lead on to more advanced books about programming and interfacing microcomputers. New versions of my other book *Microcomputers in Science Teaching* are in preparation for each of the more popular machines in schools, such as the ZX Spectrum and the BBC microcomputer. These treat the topics of interfacing and machine code programming in detail and are intended to help those wishing to delve more deeply into microelectronics.

As with the previous *Electronics* this present book is not just to be read in an armchair. I cannot stress too much that it is a *practical* guide to microelectronics. Every effort should be made to acquire and use the recommended equipment. Full design details for this are given in Chapter 6 and a list of commercial suppliers is given too. A large number of practical investigations is suggested and without these progress will be severely limited. Where these investigations require special equipment that is not easily available (such as a cathode ray oscilloscope) the results of the investigations are discussed in more detail.

The aim of this book is to provide the teacher with a resource, which may be used in devising microelectronics modules or courses. I believe that all pupils should have some introduction to microelectronics and I hope that this book will show teachers possible approaches. As written I believe that Chapters 0 to 3 could be followed by an average student, whereas Chapters 4 and 5 require greater ability. I feel that practical activity is vital for understanding and for maintaining interest and I have tried to indicate the sort of practical work that can be done. For this purpose certain sections have been designated as Investigations. These adopt a more familiar style of language, because they are intended to give directions. Teachers are welcome to select from these investigations and adapt them to suit the abilities of their own pupils. Throughout the book there are questions, practical exercises and problems. These are designed to indicate ways of assessing what pupils learn.

We are constantly urged to introduce pupils to microelectronics, indeed the Government has spent more than twenty million pounds to this end. We have had many decades to find the right approaches to the teaching of, say, mathematics and physics (and even there we change our minds every twenty years or so). Because of its rapid progress, we do not know how to go about teaching microelectronics in schools. This book is an attempt to find a way.

0 Before electronics

'If your Majesty will only tell me the right
way to begin, I'll do it as well as I can.'
(Lewis Carroll, *Through the Looking Glass*)

Introduction

If schools should be teaching about modern microelectronics – the world of computers and microprocessor control – where should they begin?

An electric light switch can be up or down. An electromagnetic relay can be on or off. A valve can be open or closed. These are all examples of **digital devices.** They have two states, one called the **on state** and the other called the **off state.** Most computers are digital too, so they can easily control digital devices like those above. Chapter 5 deals with switching digital devices on or off with a microcomputer.

Some other devices have more than two states. For example, the sound from a loudspeaker can be very loud or very quiet, or it can have any value between these two. A thermometer reading can be high or low or any value in between. A device that can have a range of values is called an **analogue device.** When electrical circuits are being taught, analogue devices may easily be introduced through the variable resistor. Although young pupils find Ohm's law quite complicated, they are able to get some appreciation of analogue systems by using a variable resistor in a potential divider circuit: the larger the resistor, the bigger share of the voltage it takes. This idea can form the basis of understanding transducers as well as transistors, as we shall see in the next chapter. This is the traditional starting point for electronics, leading on to radio receivers and amplifiers, but it is not here that microelectronics has its greatest impact. The best place to begin is with digital devices, the easiest of which is the switch.

This chapter is an introduction to the basic concepts of microelectronics: memory, the astable and logic. These can all be taught to junior pupils and, in my opinion, should be included in any introduction to electrical circuits. They form a useful introduction to microelectronics through concrete experiences. Pupils can actually see switches and relay contacts close and can appreciate more readily how a similar process might occur in transistor circuits too.

The best way to learn electronics is through practical investigations. This book describes some that pupils can do for themselves. All the equipment needed is described in Chapter 6 and there are also details of where to buy it and how to make it.

Combinations of switches

You will remember how to connect lamps in series and in parallel (Figure 0.1). When

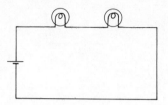

Figure 0.1 Two lamps in series

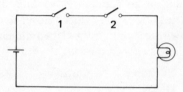

Figure 0.2 The AND combination of two switches

two lamps are in series, the same electric current passes through them both. If one of the lamps burns out, then the other lamp goes out too.

When two lamps are in parallel, the current splits into two parts. One part goes through one lamp and the other part goes through the other lamp. If one of the lamps burns out, the other lamp is not affected. The current can still get to it from the battery.

The same thing happens when two switches are connected in series to a single lamp (Figure 0.2). If one switch is opened, then the lamp goes off. We say that both switch 1 AND switch 2 must be closed to put the lamp on. This way of combining two switches is called the **AND combination.**

We can draw up a table to show the positions or states of each switch and the corresponding state of the lamp. This is called the AND **truth table.** It is a way of remembering the different states that the switches can have.

Switch 1	Switch 2	Lamp
OPEN	OPEN	OFF
OPEN	CLOSED	OFF
CLOSED	OPEN	OFF
CLOSED	CLOSED	ON

The AND combination of switches would be used as a safety device on say a spin drier. The door would have a switch that goes off if the door is opened. The spin drier could only be switched on at its main switch if its door had been properly closed. We can draw up a table to describe the state of each of these switches and the spin drier motor, which would be just like the AND truth table above.

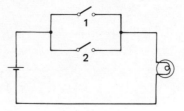

Figure 0.3 The OR combination of two switches

When the two switches are in parallel, either one of them will put the lamp on (Figure 0.3). Either switch 1 OR switch 2 can be closed and the lamp will come on. This way of combining two switches is called the **OR combination.** We can draw up an OR truth table for two of these switches showing the state of each switch and the lamp.

Switch 1	Switch 2	Lamp
OPEN	OPEN	OFF
OPEN	CLOSED	ON
CLOSED	OPEN	ON
CLOSED	CLOSED	ON

This would be useful for operating a doorbell from two separate bell-pushes, one at the front door and the other at the back. Note that you could not use this arrangement for switching on the electric light in a hallway, so that the light could be put on or off at either switch. With the OR combination the light could only be switched off with the same switch that was used to put it on.

A two-way switch introduces the concept of **NOT.** When the switch is up, a connection is made via the top contact. We normally call this the off position. When the switch is down, it is in the on position. Now a connection is made through the bottom contact. If two lamps are connected as in Figure 0.4, one will be on when the other is off and vice versa. We say one lamp is the **inverse** of the other, if one lamp is called A, the other is NOT A.

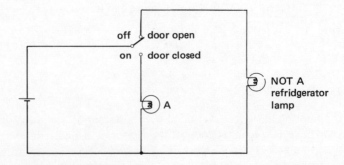

Figure 0.4 The NOT arrangement

A NOT switch would be used inside a refridgerator, so that when the door is opened the switch comes on. Thus the inside lamp comes on, when the door opens and goes off, when the door closes. It is useful now to concentrate on the position of the door rather than the position of the switch. This gives the following truth table.

Door	Lamp
OPEN	ON
CLOSED	OFF

Using the NOT contacts of two switches allows the introduction of two other combinations. These are more difficult to visualize, because it is only our point-of-view that has changed, we have turned the switch upside-down. Nevertheless it is possible to discuss the truth tables that result and to give a practical demonstration of one quite important idea in mathematics, known as **De Morgan's laws.**

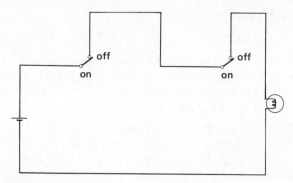

Figure 0.5 The NOR combination

Two NOT switches in series give a truth table which is opposite to that of the OR combination (Figure 0.5). This is known as the **NOR combination** (because neither A nor B must be on to switch the lamp on). It can be seen that the NOR truth table is the opposite of the OR truth table.

Switch 1	Switch 2	Lamp
OFF	OFF	ON
OFF	ON	OFF
ON	OFF	OFF
ON	ON	OFF

Thus the NOR combination is made by combining two NOT switches with the AND (series) arrangement. In terms of logic NOT A AND NOT B = A NOR B. This is a statement in propositional logic as we shall see later.

Two NOT switches in parallel give the **NOT-AND** (or **NAND**) combination (Figure 0.6). This has a truth table which is the inverse of the AND combination. In terms of logic NOT A OR NOT B = A NAND B.

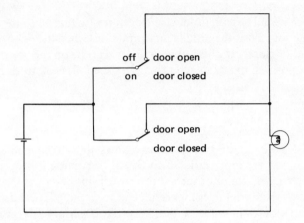

Figure 0.6 The NAND combination of switches

This combination of switches is used in a motor car to operate the inside light of the car. This 'courtesy' light comes on when any door is opened. There is a small switch in each door of the car, which comes on if the door is opened. All these switches are in parallel, so if any door is opened the lamp will come on.

Door 1	Door 2	Lamp
OPEN	OPEN	ON
OPEN	CLOSED	ON
CLOSED	OPEN	ON
CLOSED	CLOSED	OFF

I usually set a 'hall lights' problem as a practical investigation for pupils who have finished a worksheet on switches in series and parallel. How can you switch the hall lights on or off at either of two switches? Very few can solve it, although many produce arrangements that work to some extent (for example, with one switch across the battery!). The true solution is to combine two two-way switches in the arrangement of Figure 0.7.

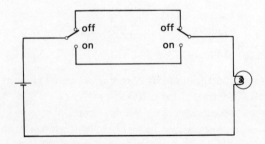

Figure 0.7 The EQUIVALENCE combination

The **EQUIVALENCE** combination gives this truth table.

Switch 1	Switch 2	Lamp
OFF	OFF	ON
OFF	ON	OFF
ON	OFF	OFF
ON	ON	ON

Relays

Unless a computer has a robot arm, it will not be able to operate ordinary switches. A different way must be found. One way is to use an electromagnetic relay (Figure 0.8). This is like a switch that can be opened or closed by applying a voltage to it. The relays we use can be operated by a voltage of just 5 V.

When an electric current passes through the coil of the electromagnet, it is said to be energized. It becomes a magnet and pulls the armature in. This is hinged, so its top part swings up and pushes the pair of contacts together. This is just like closing a switch. When the current to the coil is stopped, the armature is released and the contacts open (Figure 0.9).

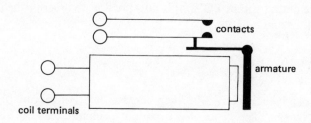

Figure 0.8   An electromagnetic relay

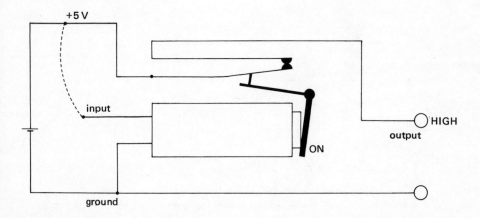

Figure 0.9   The relay as a switch

The current to the coil may come from a voltage connected to one of the terminals of the coil. This terminal is called the **input.** The other terminal is connected to the 0 V line of the battery, which is often called the **ground** or **earth.** If 5 V is applied to the input, the relay will be energized (it will be on). If the input voltage is removed, the coil will release the armature and the relay will be off.

TTL levels

Although 5 V is enough to switch on some relays, it may not be enough for others. So that we don't have to bother with the actual voltages, we usually just use the terms HIGH and LOW. Now our description will be true for *any* relay. Of course, to use any particular relay, we shall need to know what its HIGH and LOW voltages are, but that is a problem we can leave till later. One important standard in electronics is **TTL levels.** Here HIGH means a voltage between 2.4 V and about 5 V. LOW means less than 0.4 V. In between, from 0.4 to 2.4 V, is the transition region, where we are not sure if we have a HIGH or a LOW voltage. Because of this, we try to avoid this region. In the investigations that follow, we shall use the terms 'HIGH' and 'LOW' in this way.

If one of the contacts of the relay is connected to the power supply (Figure 0.9), then the other contact is called the **output.** If the relay is on, this output will be HIGH. If the relay is off, the output will be LOW. It is now possible to describe the relay solely in terms of its inputs and outputs.

Input	Output
LOW	LOW
HIGH	HIGH

Two relays can be connected with their contacts in series (Figure 0.10). This will produce an AND gate. This system has two inputs; A and B but only one output. We can see that this output will only be connected to the + 5 V line if **both** pairs of contacts are closed; that is, if both relays are on. This will only happen if both A AND B are HIGH. Again, we use the truth table to describe this system.

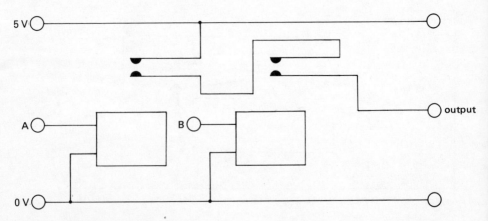

Figure 0.10 The relay AND gate

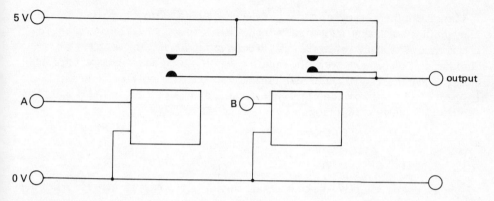

Figure 0.11   The relay OR gate

Input A	Input B	Output
LOW	LOW	LOW
LOW	HIGH	LOW
HIGH	LOW	LOW
HIGH	HIGH	HIGH

If the relays are connected in parallel, we get the OR gate (Figure 0.11). Now the output will be HIGH if either relay is energized. This system too can be described by its truth table.

Input A	Input B	Output
LOW	LOW	LOW
LOW	HIGH	HIGH
HIGH	LOW	HIGH
HIGH	HIGH	HIGH

Electronic circuits, which behave just like these relays, are used a great deal in digital circuits. Since we are usually only interested in the inputs and outputs, we do not bother to show all the internal connections. Figure 0.12 gives the symbols for the AND and OR gates. As you can see, they only include relevant information, such as the number of inputs and the type of gate.

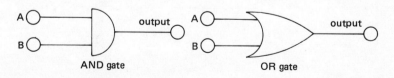

Figure 0.12   AND and OR gate symbols

There is another sort of relay that is also important. So far we have only looked at relays with contacts that are normally open. That is, the contacts close when the relay is energized. Normally, when the relay has no input voltage, the contacts are open. Another sort of contacts work the opposite way to this. The contacts are normally closed. When the relay is energized, the armature is pulled in and the contacts are made to open. This gives a very important system, called an **INVERTER** or a **NOT gate**. The INVERTER has this truth table.

Input	Output
LOW	HIGH
HIGH	LOW

When the input is LOW, the contacts are closed, so the output is HIGH. When the input is HIGH, the relay is energized. The contacts open and the output goes LOW. Clearly by wiring the normally closed contacts together, we obtain the inverse relationships as we did with switches. Normally closed contacts in series give the NOR combination.

Input A	Input B	Output
LOW	LOW	HIGH
LOW	HIGH	LOW
HIGH	LOW	LOW
HIGH	HIGH	LOW

Normally closed contacts in parallel give the NAND combination.

Input A	Input B	Output
LOW	LOW	HIGH
LOW	HIGH	HIGH
HIGH	LOW	HIGH
HIGH	HIGH	LOW

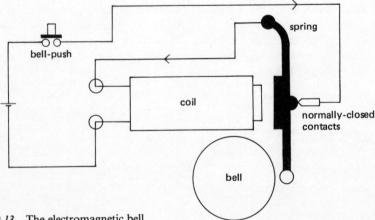

Figure 0.13 The electromagnetic bell

An important use of the NOT contacts is in making an electromagnetic buzzer or bell (Figure 0.13). When the bell switch is pressed, current flows round the circuit. This energizes the relay so the contacts open, causing the current to stop flowing. The relay thus releases the armature and the contacts close again. So the whole process repeats. The armature vibrates rapidly back and forth and makes the hammer strike the bell each time. Although such systems are now old-fashioned, they do teach us about one important circuit in electronics, the **astable.**

As its name implies the astable is 'un-stable' (in the same way that 'asymmetric' means not-symmetric). It vibrates back and forth because it has no stable state in which to rest. Electronic astable circuits are used a great deal in microelectronics as we shall see.

The relay with normally open contacts also makes an important electronic circuit, called the **bistable.** This has two stable states. It will remain in one state or the other as long as power is supplied to it. Its main use is as a latch to remember which state it is in. Figure 0.14 shows one application. When switch 1 is pressed, current reaches the relay, which is energized. This causes both sets of contacts to close. But the A contacts are in parallel with switch 1, so they continue to supply current to the relay, even if switch 1 is opened again. Now the relay is on and it will stay on: it is in a stable state. The B contacts can be used to supply power to another system, for example a high-voltage X-ray machine. This means that the operator, who pressed switch 1, is in no danger of getting a shock from the high voltage. Switch 1 is probably connected to a smaller voltage, since it only has to supply the relay.

To switch the X-ray machine off, the relay must be de-energized. Switch 1 is no good for this, because the A contacts are in parallel with it, and they are already closed. But switch 2 is in series with the A contacts. Of course, this means that switch 2 is normally closed. So when switch 2 is pressed, the current stops and the relay is de-energized. Both pairs of contacts open again and the X-ray machine is turned off. When switch 2 is released again, the relay will not be re-energized, because the A contacts are now open. The system is in its other stable state.

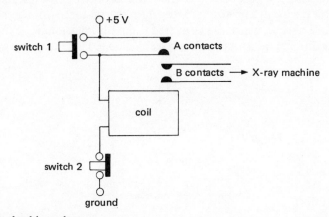

Figure 0.14 The latching relay

Electronic bistable circuits are very important in computers, because they are used as memory devices. They can remember whether they are on or off. Of course they are no use if they need switches to make them change state. Later we shall see how a **voltage** can be used to switch the bistable on or off.

Analogue devices

Now we must look at analogue devices – ones that produce a whole range of voltages. The simplest of these is the **voltage divider.** This consists of two resistors in series (Figure 0.15). The input voltage to this circuit is 5 V. The combined resistance of the two resistors is R1 + R2, so the electric current flowing through them is 5/(R1 + R2), (obtained by using Ohm's law). V is the voltage across the resistor R2, which is thus 5 x R2/(R1 + R2).

With the resistor values R1 = 300 ohms and R2 = 100 ohms, V can be calculated, giving a value of 1.25 V. There is, however, an entirely different way of finding this value; by **measuring** it with a voltmeter.

This demonstrates the essential difference between the scientific approach to electronics, where you study the physics of the circuit, and the systems approach. In the latter the attention is focussed on the terminal properties; what goes into the circuit and what comes out. There is no doubt that the first way gives the greater understanding, but the second way is very much easier and often gives enough information for making practical use of the circuit. That is what engineering is all about.

Investigation 0.1   The voltage divider
The size of the output voltage depends upon the sizes of the two resistors. One way to see this is to use a circuit, in which the values of R1 and R2 can be changed. The output voltage is measured with a voltmeter. In Figure 0.16 R1 is two resistors, a fixed 100 ohms resistor (acting as a protector to stop the total resistance from becoming too low) and a variable resistor, which can be altered from 0 to 100 kilohms. R2 can be changed by plugging different resistors into the space available. There are two ways of changing

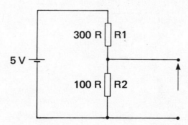

Figure 0.15   Voltage divider

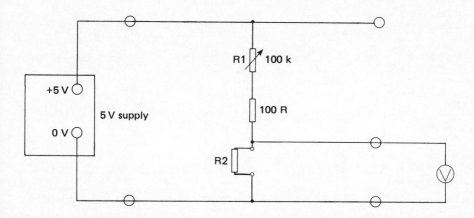

Figure 0.16 Voltage divider board

the output voltage in this circuit by changing R1 or by changing R2. First of all let us keep R1 constant and change R2.

1 Begin by making R1 as small as possible, by turning the variable resistor fully anti-clockwise.
2 Plug the 1000 ohms resistor (coloured brown-black-red) into the space for R2. What is the voltmeter reading?
3 Plug the 100 ohms resistor (coloured brown-black-brown) into the space for R2. What is the new voltage reading?
4 Do this for R2 equal to 0 ohms (by connecting a short lead into the space for R2). What output voltage do you get in each case?
5 The value of R1 was fixed at 100 ohms in this investigation. Copy out this table and enter your results into it.

R1	R2	Output voltage
100	1000	
100	100	
100	0	

You should observe that the voltage increases as R2 increases.

6 Now keep R2 fixed; put the 1000 ohms resistor into the place for R2. Change R1 by turning the variable resistor slowly clockwise. What happens to the output voltage?

You should observe that the voltage decreases as R1 increases.

Investigation 0.2 The potentiometer

The potentiometer (Figure 0.13) is made up from a single resistor with a central slider that can be moved from one end of the resistor to the other. The resistance of this resistor is always 100 ohms, but the central slider divides it into two parts, resistors R1 and R2. The values of R1 and R2 can be altered by turning the shaft of the

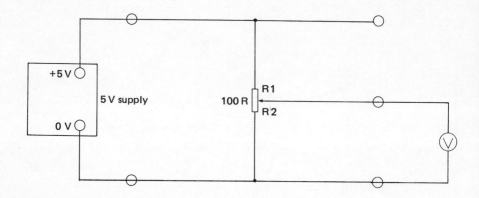

Figure 0.17   The potentiometer

potentiometer. The input voltage to the potentiometer is fixed at 5 volts. When the shaft is turned fully anti-clockwise, R2 is very small and R1 is large, so the output voltage is small. As the shaft is turned more and more clockwise, R2 gets bigger and R1 gets smaller, so the output voltage gradually increases. When the shaft is turned fully clockwise, the output voltage reaches its maximum of 5 V.

This is such a useful way of producing a variable voltage, that we shall use it whenever we want a voltage that can be changed. Set up the potentiometer as in Figure 0.17 and adjust it to get an output voltage of exactly 1 V.

The voltage divider (Figure 0.16) also uses a potentiometer, but in a different way. Only the central wiper and one end of the resistor are used. As the shaft is turned the resistance between these two terminals changes, thus giving a *variable* resistance from 0 to 100 kilohms (Figure 0.18). The fixed 100 ohms resistor of the voltage divider unit is used for protection. it prevents the total resistance of R1 from becoming zero. Otherwise there could be too large a current for some of the circuits we shall use later.

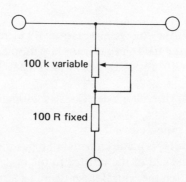

Figure 0.18   The potentiometer as a variable resistor

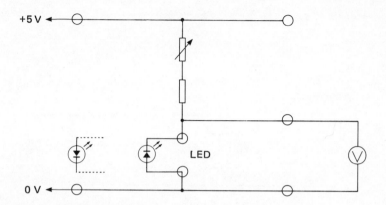

Figure 0.19   The light emitting diode

Investigation 0.3   The light emitting diode

The special property of a diode is having a 'forward' and a 'reverse' direction. In the forward direction its resistance is small and in the reverse direction its resistance is large. So if a diode is put into the space for R2, the ouput voltage will change, depending upon which way round it is plugged in. Figure 0.19 shows the two ways of plugging it in.

The particular diode used emits light when the current flows through it in the forward direction. It is called a **light emitting diode** or **LED.** LEDs are very useful as indicator lamps because only a small current is needed to switch them on.

Change the value of R1 (Figure 0.19) by altering the variable resistor. Note when the LED is on and off. Then turn the LED round the other way and again alter R1. In each case measure the output voltage. Can you see which is the forward direction and which is the reverse direction for the LED?

Investigation 0.4   The light dependent resistor

Another important device in electronics is the **light dependent resistor** or **LDR.** As its name suggests, this device changes its resistance depending on the amount of light falling upon it. In a voltage divider, this change of resistance becomes a change in voltage. If the light level is high, the resistance of the LDR is low, so the output voltage is low.

As the light gets less bright, the resistance of the LDR increases, so the output voltage increases too. With a suitable voltmeter, this can be measured. The overall effect is a meter that indicates how much light there is: a photographer's light meter (Figure 0.20).

Make sure that a bright light falls upon the LDR. Then adjust the variable resistor until the output voltage is about 1 V or more. Now put your hand over the LDR. You should see that the voltage goes up. When you remove your hand, the voltage goes down again.

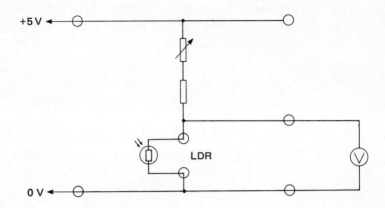

Figure 0.20   A light meter circuit

The resistance of the LDR increases in the dark. Because of this R2 becomes bigger so the voltage increases. In the light the resistance of the LDR gets less, so the output voltage gets less too.

Investigation 0.5   The thermistor

If the LDR is replaced by a thermistor, the same circuit can be used as a thermometer. A thermistor changes its resistance as the temperature changes. The thermistor you are using (the most common type) *decreases* its resistance as the temperature rises. So the output voltage from the voltage divider will go down as the temperature goes up.

Both the LDR and the thermistor are **transducers.** A transducer changes a physical quantity like temperature or pressure or light intensity into a voltage. Since it is possible to measure a voltage with a microcomputer, these other quantities can be measured too.

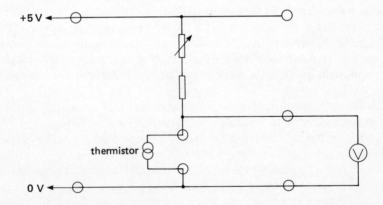

Figure 0.21   A thermistor thermometer

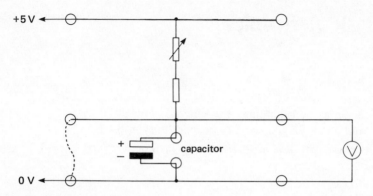

Figure 0.22 The capacitor

Investigation 0.6 The capacitor

The capacitor can be confusing, because it does not have 'resistance' at all. It has 'capacitance', which measures how much charge it can store. The size of the capacitor is measured in microfarads (μF). The capacitors used in this book range from 0.01 to 1000 microfarads. When a voltage is applied to a capacitor, it charges up. That is, electric current flows into it. But like a bucket of water, it can only hold so much. Once the capacitor is full, no more current will flow into it and it becomes like a high resistance. This gives us one way of making use of the capacitor. It can be connected as R2 in our voltage divider network. When the capacitor is empty (discharged) it has no voltage across it. As it charges up the voltage across the capacitor rises until it is fully charged.

1 Put a 1000 μF capacitor into the voltage divider circuit. Make sure that it is connected the right way round. Because of the way they are made, big capacitors have a positive end (red) and a negative end (black). If these capacitors are connected the wrong way round, they may not work properly. Smaller capacitors (usually those less than 1 microfarad) are not made like this, so they can be connected either way round.
2 Now discharge the capacitor by connecting a flying lead across it, shown in Figure 0.22 as a dotted line. When this lead is removed, the capacitor will charge up and the voltmeter reading will rise. The capacitor can be discharged again by reconnecting the flying lead.
3 The rate at which the capacitor charges up depends upon the size of R1. Alter the variable resistor to investigate this. Does a larger resistance make the capacitor charge up faster or slower?
4 The rate at which the capacitor charges up also depends upon how big it is. Use a different capacitor, say 100 μF, to observe this effect. Again make sure that it is connected the right way round. The capacitor is used a great deal for delay circuits (because it takes time to make the capacitor charge up). Such timing systems will be studied later.

1 Basic electronics

'Begin at the beginning,' the King said gravely,
'and go on till you come to the end; then stop.'
(Lewis Carroll, *Alice's Adventures in Wonderland*)

Introduction

It is usual for pupils to reach the transistor only after a long introduction by way of
holes, electrons and p-n junctions. The systems approach allows us to go straight to the
important heart of the transistor without bothering about how it works. Some
introductions treat the transistor as a current amplifier, concentrating on the
relationship between the base current and the collector current. While this might be
useful for dealing with amplifiers, it is less so when dealing with the transistor as a
switch. I much prefer to introduce this device by means of the voltage divider network,
treating the transistor as a sort of variable resistor, whose resistance is altered by the
voltage applied to its base terminal. It is then a simple step to talk about its input and
output voltages and its use as an INVERTER.

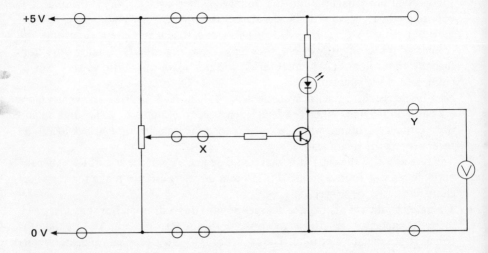

Figure 1.1 The transistor

Investigation 1.1 The transistor

The voltage divider circuit can be used with a transistor in place of R2. The simplest way of thinking about the transistor is to regard it as a resistor, which can change its resistance. However, the cause of this resistance change is not light or temperature but the voltage applied to the input of the transistor.

A low voltage applied to the input makes the transistor have a high resistance, so the output voltage will be high. A bigger voltage applied to the base makes the transistor have a lower resistance, so the output voltage is also less. Thus the voltage applied to the input (the input voltage) controls the output voltage.

Set up the circuit of Figure 1.1 and use the potentiometer to change the input voltage. You can measure both the input and the output voltage with the same voltmeter. When the voltmeter is connected to point X, it is measuring the input voltage. When it is connected to point Y, it is measuring the output voltage. Watch how the output voltage changes, when the input voltage is changed. You should notice that the output voltage goes HIGH, when the input voltage is LOW. The output goes LOW, when the input is HIGH. In fact the transistor is working like an INVERTER.

Investigation 1.2 Voltage ratio

So far we have kept the input voltage to the voltage divider fixed at 5 V. Now we shall investigate what happens if this voltage is varied. We shall use the potentiometer to change the voltage. Connect the potentiometer to the input of the circuit as in Figure 1.2. The size of this voltage can be measured with the voltmeter connected to point X. This is the input voltage Vi. The output voltage Vo can be measured by connecting the voltmeter to point Y.

1   The potentiometer allows any voltage from 0 to 5 V to be produced just by turning the shaft of the potentiometer. Turn it to get an input voltage of 0 V and measure the output voltage on the voltmeter.

2   Turn the potentiometer until Vi is 1 V and note the output voltage again.

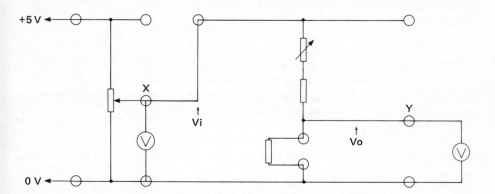

Figure 1.2   The voltage ratio of the voltage divider

3 Do this for input voltages of 0, 1, 2, 3, 4 and 5 volts. Put your results into a table like this:

Input voltage	Output voltage
0 V	
1 V	
2 V	
3 V	
4 V	
5 V	

4 Plot a graph of your results (called the **voltage characteristics** of the circuit), it will look something like Figure 1.3.

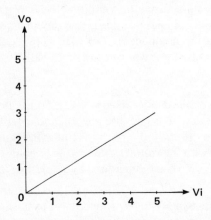

Figure 1.3 Voltage characteristics of the voltage divider circuit

The circuit of Figure 1.2 is known as a linear network, because the voltage characteristics give a straight line. The slope of this line is the fraction Vo/Vi and it is a constant. As the input voltage changes the output voltage changes in exactly the same direction. Mathematically,

$$Vo = f \times Vi$$

where f is a fraction between 0 and 1. This fraction depends on the two resistors R1 and R2. If R1 is small and R2 is large then the fraction will be large and Vo will be nearly equal to Vi. If R1 is much bigger than R2, then the fraction will be small and Vo will be much smaller than Vi. The exact fraction is given by the equation:

$$f = R2/(R1 + R2)$$

although, as we have seen, it is not necessary to be able to prove this in order to make use of it.

Investigation 1.3 Transistor characteristics
In investigation 1.1 we saw how a transistor behaves. When the input voltage is low,

the transistor has a high resistance. This means that R1 is smaller than R2. We know that the output voltage will therefore be high. When the input voltage is made bigger, the resistance of the transistor gets less. So the output voltage will fall. Finally, when the input voltage is made high, the transistor has a low resistance. So R1 is now bigger than R2 and the output voltage is therefore low. To investigate this, set up the circuit of Figure 1.1 again.

As the potentiometer is varied, the input voltage to the transistor changes too. If the voltmeter is connected to point X, it will measure this input voltage Vi. The output voltage Vo will also change. This can be seen by connecting the voltmeter to point Y.

The current flowing through the transistor will cause the light emitting diode (LED) to light up. But instead of thinking about the current, concentrate on the voltage at each end of the LED. The 'top' end of the LED is connected to 5 V. If the other end of the LED is also at 5 V, then there is no voltage across it and it will not light up. If, however, this other end of the LED is nearer to 0 V, there *will* be a voltage across it, so the LED will light up.

1 Turn the potentiometer fully anti-clockwise.
2 Connect the voltmeter to point X and measure Vi.
3 Connect the voltmeter to point Y and measure Vo.
4 Enter these results into the following table.

Input voltage Vi	Output voltage Vo	LED off, dim, or bright

5 Now connect the voltmeter to point X again. Turn the potentiometer until Vi goes up a little.
6 Note whether the LED is off, dim or bright. Enter this into the table too.
7 Go back to step 2 and repeat this until you have about ten sets of readings for Vi and Vo. The readings should cover the whole range from 0 to 5 V.
8 Plot these readings on a graph of Vo against Vi. This graph is called the voltage characteristic of the transistor.

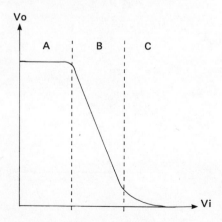

Figure 1.4 Voltage characteristics of the transistor

The voltage characteristic has three regions:

Region A. When the input voltage is low, the output voltage is high. In this case the voltage at both ends of the LED is the same, so it is off. In this region the transistor is said to be 'off'.

Region B. When the input voltage is between high and low, the output voltage is 2 or 3 V. The LED is dim to start with, but becomes brighter as the input voltage is made bigger. Notice that the output voltage goes from 5 V to 0 V at the same time that the input voltage goes from about 0 to 1 V. The change in the output voltage is bigger than the change in the input voltage. This fact can be used to make an **amplifier** as we shall see later.

Region C. When the input voltage is high, the output voltage is low. In this case the 'other' end of the LED is near to 0 V, so there is a voltage difference across the LED and it is bright. In this region the transistor is fully on and is said to be saturated.

Regions A and C are important when the transistor is used as a switch in digital electronics. In that case we are not interested in the actual voltages but whether they are HIGH or LOW. HIGH means greater than 2.4 V and LOW means less than 0.4 V. These are the TTL levels mentioned previously.

Investigation 1.4   The transistor as a switch

We have just seen how the transistor can be switched on or off by the voltage at its input. In investigation 0.4 we saw how to use an LDR to make a voltage change when the light intensity changes. Figure 1.5 puts these two ideas together.

1   Plug the LDR into the voltage divider unit and connect to the transistor. Make sure that bright light is falling upon the LDR.
2   Turn the variable resistor until the LED comes on. Then turn the variable resistor clockwise until the lamp just goes off. The circuit is now ready.

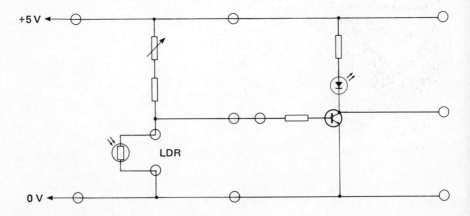

Figure 1.5   An automatic parking light

3   Place your hand over the LDR. The LED will come on. Take your hand away and the LED goes off. What is the effect if the variable resistor is turned too far clockwise? What is the effect if the variable resistor is turned too far anti-clockwise?

Applications

We have a system that will turn on a lamp when the LDR becomes dark. We could use this for the automatic parking lights of a motor car. The parking lights will come on automatically at night-time.

Alternatively we can replace the LED by an alarm or siren. A light beam from a lamp can shine on the LDR across the entrance to a room. If a burglar crosses in front of the LDR, he will make it go dark, so the alarm will sound. Do you think that this would make a good burglar alarm?

If the transistor switches an electronic 'clock' on and off, instead of the LED, we can use this system to measure speed. A card stuck onto a trolley can pass in front of the LDR. As it does so, it starts and stops the clock. This gives the time taken for the card to cross the LDR and the speed of the trolley can be calculated from this measurement.

The opposite effect can be obtained by changing over the positions of the variable resistor and the LDR. To do this, disconnect the power supply lines and turn the voltage divider unit upside-down. Then reconnect the power supply lines so that the black terminals are at + 5 V and the red terminals are at 0 V. This gives a system where the LED is on when the LDR is in bright light. The LED goes off when you pass your hand in front of the LDR.

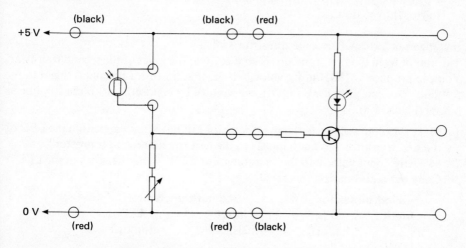

Figure 1.6 A light operated switch

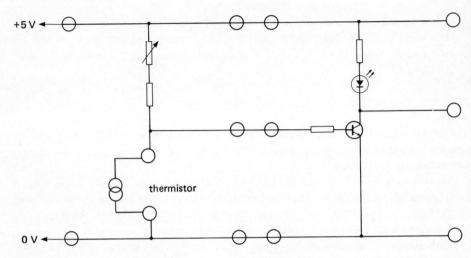

Figure 1.7 Temperature switch

Investigation 1.5 A temperature switch

Replace the LDR with the thermistor (Figure 1.7). You now have a system that switches the LED when the *temperature* changes. Adjust the variable resistor so that the LED switches off when you warm up the thermistor. Now turn the voltage divider unit upside-down to make a system, that turns the LED on, when the thermistor is heated.

Which of these systems could you use for a fire alarm?
Which could you use for a frost warning system?
Which could you use to control the temperature of the water in a tropical fish tank?
How could you do this?

Investigation 1.6 A two-stage transistor switch

The output from the first transistor is connected to the input of the second transistor. You can produce a HIGH input voltage to the first transistor by connecting it to the 5 V line. You can produce a LOW input voltage by connecting it to the 0 V line as before (Figure 1.8).

1   Make the input voltage to the first transistor HIGH. What happens to the LED of the first transistor ? What happens to the LED of the second transistor?
2   Make the input voltage to the first transistor LOW. What happens to the LEDs?
3   Copy out and complete this table.

First transistor		Second transistor	
Input	**LED** (on/off)	**Input** (HIGH/LOW)	**LED** (on/off)
LOW			
HIGH			

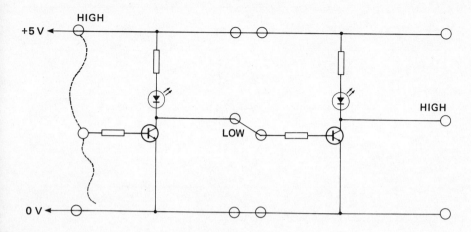

Figure 1.8 A two-stage transistor switch

Note two things:
1 When the input to a transistor is HIGH, its LED is on.
2 The two transistors are always in the opposite state. When one is on the other is off. You can see why this happens if you remember Investigation 1.3. The input to the second transistor must always be the same as the output from the first.

First transistor		Second transistor	
Input	**Output**	**Input**	**Output**
LOW	HIGH	HIGH	LOW
HIGH	LOW	LOW	HIGH

Observe that it is not possible for both LEDs to be on at the same time. The second transistor acts as an INVERTER. It will always have the opposite state to the first transistor.

Applications
We can use these two transistors in the switching circuits we investigated above. The output of the first transistor is connected to the input of the second as before. Because the first transistor *inverts* the voltage levels, you will find these circuits work the opposite way to when there was only one transistor. Note also that the circuits are now much more sensitive. The second LED operates with smaller changes in temperature (or smaller changes in light intensity). The LDR and the thermistor are used exactly as before, for example Figure 1.9 shows a light operated switch. How will this switch operate, will the second LED come on in the dark or in the light?

1 Make a burglar alarm so that the second LED comes on if you pass your hand across the LDR.
2 Turn the voltage divider unit round, to make the circuit work the other way.

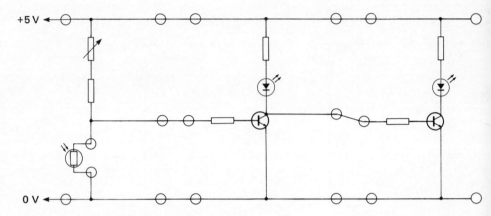

Figure 1.9 A two-stage light operated switch

3 Make a fire alarm so that the second LED comes on if you warm up the thermistor.
4 Turn the voltage divider unit upside-down to make a frost warning system.

Investigation 1.7 The bistable
Connect the output from each transistor to one of the resistor inputs of the other transistor as in Figure 1.10. You will find that one transistor is on and the other is off. But both transistors are identical, so why do they behave differently?

Each transistor has two resistor inputs. Connect a flying lead to the 5 V line. Now use this to apply a HIGH voltage to each of the other inputs in turn (dotted lines in Figure 1.10). What happens?

You should see that the system has two states. The first transistor can be on or off. The second transistor can be off or on. Because the two transistors are connected

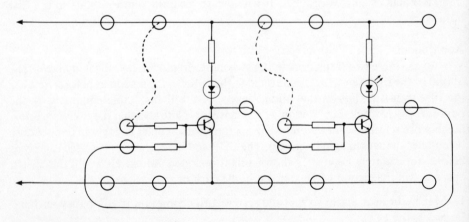

Figure 1.10 The transistor bistable

output-to-input, output-to-input, they are always opposite to each other, because they invert each other.

These are the two states:

1 The first transistor has a HIGH output. This makes the input to the second transistor HIGH also. So the second transistor has a LOW output. This is fed back to the first input, so that is LOW too. So the output from the first transistor must be HIGH (which it is).
2 The first transistor has a LOW output. This makes the input to the second transistor LOW also. So the second transistor has a HIGH output. This is fed back to the first input, so that is HIGH too. So the output from the first transistor must be LOW (which it is).

Because of these two states, this circuit is called a bistable. In the first state (when the second transistor output is LOW), the bistable is said to be OFF. In the second state (when the second transistor output is HIGH), the bistable is said to be ON.

The bistable can be switched from one state to the other by momentarily connecting the flying lead from the 5 V line to each input in turn. If the bistable is off, how do you turn it on? If the bistable is on, how do you turn it off?

Applications

The burglar alarm of Investigation 1.4 is a very poor system. The alarm only sounds while the burglar is in front of the LDR. Using the bistable you can make an alarm that comes on, and stays on, even if the burglar moves away again. Figure 1.11 shows how to do this. Can you explain how this works?

The bistable is the most important circuit in the whole of electronics; it can *remember*. If it has been turned on, it stays on; if it has been turned off, it stays off. It can remember which state it is in for ever (or until the power is turned off). So it is used in computers to store information. Even a small computer like the PET has many thousands of bistables in it.

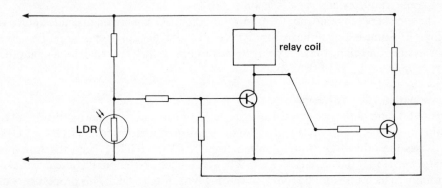

Figure 1.11   An improved burglar alarm

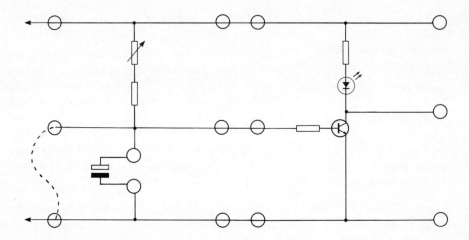

Figure 1.12   Time switch

Investigation 1.8   Timing circuits

The circuits we have looked at so far operate very quickly. Sometimes we want circuits to operate more slowly. For example, an electronic kitchen clock will need to tick away in one second intervals. We use the capacitor for this (Figure 1.12). When we looked at the capacitor in Investigation 0.6, we saw that the voltage across the capacitor rises slowly as the capacitor charges up. We saw that a big capacitor takes longer than a smaller capacitor and we noted that the charging rate also depended upon the variable resistor. A larger resistance caused the voltage to rise more slowly.

Figure 1.12 shows this arrangement connected to the transistor unit. When you connect these units together, make sure that the capacitor is connected the right way round. When the capacitor is 'shorted', the input voltage to the transistor is LOW, so the LED is off. When the 'short' is removed, the voltage rises until it is high enough to switch the transistor and the LED comes on.

The time between removing the 'short' and the LED coming on depends upon two things. The time is long if the resistor R1 is high and if the capacitor is large. This gives us a way of controlling the time delay to make a time switch. We shall look at another sort of time switch in Investigation 1.10.

Investigation 1.9   The astable

Figure 1.13 shows the two transistors connected by capacitors. Make up this circuit by connecting leads as shown. When one of the transistors switches from HIGH to LOW, it causes the other transistor to switch from LOW to HIGH. The capacitor then charges up slowly through its resistor. When it reaches a big enough voltage, it makes the input to its transistor go HIGH, so causing it to switch again. This process goes on continuously. First one capacitor charges up and then the other. The circuit thus switches on and off continuously. It has no stable state and oscillates from one to the

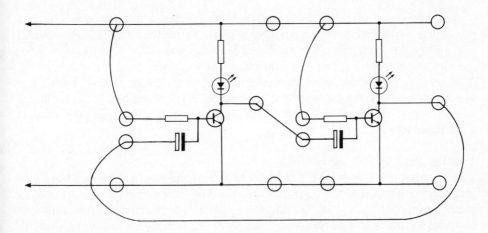

Figure 1.13   The astable

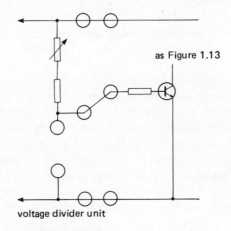

voltage divider unit

Figure 1.14   Altering the frequency

other, just like the electromagnetic bell. The rate at which it oscillates (its **frequency**) depends upon the resistors and capacitors in the circuit.

The resistance can be changed for the first transistor by adding the variable resistor as in Figure 1.14. What is its effect? If the capacitors could also be changed to a smaller value, the switching rate would be raised to a higher frequency. If the frequency were high enough it could be fed into an earpiece to produce sound.

Applications
The hazard warning lights of a motor car use an astable circuit (although not usually an electronic circuit). The indicators flash on and off at regular intervals.

An astable circuit is often used to produce oscillations, which can then be turned into sound. To do this the capacitors must be small, so that the astable switches on and off quickly. An electronic organ can be made in this way.

In a computer there is one very important astable that is called the system clock. This acts like the conductor of an orchestra, who keeps all the players in step. The system clock sends out a stream of clock pulses, and every component of the computer has to keep in step with them. These clock pulses are very rapid, usually about a million per second.

Investigation 1.10   The monostable

The monostable in Figure 1.15 is a mixture of astable and bistable. The first transistor is connected to the second through the capacitor. The second transistor is connected to the first transistor through the resistor. Because of this connection, the first transistor imagines it is part of a bistable. When the flying lead from the 5 V line is momentarily connected to its input, the first transistor switches on (its LED goes on). The second transistor is switched off.

After a short time (depending upon the sizes of its resistor and capacitor) the second transistor acts like an astable and switches back again. The circuit then remains in this state until it is once more triggered into action. Because there is only one stable state, it is called a monostable.

Applications

The monostable can be used as a time switch. After switching it on, it remains on for some time and then switches itself off again automatically. Some electronic calculators are like this. If you forget to switch them off, they switch themselves off after a few minutes. This helps to conserve their batteries. Every time you press a key of the calculator, it re-triggers the monostable, which then starts to measure its time interval again. So if you press the keys fairly often, the calculator will not switch itself off.

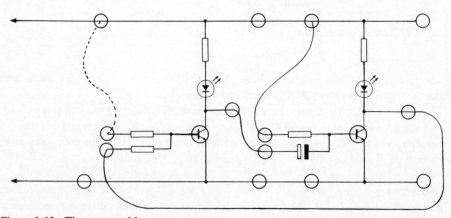

Figure 1.15   The monostable

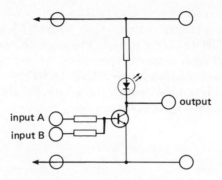

Figure 1.16   A transistor logic gate

Investigation 1.11   Electronic logic

We saw how an OR gate can be made from two relays with their contacts connected in parallel. We have also seen that transistors can act as switches. By giving a transistor two inputs in parallel, it can also carry out this OR gate combination. The transistor in Figure 1.16 has two input terminals A and B and if either input A or input B is connected to the + 5 V line (HIGH), then a current flows through the transistor and the LED comes on.

1   Connect both input A and input B to the 0 V line, so that they are both LOW. The LED is off.
2   Connect input B to the 5 V line (HIGH) and input A to the 0 V line (LOW). Is the LED on or off?
3   Make input A HIGH and input B LOW. What is the state of the LED?
4   Make both inputs HIGH by connecting them to the 5 V line. What is the state of the LED?
5   Copy and complete this table:

Input A	Input B	LED
LOW	LOW	
LOW	HIGH	
HIGH	LOW	
HIGH	HIGH	

You will see that the LED is on if either input A or input B is HIGH.

Applications
Gates like this enable computers to make decisions. For example a paint spraying robot in a car body factory would be told to stop if either of two things happened: a) if the machine had run out of paint, or b) if there were no more cars to be sprayed. This decision needs the OR function. Circuits that produce logic functions like this are called **gates**.

It is possible to put transistors together to make other kinds of gates. Because there are better ways of doing this, we shall leave this study till Chapter 2 called Electronic logic. We refer to HIGH and LOW voltages as **logic levels.** 'Logic HIGH' and 'logic LOW' are terms often used. Sometimes, however, the numbers '1' and '0' are used instead. Logic 0 is LOW and logic 1 is HIGH. This allows us to represent binary numbers by the 0s and 1s of logic circuits. This is how digital computers work and we shall be meeting these ideas again in the following chapters.

Linear electronics

Investigation 1.12   The transistor as an amplifier

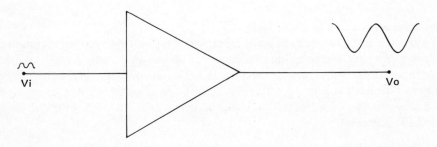

Figure 1.17   An amplifier

Speech and music and all sound consists of vibrations in the air. A microphone will turn sound into electrical signals, which are rapidly changing voltages. If these signals are fed into a loudspeaker, they are turned back into sound. The signals made by speaking into a microphone are small. In fact they are too small to make a loudspeaker work properly. They can be made bigger by putting them through an amplifier (Figure 1.17). The amplifier will then make them big enough for the loudspeaker. Our transistor can act as an amplifier, because it can turn a small input voltage into a larger output voltage.

We can put a small signal into the transistor and a larger signal will come out. But we can only do this if the transistor is in region B of its voltage characteristic (see Investigation 1.3). Putting the transistor into this region is called **biasing** the transistor (Figure 1.18).

Adjust the variable resistor until the output voltage from the transistor is about 2.5 V. This is half-way between HIGH and LOW. Now connect the microphone to the capacitor input and blow into it gently. The input voltage swings up and down by a small amount, because this blowing produces a small electrical signal. The output voltage swings down and up by a bigger amount and it may even be possible to hear the result in the earpiece. You may not see the voltage reading on the voltmeter change by

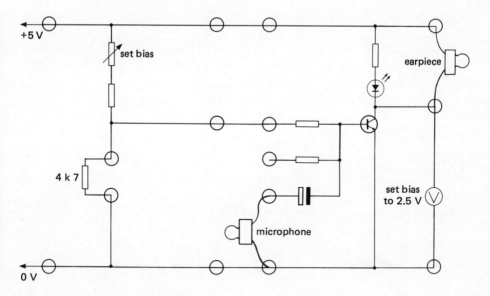

Figure 1.18 Biasing the transistor

very much. This is because the voltage is changing very rapidly. However you may notice the LED flickering rapidly.

By adding the second transistor, you would be able to get even more amplification and an even louder sound. The second transistor would first be biased correctly by adjusting its input voltage too. This two-stage amplifier is very unstable, it tends to produce sounds of its own, without any help from the microphone! For this reason the making of amplifiers from separate transistors is a very difficult task and it is usually easier to use integrated circuit amplifiers.

Investigation 1.13   Oscilloscope investigation
The way, in which the transistor amplifier works, can be seen more clearly with a dual-trace oscilloscope.

1   Set the correct biasing for the transistor as in Figure 1.19. Adjust the variable resistor until the output voltage is about 2.5 V. Leave the voltmeter connected for later investigations.
2   A small signal from the oscillator (about 1 kHz) can be input to the transistor amplifier. The amplitude of this signal should be small, about 10 mV as measured by the Y1 trace of the CRO.
3   Note the output voltage; this consists of two parts, the steady 2.5 V voltage of the biasing and the 1 kHz signal, which has been amplified.
4   Measure the amplitude of the output signal. What is the ratio of the output voltage to the input voltage ? This value is called the **voltage gain** of the amplifier.

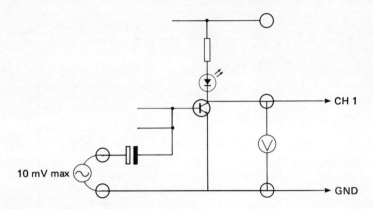

Figure 1.19   Checking bias with an oscilloscope

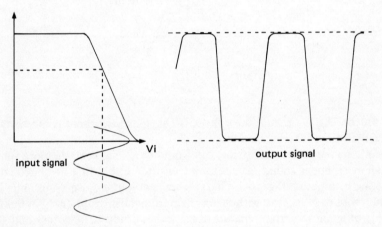

Figure 1.20   Amplitude distortion

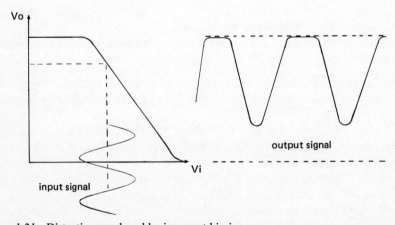

Figure 1.21   Distortion produced by incorrect biasing

5 Increase the amplitude of the input signal until the output is no longer a smooth sine waveform. This effect is called **amplitude distortion.** Can you explain why it occurs?

6 Reduce the amplitude until the output waveform is a smooth sine waveform again, but keep it as large as possible. Now alter the bias with the variable resistor. What happens if the bias is too low or too high? Why does this happen? Use the diagrams in Figures 1.20 and 1.21 in your explanation.

In dealing with amplifiers, we have had voltages that change over a whole range; they are not just HIGH or LOW. The voltages have more than one value and may be alternating (a.c.) or direct (d.c.). This is the other branch of electronics, called **linear** or **analogue** systems. We shall look at this again in Chapter 4.

The operational amplifier

When studying the transistor we did not look inside it to see how it was constructed and how it works. We investigated it by applying voltages to its input terminals and watching its output terminals (or the LED). This is the **systems** approach to electronics. It *is* possible to find out how a transistor works, such a study is in many A level physics courses. But more complicated circuits do not lend themselves to this scientific analysis very well. The systems approach can be used with almost any circuit, no matter how complex. It can even be used with a complete microcomputer! Let us use the techniques of the systems approach in studying one very complicated device, the **operational amplifier** or **op.amp.**

Figure 1.22 shows an op.amp. with two input terminals called its **inverting input** and its **non-inverting input** (these names will make more sense later.) It has one output terminal and the voltage from this can vary from 0 V to 5 V (or to whatever voltage is supplied to it). The output voltage depends on the voltage applied *between* its two inputs. The formula describing this is

$$Vo = G \times Vi$$

where G is a very large number, usually several thousands. The voltage characteristics of the op.amp. are described in Figure 1.23. It can be seen from this that the amplifying region of the op.amp. is limited to when the input voltage is very small, a few millivolts at most. If the input voltage exceeds this, the output voltage simply goes HIGH (to 5 V or thereabouts).

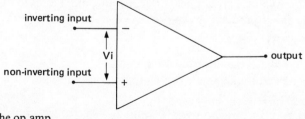

Figure 1.22   The op.amp.

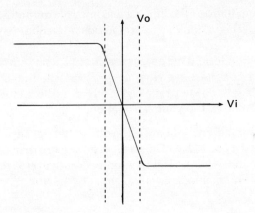

Figure 1.23   Voltage characteristics of the op.amp.

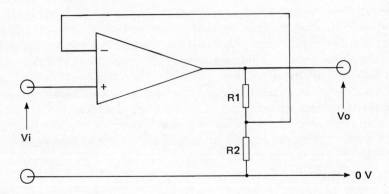

Figure 1.24   Negative feedback

By taking some of the output voltage and feeding it back to the inverting input, a special effect is created (Figure 1.24). This can be investigated using the ideas of the voltage divider network studied at the beginning of this chapter. The output voltage Vo is applied to the voltage divider network consisting of R1 and R2. We have already noted that the voltage produced by the voltage divider is

$$Vo \times R2/(R1 + R2)$$

and this is the voltage at the inverting input (V2).

The voltage applied to the non-inverting input is called Vi so $V1 = Vi$. The input voltage to the op.amp. is thus

$$(V1 - V2) = Vi - Vo \times R2/(R1 + R2)$$

But the op.amp. formula above is

$$Vo = G \times (V1 - V2)$$

or

$$Vo/G = V1 - V2$$

Combining these equations gives

$$Vo/G = Vi - Vo \times R2/(R1 + R2)$$

or

$$Vo(1/G + R2/(R1 + R2)) = Vi$$

Now if G is several thousands, then $1/G$ is very small, much less than 1, so we can ignore it for most purposes. The last equation thus reduces to

$$Vo \times R2/(R1 + R2) = Vi$$

which is the same as

$$Vo = Vi \times (1 + R1/R2)$$

Thus the amplification produced by this system does not depend upon the gain of the op.amp., provided this is large. The amplification depends solely upon the sizes of the two resistors R1 and R2. There are very many advantages in this, for one thing the amplification will be frequency independent. It will amplify direct voltages as well as alternating voltages and different op.amps. in the circuit will still give the same voltage gain.

Investigation 1.14   The op.amp. as a fixed gain amplifier

Connect the op.amp. board as in Figure 1.25 and measure the output voltage for various input voltages from 0 to 5 V. The voltage gain of this system should be about two (since R1 = R2). You should therefore get a graph like that in Figure 1.26.

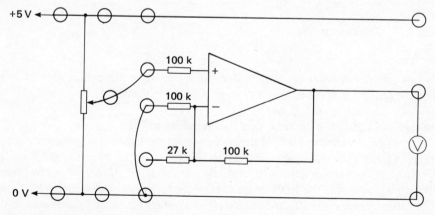

Figure 1.25   The op.amp. amplifier

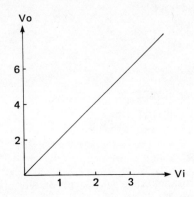

Figure 1.26   Voltage characteristics

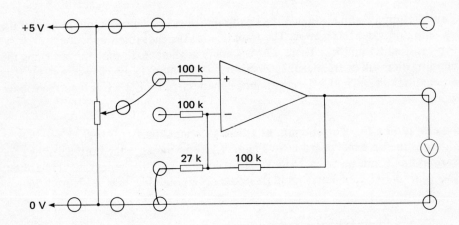

Figure 1.27   The op.amp. amplifier

Now connect the other resistor in place of R2 giving a theoretical gain of three (Figure 1.27). What is the actual voltage gain that you measure?

Investigation 1.15   The op.amp. as a transducer amplifier

This circuit can be used in place of the transistor for the lightmeter and thermometer circuits. Figure 1.28 shows the general arrangement, with either the LDR or the thermistor in the voltage divider unit. Again the voltage divider unit can be turned upside-down to enable the LDR or the thermistor to work the opposite way round. Devices that change some physical quantity into a voltage are called **transducers,** so the op.amp. is acting as a transducer amplifier.

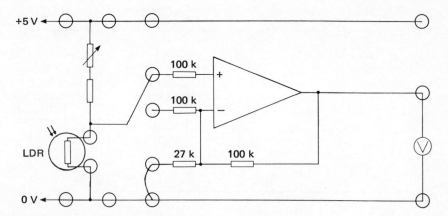

Figure 1.28   The op.amp. light meter

One particular transducer is a resistor itself. This converts the current flowing through it into a voltage. Thus a simple resistor can be used to turn the op.amp. transducer amplifier into an ammeter.

The problem with these simple devices is that they are not linear. For example if the amount of light is doubled, the voltage does not increase by a factor of two. Practical circuits use devices that are more linear. Such circuits are invaluable when using a microcomputer as an automatic measuring instrument. There are several other transducers that could be used in this circuit, such as a Hall effect device for measuring magnetic fields or a strain gauge for measuring the amount that a piece of metal is stretched or compressed. Since the strain is directly proportional to the applied force, this gives a force meter and hence a means of measuring weight.

Investigation 1.16   The op.amp. as a differential amplifier
The arrangement in Figure 1.29 is an extension of the previous ideas, the op.amp. amplifies the *difference* between V1 and V2. In this circuit if V1 is bigger than V2 then the output voltage is HIGH. If V1 is less than V2 then the output voltage is LOW. One

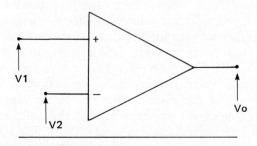

Figure 1.29   The differential amplifier

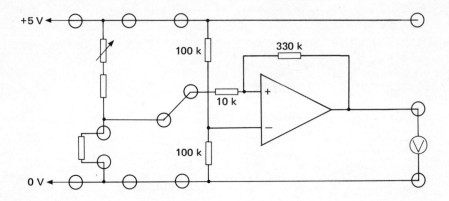

Figure 1.30   The op.amp. switch

particular use of this circuit will be described in Chapter 4 as an element of an analogue to digital converter. For the moment we can put the idea to practical use to make the op.amp. into a switch. To do this we fix the value of V2 to be 2.5 V, by connecting it to a voltage divider network with equal resistors.

The arrangement of the op.amp. in Figure 1.30 turns it into a switch. The best way of looking at this circuit is to note that the inverting input is now held half-way between 0 V and 5 V, that is at 2.5 V. If the non-inverting input is taken a few millivolts above 2.5 V then the output voltage will go HIGH to nearly 5 V. If the voltage applied to the non-inverting input is slightly less than 2.5 V, then the output will go to 0 V.

In this rearranged circuit the 330 kilohm resistor is connected to the non-inverting input instead. The effect of this is to increase the switching effect of the op.amp. When the input starts to go above 2.5 V, the output starts to go HIGH. An extra positive voltage is then fed back through the 330 kilohm resistor to the non-inverting input, making it go even more positive. The effect is to force the output right up to the 5 V level. Similarly if the input voltage starts to go below 2.5 V, this **positive feedback** forces the output to go to 0 V. The output cannot thus hover in the indeterminate place between HIGH and LOW, it is now a *digital* system.

This can be checked with the circuit of Figure 1.30, changing the input voltage with the output of the voltage divider unit. Measure the input voltage that just makes the output go HIGH (as shown by the LED of the transistor board, which is acting as a voltage indicator). Then reduce the input voltage slowly, using the variable resistor until the LED switches off. Note the input voltage at which this occurs. You should observe that the switch-on voltage is about 0.25 V higher than the switch-off voltage. This effect is very useful for ensuring that the switch cannot remain in the indeterminate mid-way position between on and off. It is called **hysteresis.**

By replacing the 4.7 kilohm resistor on this unit with the LDR, the thermistor or the 1000 μF capacitor, the light switch, temperature switch and time switch circuits can be made and investigated as before.

Many electronics textbooks give other applications of the op.amp., for example it can be a bistable, an astable or a monostable. Since digital integrated circuits do these jobs faster, these applications of op.amps. have not been described in this book.

Investigation 1.17   The voltage follower

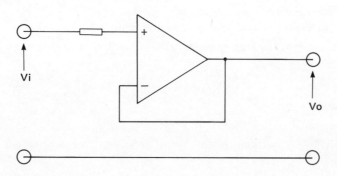

Figure 1.31   The voltage follower

The last investigation of this chapter is reserved for a very useful circuit, the **voltage follower.** In this arrangement (Figure 1.31) the whole of the output voltage is fed back to the inverting input, so V2 = Vo. Thus

Vo/G = V1 – V2

or

Vo/G = Vi – Vo

or

Vo x (1/G + 1) = Vi

and ignoring 1/G as before, we get

Vo = Vi

The op.amp. is no longer an amplifier so what is the advantage of this circuit? The answer lies in the fact that an op.amp. connected like this has a very large input resistance and draws very little current from any device connected to it. However the op.amp. output is capable of delivering about 100 mA. The effect is a device that could not produce much current by itself is now able to do so, thanks to the op.amp. The op.amp. is only *following* the voltage changes at its input terminal, hence the name given to this circuit. It is also called a **buffer circuit,** because it acts like a buffer between an ouput and an input.

2 Electronic logic

'What's one and one and one and one and one
and one and one and one and one and one?'
(Lewis Carroll, *Through the Looking Glass*)

Introduction

We saw in Chapter 1 that *digital* electronics is concerned with switching things on and off automatically. Let us consider the sort of problem that can be solved with digital electronics.

Once there was a man who became rather lazy. He did not like getting out of his car to open the garage doors, so he mounted an LDR by the side of his garage drive. He used a circuit like that of Figure 1.5 to open the garage doors automatically, whenever he drove his car past the LDR. Unfortunately he found that the garage doors also opened when the postman came past to deliver letters!

After thinking about this for a bit, he realized that he would need *two* LDRs, spaced about two metres apart. He arranged that the garage doors would open only if *both* LDRs were operated at the same time. His car was long enough to do this, but the postman only passed the LDRs one after the other, not both at the same time. So the garage doors were no longer opened when the postman walked up the drive.

Now let us look at the circuit used by this man (Figure 2.1). It is called an **AND gate** and has two inputs and one output. The output is used to operate the garage doors and each input is connected to one of the LDR circuits. When the car (or postman) passes in front of an LDR, the output voltage from that LDR circuit goes HIGH. There are thus four cases to consider; either one or both or neither of the two LDR circuits may be HIGH.

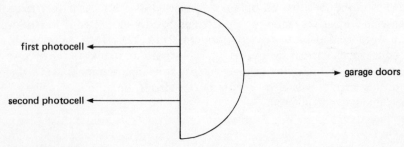

first photocell

second photocell

garage doors

Figure 2.1   The AND gate

It is possible to make up this AND gate with three transistors, but an easier way is to use a digital integrated circuit, in which the transistors have already been wired together. It is not necessary to know how the circuit is made up, since we are only interested in its input and output voltage levels. We study it with the systems approach. The AND gate is described by looking at the output voltage for the four different combinations of its two inputs. This gives us the truth table for the AND gate.

Input A	Input B	Output
LOW	LOW	LOW
LOW	HIGH	LOW
HIGH	LOW	LOW
HIGH	HIGH	HIGH

The 'HIGH' and 'LOW' in this table are voltages. In the case of integrated circuits a HIGH voltage means somewhere between 2.4 and 5 V and a LOW voltage means about 0 V. Note that the output from the AND gate is only HIGH if both of its inputs are HIGH. If only one or neither inputs are HIGH, then the output is LOW. So we can use the output from the AND gate to operate the garage doors. The reason for calling this an AND gate is now clear. The output is HIGH only if both input A *and* input B are HIGH.

There are two other ways of writing the truth table for the AND gate, as follows:

A	B	Output	A	B	Output
0	0	0	L	L	L
0	1	0	L	H	L
1	0	0	H	L	L
1	1	1	H	H	H

The 'H' and 'L' stand for HIGH and LOW voltages as before, and the '1' and '0' have the same meaning: they are called 'logic 1' and 'logic 0' to avoid confusion with the numbers 0 and 1. To describe an output as logic 1 means that it is HIGH, or is at a voltage of at least 2.4 volts (usually about 3 or 4 V). To say an output is at logic 0 means that it is LOW, or is at a LOW voltage (usually 0 V).

The easiest way to obtain a logic 0 or a logic 1 is with a switch as in Figure 2.2. When the switch is down, the output is connected to the 0 V line (called **ground**), so it will be

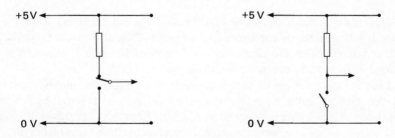

Figure 2.2   Switch logic

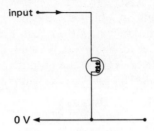

Figure 2.3 Lamp logic

LOW, or at logic 0. When the switch is up, the output is connected to the 5 V line through the 1 kilohm resistor, so it will be HIGH or at logic 1.

To find out if any output is HIGH or LOW, we could use a voltmeter, but this is rather large for the purpose. A more sensible method is to use a lamp (Figure 2.3).

When the input to the lamp is HIGH, it will be switched on. When the input is LOW, there will be no voltage across the lamp, so it will be off. So the lamp is an indicator of the HIGH or LOW output from the AND gate.

Unfortunately it isn't any good for that purpose, because it takes too much current to switch a lamp on. Even a small lamp needs a current of about 50 mA to glow, and the AND gate cannot provide that much. A light emitting diode (LED) needs less current, so it can be used like this, but even that is not satisfactory (Figure 2.4).

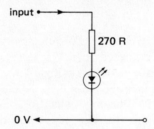

Figure 2.4 LED true logic

The LED is a true diode as well as a light emitter. It will only work if it is the right way round, with its cathode connected to the lower voltage and its anode connected to the higher voltage. The 270 ohms resistor is needed to prevent the current from becoming too large and destroying the LED.

The LED in Figure 2.4 can be turned on easily by a switch, but an AND gate would only do this with difficulty. Even though only 5 mA is needed to turn the LED on, this is more than the AND gate is designed to give out. Engineers call this 'sourcing' and the AND gate is acting as a current **source**. The current is flowing **out** from the output terminal of the AND gate, in the same way that water flows out from a source.

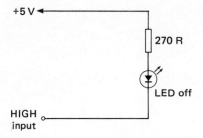

Figure 2.5 LED inverted logic

In practice this way of driving an LED works, but a better way to use an LED is shown in Figure 2.5.

In Figure 2.5 the LED will not be turned on if the input is HIGH. This is because the voltage at both ends of the LED will then be the same and there must be a difference in voltage to make a current flow.

The LED can, however, be turned on if its input is made LOW (Figure 2.6). The voltage across the LED is then enough to make it light up. Note that current flows through the LED from the 5 V supply and into the output of the AND gate. Thus the output from the AND gate is acting as a current **sink**. The current flows into the AND gate, in the same way that water sinks into a hole in the ground.

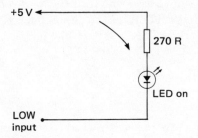

Figure 2.6 LED inverted logic

This idea of 'sinking' and 'sourcing' current is vital when devices are being connected together. It is no use expecting to turn an LED on with the circuit of Figure 2.4, if the AND gate cannot source the required current. Most integrated circuits sink larger currents than they are able to source, so the circuit of Figure 2.5 must unfortunately be used instead. It is 'unfortunate' because this circuit is the wrong way round! The LED comes on if its input is LOW and it goes off if its input is HIGH, which is the reason for calling it 'inverted' logic.

There are two ways out of this difficulty. The first is to use a special circuit, called a **driver** to turn the LED on and off, using the true LED logic of Figure 2.4. This driver is

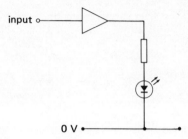

Figure 2.7 Sourcing an LED

specially designed to act as a current source. The logic board used in Chapter 5 uses a driver like this.

The other method is to use an INVERTER (Figure 2.8). We have already done this in Chapter 1, because a transistor is a natural INVERTER. The integrated circuit INVERTER behaves in the same way, having one input and one output. It has the following truth table.

Input	Output
LOW	HIGH
HIGH	LOW

It is called an INVERTER because its output is the opposite or inverse of its input. This device will sink 16 mA of current, but it can only source 0.1 mA. Since it inverts the effect of the input, it can be used with the LED to provide true logic.

When the input to the INVERTER is LOW, its output is HIGH, so the LED is off. When the input to the INVERTER is HIGH, the output is LOW, so the LED is 'pulled' on. Thus we get a true logic for the LED.

INVERTER input	LED
LOW	off
HIGH	on

Figure 2.8 is thus the circuit used to indicate whether a terminal is HIGH or LOW. It is the method employed in the electronic units used in the investigations in this chapter.

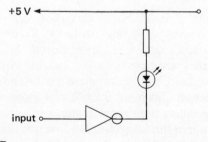

Figure 2.8 Sinking an LED

Investigation 2.1   Logic levels

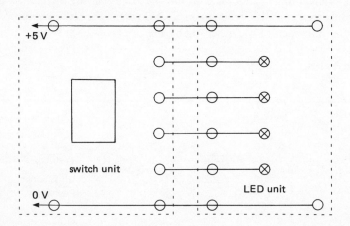

Figure 2.9   LED indicators

Connect the switch outputs to the LED inputs as shown in Figure 2.9. Make sure that the 5 V and 0 V power supply lines are connected too. When the switches are operated, the LEDs should go on and off.

What happens to an LED when its switch is pushed to the left?

What happens to the LED when its switch is pushed to the right?

Copy and complete this table.

Switch	LED (on/off)	Logic level (LOW/HIGH)
left		
right		

Disconnect one indicator input from its switch. Does the LED come on or go off? This is an important difference between these integrated circuits and the transistor logic circuits of Chapter 1. In those circuits any input that was left unconnected was LOW. With integrated circuits any input that is left unconnected is HIGH. This is why the LEDs of the indicator unit are on, even when nothing is connected to their input terminals.

Investigation 2.2   Logic gates

The INVERTER and the AND gate are examples of **logic gates.** We use them to combine together HIGH and LOW logic levels for different purposes. In investigating logic gates, we do not attempt to see how these are constructed from individual transistors. There is no need for this. As long as we know the truth table for each logic gate, we have all the information needed to make use of it.

In these investigations on logic gates we shall only use one set of four NAND gates (called the NAND unit). This saves us having to buy all the different types of logic gates, because they can all be made from NAND gates. The connections needed to turn NAND gates into each of the other logic gates are given each time.

The INVERTER

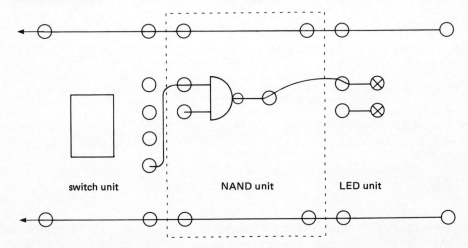

Figure 2.10 The INVERTER

Join the units together as in Figure 2.10. The INVERTER is made by using only one of the inputs of a NAND gate. The other input is not used. The switch is used to make the INVERTER input HIGH or LOW. The LED unit is used to see if the INVERTER output is HIGH or LOW.

Now make the INVERTER input HIGH or LOW (using the switch) and see what happens to its output (using the LED as an indicator). Copy and complete this table.

Input	Output (HIGH/LOW)
LOW	
HIGH	

The AND gate

Join the units together as in Figure 2.11. The AND gate is made by connecting two NAND gates together as shown. Two switches should be used to make the inputs of the AND gate HIGH or LOW. These will be called input A and input B of the AND gate. The output of the AND gate is connected to an LED indicator, to see if it is HIGH or LOW.

First make both inputs of the AND gate LOW and check on its output. Then make input B HIGH and input A LOW. Then make input A HIGH and input B LOW.

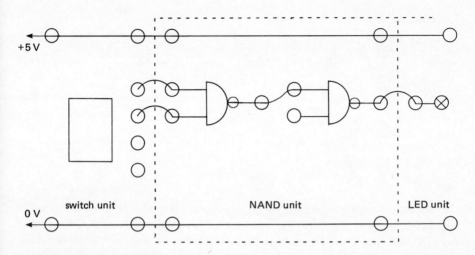

Figure 2.11   The AND gate

Finally make both inputs HIGH. Copy and complete this table.

Input A	Input B	Output
LOW	LOW	
LOW	HIGH	
HIGH	LOW	
HIGH	HIGH	

The NAND gate

Join the units together as in Figure 2.12. Two switches are needed to provide the inputs to the NAND gate, they are called input A and input B. An LED indicator should be used to find the logic level of the NAND gate output. Try different combinations of inputs A and B and note the effect on the output each time. Copy and complete this table.

Input A	Input B	Output
LOW	LOW	
LOW	HIGH	
HIGH	LOW	
HIGH	HIGH	

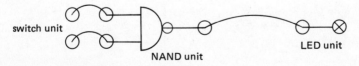

Figure 2.12   The NAND gate

63

The OR gate

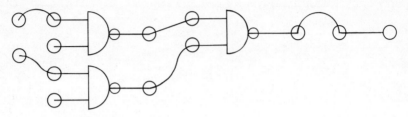

Figure 2.13 The OR gate

Join the units together as in Figure 2.13. This combination is called an OR gate. Two switches are needed to provide the inputs to the OR gate, called input A and input B. An LED indicator should be used to find the logic level of the OR gate output. Try different combinations of inputs A and B and note the effect on the output each time. Copy and complete this table.

Input A	Input B	Output
LOW	LOW	
LOW	HIGH	
HIGH	LOW	
HIGH	HIGH	

The NOR gate

Combine the units together as in Figure 2.14. In this combination they form a NOR gate. Two switches are needed to provide the inputs to the NOR gate, called input A and input B. An LED indicator should be used to find the logic level of the NOR gate output. Try different combinations of inputs A and B and note the effect on the output each time. Copy and complete this table.

Input A	Input B	Output
LOW	LOW	
LOW	HIGH	
HIGH	LOW	
HIGH	HIGH	

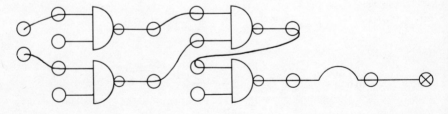

Figure 2.14 The NOR gate

The EXCLUSIVE-OR gate (*parity*)

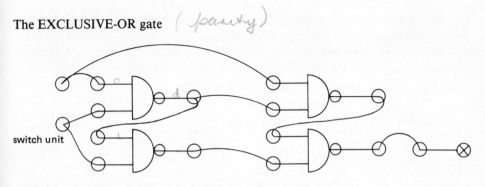

Figure 2.15 The EXCLUSIVE-OR gate

Join the units together as in Figure 2.15 to form the EXCLUSIVE-OR gate. This is quite a complicated arrangement and care must be taken. Two switches are needed as before for inputs A and B and an LED indicator should be used to check the output. Try different combinations of inputs A and B and note the effect on the output each time. Copy and complete this table.

Input A	Input B	Output
LOW	LOW	
LOW	HIGH	
HIGH	LOW	
HIGH	HIGH	

Logic symbols
In this investigation we have looked at six different types of logic gate. Each has its own truth table. The symbols for these gates are given in Figure 2.16. These symbols are used when drawing diagrams of digital systems.

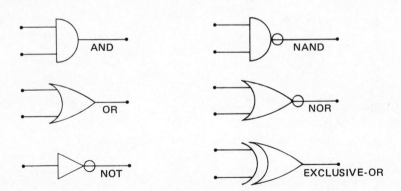

Figure 2.16 Logic symbols

It can be seen from this that the symbol for the NAND gate is a combination of the AND symbol and the INVERTER symbol (the small circle signifies inversion). In fact a NAND gate can be made in just this way, by taking the output from an AND gate and connecting it to an INVERTER. The truth table shows this quite well.

A	B	AND output	NAND output
LOW	LOW	LOW	HIGH
LOW	HIGH	LOW	HIGH
HIGH	LOW	LOW	HIGH
HIGH	HIGH	HIGH	LOW

The third column is the truth table for the AND gate. This is inverted by the INVERTER to give column four. This fourth column is the truth table for the NAND gate.

Use this truth table method to show that the NOR truth table can be obtained by inverting the output from an OR gate.

Boolean algebra

We have seen that some gates can be made by combining others. In the investigations we used only NAND gates to make the others. We also saw that the NAND gate could itself be made by combining an AND gate with an INVERTER. The truth table is one way of proving these relationships, but it is rather cumbersome if a large number of inputs is used. Gates with three separate inputs need a truth table of eight lines to cover all possible states. Later we shall be using gates with eight inputs, giving a total of 256 states. A truth table of this length would be of little practical use; we need a more compact language called Boolean algebra.

In this algebra only three relationships are used: AND, OR and NOT. 'NOT' refers to the INVERTER. If the input to an INVERTER is called 'A' then its output is 'NOT A'. It is also more usual to use the logic levels 0 and 1 in place of the LOW and HIGH that we have used so far.

A	NOT A
0	1
1	0

The AND gate

The two inputs to the AND gate are called 'A' and 'B'. The output from the AND gate is called 'A AND B'.

A	B	A AND B
0	0	0
0	1	0
1	0	0
1	1	1

The OR gate

The inputs are 'A' and 'B' as before and the output is 'A OR B'.

A	B	A OR B
0	0	0
0	1	1
1	0	1
1	1	1

The NAND gate

To describe the remaining gates we use a combination of these terms. Thus the NAND gate can be described by NOT(A AND B). The brackets are used to show that everything inside the bracket is to be 'NOTTED'. Without them there could be confusion with NOT A AND B, which is a different thing altogether. The rule is that 'NOT' takes precedence over 'AND'. (In the same way 'multiply' takes precedence over 'add' in ordinary arithmetic. For example 2 x 3 + 5 is not the same as 2 x (3 + 5). If you mean the latter, then the brackets are essential.)

The Boolean functions NOT(A AND B) and NOT A AND B are obtained by combining gates as shown in Figure 2.17.

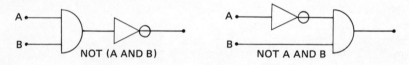

Figure 2.17   NOT(A AND B)   NOT A AND B

The truth tables of the two gates also show their differences.

A	B	NOT(A AND B)	A	B	NOT A AND B
0	0	1	0	0	0
0	1	1	0	1	1
1	0	1	1	0	0
1	1	0	1	1	0

The NOR gate

The NOR gate can be described by NOT(A OR B). Again the brackets are essential, because NOT A OR B actually means (NOT A) OR B and is something different.

A	B	NOT(A OR B)
0	0	1
0	1	0
1	0	0
1	1	0

Write out the truth table for NOT A OR B.

The EXCLUSIVE-OR gate

The EXCLUSIVE-OR gate is the most difficult (of those we have studied) to represent with Boolean algebra. It is actually:

(NOT A AND B) OR (A AND NOT B)

We clearly need some way of working out the truth tables for the different functions. This 'way' consists of building up to the final function stage by stage. The EXCLUSIVE-OR gate gives a good opportunity of demonstrating this method. The function consists of the two parts (NOT A AND B) and (A AND NOT B), which are then ORed together.

A	B	NOT A	NOT A AND B	A	B	NOT B	A AND NOT B
0	0	1	0	0	0	1	0
0	1	1	1	0	1	0	0
1	0	0	0	1	0	1	1
1	1	0	0	1	1	0	0

These two tables can be combined as follows:

NOT A AND B	A AND NOT B	(NOT A AND B) OR (A AND NOT B)
0	0	0
1	0	1
0	1	1
0	0	0

giving the final table:

A	B	EXCLUSIVE-OR
0	0	0
0	1	1
1	0	1
1	1	0

By comparing the two tables, we see that the EXCLUSIVE-OR function is the same as (NOT A AND B) OR (A AND NOT B).

In spite of its apparent complexity, the EXCLUSIVE-OR function is used a great deal in microelectronics. A look at the final truth table shows that there is a 'logic 1' in the final column, only where the inputs A and B are *different*. It can be used to compare two logic levels to see if they are the same or different. The output from the gate is HIGH if its two inputs are different; the output is LOW if the two inputs are the same.

The difference between the EXCLUSIVE-OR function and the simpler OR function is as follows. If you are asked 'Would you like to buy some fish or some chips?', you are clearly allowed to buy both. This is the normal (INCLUSIVE) OR, it includes the possibility that both A and B may be chosen.

On the other hand if asked 'Are you male or female?', the reply of 'both' is excluded. This is the EXCLUSIVE-OR function, where A and B cannot both be chosen at the same time. Thus there can only be a 'logic 1' output from the EXCLUSIVE-OR gate if its two inputs are different.

Draw truth tables for the following functions, using the method shown above. Answers are given at the end of the chapter.
i)   NOT (NOT A)
ii)   NOT A AND NOT B
iii)   NOT A OR NOT B
iv)   NOT (NOT A AND NOT B). Compare this truth table with that of the OR function.
v)   NOT (NOT A OR NOT B). Compare this truth table with that of the AND function.

Making a logic system

So far we have seen how the different gates can be made from different combinations of NAND gates. We have also seen how to work out the truth table for a particular combination of gates. But how do we do the opposite of this; that is, choose a combination of gates for a particular purpose? As an example let us see how to make a system which compares two inputs and tells us if they are the same. This system has the following truth table.

A	B	Output
0	0	1
0	1	0
1	0	0
1	1	1

When A is the same as B, the output is at logic 1. When A is different from B, the output is at logic 0. This function is called the **EQUIVALENCE function.** It is often used in microcomputers to compare two numbers.

We first look at each line of the truth table and pick out those lines for which the output is at logic 1. These are lines 1 and 4.

line 1   A = 0 AND B = 0

Both A and B are at logic 0. In Boolean algebra we write this as

output = NOT A AND NOT B
line 4   A = 1 AND B = 1

Both A and B are at logic 1. We write this as

output = A AND B

We combine these two together with the OR function. We can obtain 'output = 1' with either line 1 OR with line 4. The Boolean function from the truth table is thus

output = (NOT A AND NOT B) OR (A AND B)

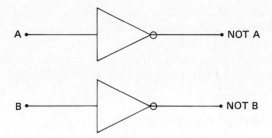

Figure 2.18   NOT A and NOT B

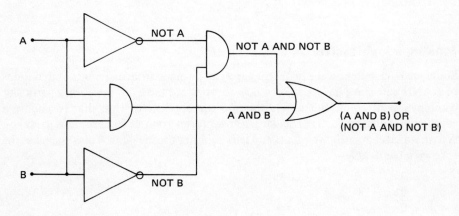

Figure 2.19   First attempt at the EQUIVALENCE gate

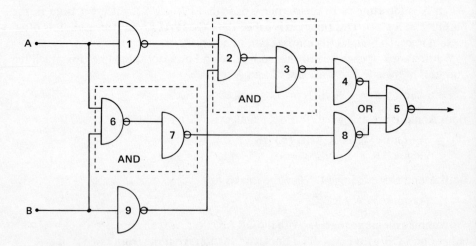

Figure 2.20   Second attempt at the EQUIVALENCE gate

How do we produce this function with electronic gates?

We need to make NOT A, this is done by putting A through an INVERTER. NOT B is made by putting B through another INVERTER as in Figure 2.18.

A AND B is made by putting A and B through an AND gate. Similarly NOT A AND NOT B is made by putting NOT A and NOT B into another AND gate. The outputs from these two gates are then ORed together as in Figure 2.19.

The next step is to replace each of these gates by its equivalent gate made from NAND gates. Figure 2.20 shows this.

This suggests that nine NAND gates are needed. Note however that gates 3 and 4 are not necessary. Gate 3 is an INVERTER and so is gate 4 and since NOT (NOT X) is the same as X, gates 3 and 4 can be removed entirely. Similarly gates 7 and 8 just cancel each other out too and may also be removed. So to make this system we only need five gates. However there are four NAND gates in each of the 7400 integrated circuits that we are using, so two of these devices are still required.

Electronic engineers, who are clever at Boolean algebra, may try to make the EQUIVALENCE function with even fewer gates. One way is to notice that the EQUIVALENCE function is the exact opposite of the EXCLUSIVE-OR function:

A	B	EQUIVALENCE	EXCLUSIVE-OR
0	0	1	0
0	1	0	1
1	0	0	1
1	1	1	0

So another way to make the EQUIVALENCE function is to put the output from an EXCLUSIVE-OR gate through an INVERTER (Figure 2.21).

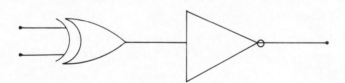

Figure 2.21   Third attempt at the EQUIVALENCE gate

In practice this still needs two SN7400 integrated circuits, so we have not gained anything. Redesigning a system does not always make it cheaper to produce!

Design NAND gate combinations to make each of the following functions. Solutions are given at the end of the chapter.

i)   NOT A AND NOT B
ii)   NOT A OR NOT B
iii)   NOT (NOT A AND NOT B)
iv)   NOT (NOT A OR NOT B)

Case study

We can use Boolean algebra to calculate the truth table for any combination of gates, although it can get quite complicated at times. Let us see how to create a logic system for a particular purpose. The example chosen is an **implication system.** This relies on the fact that digital logic is very similar to propositional logic, which was first investigated by the Greeks.

Propositional logic

The statement 'I drink tea' may be true or false. If it is true, it can be represented by the mathematical expression:

$T = 1$

If it is false it can be represented by:

$T = 0$

Clearly the statement 'I don't drink tea' is the opposite, or inverse of the first statement. It can thus be represented by NOT T. If it is true (that I don't drink tea), then:

NOT T $= 1$

But if I do drink tea then:

NOT T $= 0$

The statements 'I drink coffee' and 'I drink no coffee' can likewise be represented by C and by NOT C. It is again true that:

if C $= 1$, then NOT C $= 0$ and
if C $= 0$, then NOT C $= 1$

If it is true that 'I drink coffee', then it is false that 'I drink no coffee'.

The inverse of NOT C is NOT (NOT C) and since there are only two states, this must be equivalent to C:

NOT (NOT C) $=$ C

(This explains the logic behind the claim of the English teacher, that 'I ain't got no coffee' is equivalent to 'I do have some coffee'.)

The two statements T and C can be combined with the AND and OR operators as follows:

T AND C $= 1$ (it is true that 'I drink tea and coffee')
T AND C $= 0$ (it is false that 'I drink tea and coffee')

In this last case, the emphasis is on the word 'both'. It is saying that I don't drink *both* tea and coffee; I may well drink one or other of them. Another way of putting it is 'I don't drink tea or I don't drink coffee'.

(NOT T) OR (NOT C) $= 1$

This verifies the mathematical relationship, known as De Morgan's law, that:

(NOT T) OR (NOT C) = NOT (T AND C)

The other of De Morgan's laws is:

(NOT T) AND (NOT C) = NOT (T OR C)

What does this statement mean in English?

Implication

There is no connection between the propositions T and C above, so the statement 'If I drink tea, then I drink coffee' is pointless. But consider the two statements P and Q as follows:

P is the statement 'I have an increase in my pay'.
Q is the statement 'There will be inflation'.

P *implies* Q is the combination of these two thus: 'If I have an increase in pay, then there will be inflation' (which may be familiar to some politicians!). This is a new statement R, for which we can draw up the truth table thus:

P	Q	R	
0	0	1	No pay increase, no inflation: R is true
0	1	1	No pay increase, but inflation: R is still true. Even politicians do not say that my pay increase is the only cause of inflation.
1	0	0	I get a pay increase, but there is no inflation so somebody is lying! R is false.
1	1	1	I get my pay increase and we all get inflation. Politicians say 'I told you so!': R is true.

We must now turn this truth table into a Boolean function. We could say that R is given by lines 1, 2 and 4 of the table, or

R = (NOT P AND NOT Q) OR (NOT P AND Q) OR (P AND Q)

but this is rather a lot. It is easier to say that R is false in line 3, thus:

NOT R = P AND NOT Q

or, by inverting both sides,

NOT (NOT R) = NOT (P AND NOT Q)

or

R = NOT(P AND NOT Q)

This example may seem a long way from electronics, but I wanted an application far removed from the usual control systems. It shows how electronic circuits are capable of 'thinking'. Now that we have a truth table we can produce a set of electronic gates which give the same table. Thus we can simulate propositional logic with electronics.

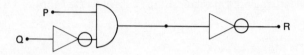

Figure 2.22   The IMPLICATION function

Figure 2.22 shows how the IMPLICATION function is realized with logic gates. But we now have to do this with NAND gates only. We have already seen how to make the AND gate from two NAND gates and how to make the INVERTERS, so our next effort is that shown in Figure 2.23.

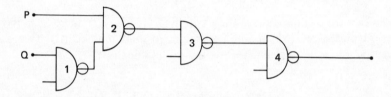

Figure 2.23   Second attempt at the implication function

Looking carefully at the last two NAND gates of this system, it is not at all clear what they are contributing, gate 4 simply inverts gate 3, which in turn inverts gate 2. They might as well not be there. Exactly the same output can be obtained from the arrangement shown in Figure 2.24.

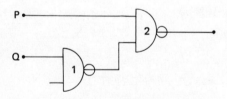

Figure 2.24   Final attempt at the implication function

This is our solution to the original problem. This method of combining a set of gates is very useful to an engineer, who must always try to reduce the number of gates needed in order to cut the cost of the finished system.

Applications of logic gates

In addition to demonstrating propositional logic and the laws of Boolean algebra, digital electronics will also demonstrate the language of 'sets' in mathematics, the principles of Venn diagrams and combinations of relays and switches in a telephone exchange. Boolean algebra has very many applications in the real world.

We started this section with a practical example, the 'garage doors' problem. This system can be made up with two light-operated switches, each acting as an input to an AND gate. The AND output could be used to open the garage doors. The doors could be closed again afterwards by a switch outside the doors.

Now, how will the man get to his car again in the morning? He could arrange with a friend to walk in front of the two LDRs at the same time, but this is not very clever. He needs to open the doors either by the two LDRs (called A and B) *or* by the switch C outside the doors. The function for this would be (A AND B) OR C and could be made from a combination of NAND gates.

This is how digital systems were built in the 1960s and 70s, from combinations of separate NAND gates. They were all wired together in the correct way to produce the desired function. If the system was sold in any great quantity, each one still had to be built up on a printed circuit board, so that the different gates could be correctly wired together.

With modern technology it is now possible to set up almost any desired logic function in a single chip, called a **ULA (uncommitted logic array).** Once the final combination of gates has been agreed, a very large number of ULAs can be produced, which will therefore be very cheap. Microelectronics has become important because it is possible to make cheap programmable systems, this is why it is essential for any microelectronics course to include the study of programmable devices.

Practical exercises
1 Build a combination of gates to carry out the garage door function outlined above. Use two switches to represent the light-dependent switches and a third to represent switch C. The garage doors may be represented by an LED.
2 In a committee of three, each member has a push-button switch. When any switch is pressed, that is a 'yes' vote by that person. If the switch is not pressed, it is a 'no' vote. Design a system so that a 'yes' lamp or a 'no' lamp comes on, when a vote is taken according to the following rules: If the chairman's vote is 'yes' then the overall decision is always 'yes'. If the chairman votes 'no' then *both* of the other committee members must vote 'yes', otherwise the decision is 'no'.

Addressing

Combinational logic is used a great deal in microcomputers to select one particular device from among the many available; this is known as **addressing.** For example a microprocessor might have fifty thousand different memory locations to inspect. The

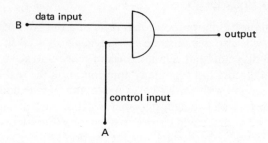

Figure 2.25   The AND gate as a gate

problem is solved by giving each memory location a special number, called its **address.** To simplify matters we shall consider a memory consisting of only four locations (Figure 2.26).

When a logic 1 is applied to one input (say input A) of the AND gate in Figure 2.25, the output will always have the same logic level as input B. If B is HIGH then both inputs are at logic 1 and the output is HIGH. If B is LOW, then the output from the AND gate is also LOW. On the other hand if the control input (input A) is LOW, then the output from the AND gate is always LOW, no matter what happens to B. Thus input A **controls** whether the information from B can pass through to the output; the system acts like a gate that can be opened or closed by the logic level at A.

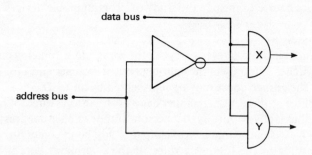

Figure 2.26   Addressing one of two locations

When the address 1 is applied to the **address bus** (Figure 2.26), the input of AND gate Y goes HIGH. This then opens the gate and allows the information (called **data**) to pass through it to its destination. Likewise the address 0 will open AND gate X, thus allowing the data to get to the other destination. In a real microcomputer system there would, of course, be more than one address line; a system with two lines is shown in Figure 2.27.

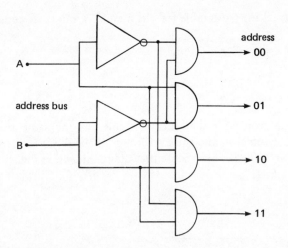

Figure 2.27 Addressing one of four locations

Two lines allow four locations to be separately addressed. Eight lines would allow 256 unique locations and sixteen address line would allow 65,536 separate locations to be maintained. It is this latter arrangement that is actually used in most microcomputers today.

When a microcomputer wishes to talk to one particular location it has to open and close all the appropriate AND gates to get at the data it contains. And the incredible thing is, that the whole process is done is less than one millionth of a second.

Investigation 2.3   Digital arithmetic
The HALF-ADDER
The binary method of counting is well known. With this system it is possible to count up to any number with just the two **binary digits** (or **bits**) '0' and '1'. Electronic logic uses just the two states HIGH and LOW, so it can be used to represent the bits 0 and 1. Hence it is possible to represent numbers by electronic circuits. This is the whole basis of microprocessors. Let us now see how digital electronic circuits can also carry out arithmetic processes (like addition).

Consider first the problem of adding together two one-bit numbers (A and B) in the binary system. This is so simple that we can even write down all the possible combinations of these two numbers.

1	1	0	0	or in	A
+1	0	1	0	general	+ B
10	01	01	00		CS

where S is the **SUM bit** and C is the **CARRY bit**.

We can construct the truth table for bits S and C from these combinations thus.

A	B	S	C
0	0	0	0
0	1	1	0
1	0	1	0
1	1	0	1

It can be seen from this that the SUM bit has the same truth table as the EXCLUSIVE-OR function and the CARRY bit is the AND function. So to build a system to add two bits together we use the gates as shown in Figure 2.28.

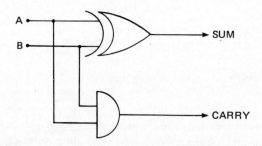

Figure 2.28   The HALF ADDER

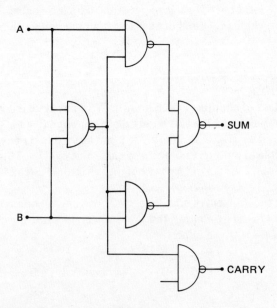

Figure 2.29   The HALF ADDER from NAND gates

NAND gates can be combined to make the AND function and the EXCLUSIVE-OR function as shown in Figure 2.29. The outputs from these gates then give the CARRY bit and the SUM bits respectively. You can make up either of these circuits with the NAND gate unit (or both at once if you have enough NAND gates). Use switches to represent A and B (the bits to be added) and use LEDs to see whether the SUM and CARRY bits are 0 or 1.

It is also possible to combine logic gates to make a **HALF-SUBTRACTOR** too but this is left as an exercise. Work out what Boolean functions are needed to make a HALF-SUBTRACTOR, that is, the value for A − B. To do this, you will need a **SUB bit** (like the SUM bit) and a **REPAY/BORROW bit** (like the CARRY bit) to hold the result. Then construct the required logic gates from NAND gates and check that your system works.

The ALU of a microprocessor

Even if these systems are expanded to cope with the addition or the subtraction of *large* binary numbers, the same principles apply and the necessary combinations of gates can be made. Inside a microprocessor is a sub-system that carries out addition and subtraction, ANDing, ORing and all the other logic functions we have studied so far. This is called the **arithmetic and logic unit** or **ALU**. Figure 2.30 gives an inside view of a primitive ALU. There are two inputs, A and B. There are three outputs, A AND B, A OR B and the SUM bit. We have looked at these functions separately already and this diagram has just put all the gates together inside one package.

In practice this ALU is of little use, it has only three functions, each with its own output. A more powerful ALU might have ten or twenty different functions and could not therefore have a different output for each. Clearly there is some way that the ALU combines the functions into a single output. We can use OR gates to do this

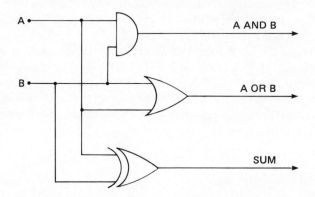

Figure 2.30 A primitive ALU

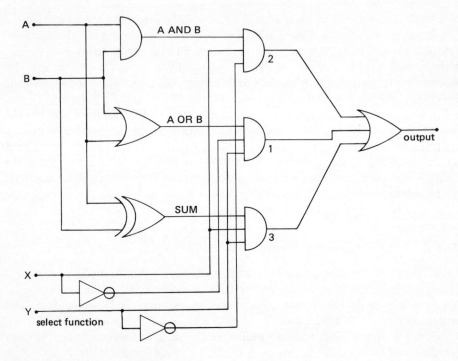

Figure 2.31 Selecting a function

'combination' for us but we then need a way of selecting the function we want. Figure 2.31 shows how this might be done with AND gates.

Inputs A and B are the data inputs. These data bits enter the ALU as before, but now there is only one output. In addition there are two control inputs X and Y. The address chosen for X and Y determines which function will be selected. The process is similar to the way we accomplished memory addressing in Figure 2.27. If X and Y are both HIGH, then gate 3 will be enabled, to open a path for the SUM bit to get through to the output. The other gates will remain closed.

If X is HIGH and Y is LOW, then gate 2 will be enabled, allowing the AND function to reach the output. If X is LOW and Y is HIGH, then gate 1 opens and the OR function is selected. Finally if both X and Y are LOW, then none of the functions will be selected. Thus the values chosen for X and Y control the function selected inside the ALU. We say that these values represent a binary **operation code** (or **op. code**) which chooses the desired function:

Code	Function
00	None
01	OR
10	AND
11	SUM

If the microprocessor wants the SUM bit of the two input bits, it proceeds as follows. First the SUM function is chosen by putting the op. code 11 onto the control lines X and Y. Then the values for A and B are put onto the data inputs and the result appears at the output.

This ALU has been greatly over-simplified to help us to understand how it might work. In reality an ALU will handle more than one bit at a time. One such ALU (the SN 74181) processes two sets of four bits at once. Each set can be thought of as a binary number from 0000 to 1111 and each can represent a decimal number or any other information. The two numbers can be added or subtracted by choosing the correct operation code, of which there are thirty-two in total. Sixteen of these are arithmetic and sixteen are logic op.codes, the logic level of the L/A line being used to choose between them. The output (Z) consists of four bits and a CARRY bit (which also serves as a BORROW bit in subtraction). There is also an input CARRY bit (C) to allow the results of a *previous* addition etc. to be included. Thus a more realistic picture of an ALU is shown in Figure 2.32.

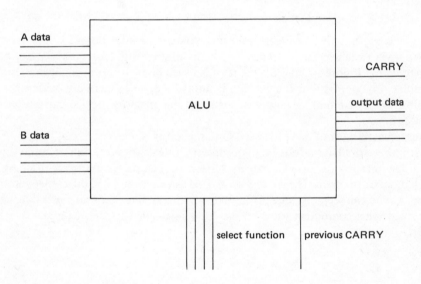

Figure 2.32 Block diagram of an ALU

We have not shown the 'inside' of the ALU this time, because it is too complicated. It would look like a mass of interconnected gates, and would not mean very much. But the systems approach means that we do not need to know what is inside. We only need to know what inputs are needed and what op.codes are required to produce each of the given functions. This information is given in the data sheet that is supplied with the

ALU. Here is the sort of information about the op.codes that might be supplied in such a data sheet.

Op.code	L/A=1 (logic)	L/A=0 (arithmetic)
0000	Z = NOT A	Z = A + C
0001	Z = NOT(A OR B)	Z = A + B + C
0010	Z = NOT A AND B	
0011	Z = 0000	Z = 1111 + C
0100	Z = NOT(A AND B)	
0101	Z = NOT B	
0110	Z = A EXCLUSIVE-OR B	Z = A – B – NOT C
0111	Z = A AND NOT B	
1000	Z = NOT A OR B	
1001	Z = A EQUIVALENCE B	Z = A + B + NOT C
1010	Z = B	
1011	Z = A AND B	
1100	Z = 1	Z = A + A
1101	Z = A OR NOT B	
1110	Z = A OR B	
1111	Z = A	Z = A – NOT C

It would be perfectly feasible to make up a board containing this ALU and to input data to it via switches. The outputs could be monitored with LEDs and the op.codes selected with yet more switches. Whether it is worth doing this practically at school is debatable, my view is that the expense is unjustified, since there are other ways of introducing programmable systems, such as the memory device introduced in Chapter 3.

The actual number of bits processed simultaneously is one measure of the power of a microprocessor. Thus a four-bit microprocessor deals with four bits at a time and a sixteen-bit microprocessor with sixteen. Most microcomputers use an eight-bit ALU, which processes data that is eight bits wide. This can have up to 256 different operation codes. As you can see, it is quite difficult to talk to a system that uses codes like these, so instead most computers use a special language called BASIC to make the task easier.

Solutions to problems on page 69.

i)

A	NOT A	NOT NOT A
0	1	0
1	0	1

ii)

A	NOT A	B	NOT B	NOT A AND NOT B
0	1	0	1	1
0	1	1	0	0
1	0	0	1	0
1	0	1	0	0

NOT A AND NOT B gives the same truth table as NOT(A OR B)

iii)

A	NOT A	B	NOT B	NOT A OR NOT B
0	1	0	1	1
0	1	1	0	1
1	0	0	1	1
1	0	1	0	0

NOT A OR NOT B gives the same truth table as NOT(A AND B)

iv)

A	B	NOT (NOT A AND NOT B)
0	0	0
0	1	1
1	0	1
1	1	1

The truth table is the inverse of (ii) above. NOT (NOT A AND NOT B) gives the same truth table as A OR B.

v)

A	B	NOT (NOT A OR NOT B)
0	0	0
0	1	0
1	0	0
1	1	1

The truth table is the inverse of (iii) above. NOT (NOT A OR NOT B) gives the same truth table as A AND B.

Solutions to problems on page 71.

i)   Figure 2.33

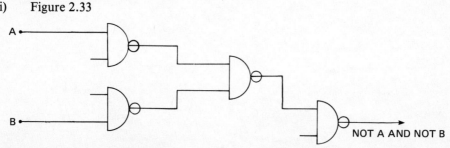

Figure 2.33   NOT A AND NOT B

83

ii)   Figure 2.34

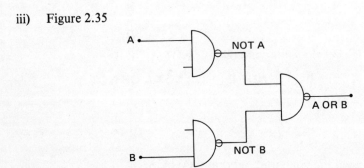

Figure 2.34   NOT A OR NOT B

iii)   Figure 2.35

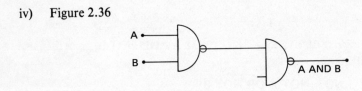

Figure 2.35   NOT (NOT A AND NOT B)

iv)   Figure 2.36

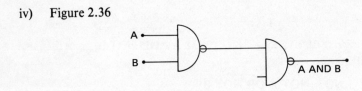

Figure 2.36   NOT (NOT A OR NOT B)

3 Digital systems

'We cannot do with more than four
To give a hand to each.'

(Lewis Carroll, *Through the Looking Glass*)

Investigation 3.1 The bistable

In Chapter 1 we looked at ways of connecting two transistors together to make the bistable. It is also possible to do this with two NAND gates (Figure 3.1). The gates are labelled A and B to identify them. The output of A is connected directly to B and vice versa. The other inputs are labelled CLR and SET; these are normally HIGH. Suppose that A has a HIGH output. The other input of B is thus HIGH and B has a LOW output. Thus the other input to A is LOW and A has a HIGH output (as we supposed).

If SET is now made temporarily LOW, then the output from B will go HIGH. This will make the other input of A go HIGH, so the output of A will go LOW. This 'LOW' will then appear at the input of B, so even if the temporary LOW to SET is removed, the output from B will still be HIGH. The bistable has switched over. This state of affairs is shown in Figure 3.2.

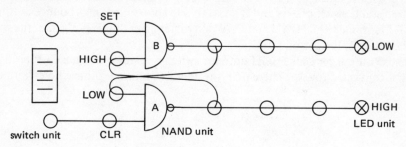

Figure 3.1   The NAND gate bistable

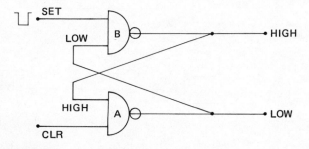

Figure 3.2   The bistable in its other state

To get the bistable to switch back again, CLR must be taken temporarily LOW. This gets us back to Figure 3.1. In this state the bistable is said to be off. The output from B is called the Q output of the bistable and it is now LOW. The output from A is now HIGH, and is called the NOT Q output. Clearly the NOT Q output is the inverse of the Q output.

If SET is taken LOW momentarily, the bistable will switch on. Q will go HIGH and NOT Q will go LOW. This is called setting the bistable. If CLR is taken LOW, the bistable will be reset or cleared and its Q output will go LOW. This explains the names of these two terminals.

Connect two NAND gates together as in Figure 3.1 and verify that it works in the way described.

One useful application of this simple bistable is in making a bounce-free switch. Normally when a switch is closed, the contacts make and break very many times as they bang together. This can create a series of pulses and, in a counting circuit, would cause counting errors. Figure 3.3 shows a way of avoiding these unwanted pulses.

1   Before the switch is operated, the CLR terminal is LOW so the bistable is OFF and Q is LOW. The SET terminal is HIGH because of the resistor to the 5 V line. (In fact, it would be HIGH without this resistor, because an unconnected terminal is almost always HIGH in TTL devices. The resistor makes certain of this fact.)
2   When the switch begins to be pressed, both terminals become HIGH, but this does not affect the bistable, which remains off.
3   When the contacts of the switch first close to connect the SET terminal to ground, the bistable switches over and Q goes HIGH. The contacts may bounce causing the SET terminal to go HIGH and LOW alternately, but this does not alter the state of the bistable, it stays on.
4   The Q output remains HIGH until the switch is released and the CLR terminal is first connected to 0 V. Thereafter any contact bounce will have no effect.

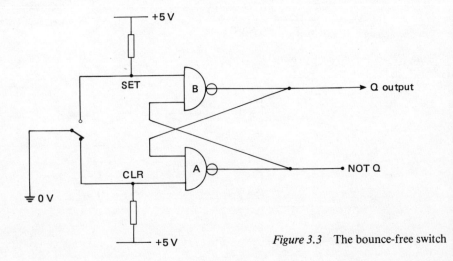

Figure 3.3   The bounce-free switch

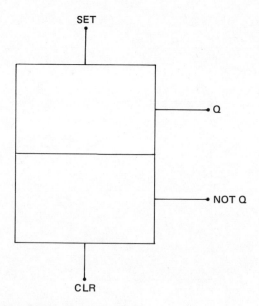

Figure 3.4   Black-box description of the bistable

Thus a single pulse will emerge from the Q output, despite the contact bounce. The push-button unit, which we shall be using in this chapter, is constructed exactly like this, using a pair of NAND gates to form the bistable.

In the systems approach we are not particularly interested in how the bistable is constructed, only in the properties of its terminals. So it is convenient to represent the bistable by a 'black box', showing only its terminals (Figure 3.4).

The description of the bistable above is not very concise, we need some form of truth table to summarize the information. The type of truth table used for logic gates is not really useful, though, because the data changes during the operation. The following data chart is a more useful way of describing it:

SET	CLR	Q	NOT Q
LOW	HIGH	LOW	HIGH
HIGH	LOW	HIGH	LOW
HIGH	HIGH	no change	
LOW	LOW	not allowed	

This data chart shows that the Q output can be set to 1 by a temporary LOW at the SET terminal. It can be cleared to 0 by a LOW at the CLR terminal. In both cases the NOT Q output will be the inverse of this. If both SET and CLR are HIGH, then the outputs will be unchanged.

The other possibility of having both SET and CLR LOW is meaningless to the bistable. Since it cannot do both things at once, it will do one or the other. There is no way of knowing which will happen, so this condition should not be allowed to occur.

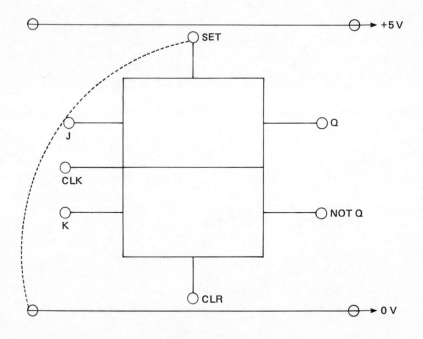

Figure 3.5   Practical connections to the bistable unit

The SN 7476 integrated circuit contains two bistables. Each has a Q output, a NOT Q output, a SET terminal, a CLR terminal and three others which we shall ignore in Figure 3.5. The logic state of the Q output is shown with an LED, which comes on when the bistable is set (when the Q output is HIGH).

Connect a flying lead from the 0 V line to the SET and CLR terminals in turn. Try also the effect of having both terminals HIGH, or both LOW and see what happens. Check the truth of the data chart above.

The J-K bistable

We have already mentioned the need of a computer to keep everything in step. The main reason for this is to prevent some bistables from switching over before other, slower ones, have had time to do so. If this happens the microprocessor will not know whether a particular bistable has already changed over or is still in the process of doing so. The clock pulses from the system clock are used to ensure that everything happens simultaneously. For this reason the simple bistable we have just investigated is no good, it has no input for clock pulses. Instead the more sophisticated J-K bistable is used (Figure 3.6), which has the following data chart:

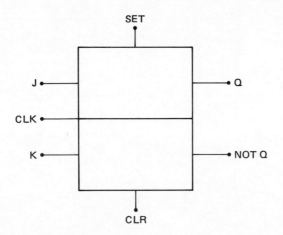

Figure 3.6 The J-K bistable

J	K	Q output
LOW	LOW	no change
LOW	HIGH	LOW
HIGH	LOW	HIGH
HIGH	HIGH	changes over

This chart is not complete because it does not show what happens to the CLK terminal. This is the terminal to which the clock pulses are applied. Unless there is a clock pulse, nothing will happen. A clock pulse is applied when the CLK terminal goes HIGH and then LOW again. Usually this clock pulse lasts for less than a microsecond, but that is sufficient. The Q output will change according to the logic states of its J and K inputs.

1   If J and K are both LOW, then Q will not change, no matter how many clock pulses there are.
2   If J is HIGH and K is LOW when the clock pulse arrives, then the bistable will be set (Q = 1).
3   If J is LOW and K is HIGH, then the bistable will be cleared when the clock pulse arrives.
4   The last case is the most interesting. When the clock pulse arrives and both J and K are HIGH, the Q output changes over. If it was 1 it becomes 0 and if it was 0 it becomes 1. The NOT Q output does the opposite. We shall see how useful this is in Investigation 3.2.

In addition to the J and K inputs, the J-K bistable also has the SET and CLR terminals, which work in exactly the same way as described above. In fact the bistable used in Investigation 3.1 was a J-K bistable.

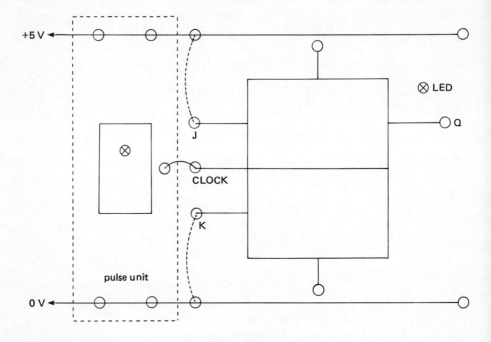

Figure 3.7 Practical connections for the J-K bistable

Investigation 3.2   The J-K bistable
Verify the data chart for the J-K bistable in the way shown in Figure 3.7. Connect the push-button switch to the CLK terminal of the bistable. Connect the J and K terminals to 0 V to make them LOW, or leave them unconnected (for HIGH). Leave the SET and CLR terminals unconnected (for HIGH). Apply a single clock pulse and check that the Q output of the bistable behaves as the data chart predicts.

Figure 3.8 shows four J-K bistables. By connecting the SET and CLR lines to 0 V, each bistable may be switched on or off. The four bistables can represent the four bits of a binary number. If the binary number 1010 is stored in the bistables, it remains

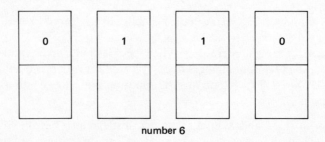

Figure 3.8 Representing data with bistables

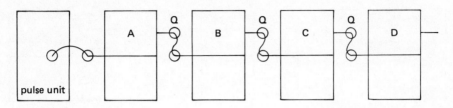

Figure 3.9   The binary counter

there indefinitely (or until the power is disconnected). This illustrates the most important use of the bistable; as a memory circuit.

Now connect the Q output of each bistable to the CLK input of the following bistable as in Figure 3.9. The CLK input of the first bistable should be connected to the pulse unit. Repeated pressing of the push-button causes a series of pulses to go to this bistable. Since its J and K inputs are HIGH (unconnected), each pulse makes the Q output of this bistable change over, from 0 to 1 or from 1 to 0.

Note that two pulses from the push-button produce one pulse from the Q output of the first bistable. It has divided the number of input pulses by two, hence the bistable is often called a **divide-by-two circuit.**

Each succeeding bistable also divides the number of pulses by two. The result is that the bistables form a binary counter. This would be more obvious if the bistables were all the other way round, with the first bistable on the extreme right, so that it represents the least significant bit (A) of the binary number. To make this more obvious we shall use 0 and 1 in the following table to represent the LOW and HIGH outputs from the four bistables.

Pulse number	D	C	B	A
0	0	0	0	0
1	0	0	0	1
2	0	0	1	0
3	0	0	1	1
4	0	1	0	0
5	0	1	0	1
6	0	1	1	0
7	0	1	1	1
8	1	0	0	0
9	1	0	0	1
10	1	0	1	0
11	1	0	1	1
12	1	1	0	0
13	1	1	0	1
14	1	1	1	0
15	1	1	1	1
16	0	0	0	0
etc.				

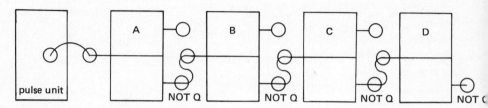

Figure 3.10   Counting down with bistables

Now connect the CLK input of each bistable to the NOT-Q output of the next bistable instead (Figure 3.10). How does it count now?

These binary counter circuits are not actually used in computer circuits, because they do not count in step. When the sixteenth pulse arrives, the Q output from bistable A changes first, then B, then C and finally D. This can cause problems in high speed computers, because the next pulse might arrive before D has had time to change from the previous pulse. This is overcome with a synchronous counter, where the change-over at each bistable is controlled by the clock pulse. The same clock pulse is applied to each bistable at the same time through its CLK input (Figure 3.11). This keeps all bistables exactly in step.

We shall now investigate a circuit which uses the clock pulses to shift the binary number along by one position. It will not yet be obvious what use this is, but there will

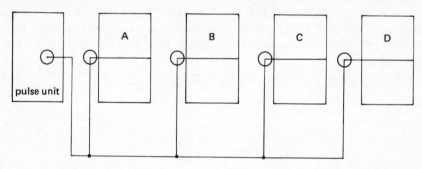

Figure 3.11   The clock inputs

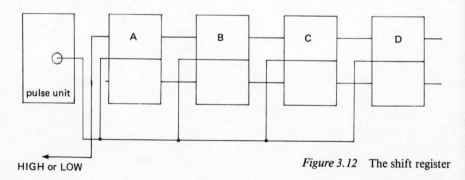

HIGH or LOW

Figure 3.12   The shift register

be several applications of it later. The clock pulses from the push-button unit are applied to all the bistables at the same time. Since each J and K input is connected to the previous Q and NOT Q outputs, the 'bit' in one bistable is transferred to the next, when this clock pulse is received. To get the table below, you will need to set all bistables to 1 before applying the clock pulses.

Pulse number	Number in the register			
0	1	1	1	1
1	0	1	1	1
2	0	0	1	1
3	0	0	0	1
4	0	0	0	0

Instead of connecting the J and K inputs of bistable A to 0 V, connect them to the Q and NOT Q outputs of bistable D. Now the binary number in this shift register cycles round repeatedly. Of course, if the number is initially 0000 or 1111, you will not see much shifting. Use the SET and CLR terminals of each bistable to put other bit patterns into the register before you start. Can you think how to connect the bistables together to make the register shift the other way?

Figures 3.13 and 3.14 show two other ways of connecting the bistables together, each of which has a particular property. These are worth investigating.

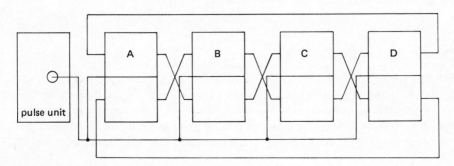

Figure 3.13   The ring counter

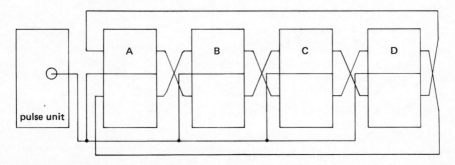

Figure 3.14   The twisted ring counter

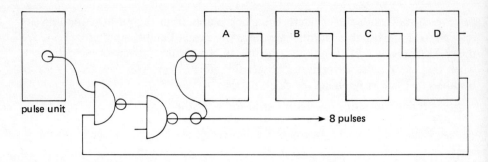

Figure 3.15　An eight-pulse unit

In a microprocessor it is sometimes necessary to produce a particular number of pulses. This application of bistables demonstrates how they are used in conjunction with logic gates to solve this sort of problem. The arrangement in Figure 3.15 will produce exactly eight pulses when the push-button is pressed repeatedly. All bistables should be cleared initially. Pulses will be allowed through the AND gate as long as its input (connected to the NOT Q output of A) is HIGH. When the eighth pulse is counted, this NOT Q output goes LOW and the AND gate closes. No further pulses can get through until the bistables are cleared.

The decade counter

Bistables are not restricted to counting only in binary. In combination with logic gates, the bistables can be reset or cleared at any desired count. Figure 3.16 shows how a decade counter can be made, which counts up to ten before resetting automatically to zero. All bistables should be cleared initially. When the tenth pulse is counted, the Q outputs of B and D are both HIGH for the first time. They are connected to a NAND

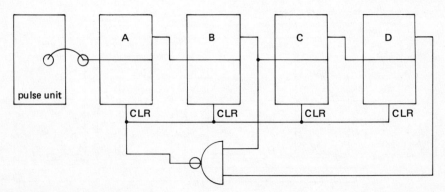

Figure 3.16　The decade counter

gate, so the output from this gate goes LOW, thus taking the CLR terminals of all bistables LOW. Thus all the bistables are cleared and the counting of the next ten pulses can begin.

Investigation 3.3 The binary counter

The binary counter is such a useful device that it is available in a single chip (SN 7493). This contains four bistables connected as in Figure 3.9. The CLR terminals of each bistable are connected together and to the output of a NAND gate. This has two inputs R1 and R2 and if both of these are HIGH, the NAND gate output goes LOW and resets the counter. To get the device to count, at least one of these inputs must be connected to 0 V. The pulses to be counted are fed into input A from the pulse unit.

By connecting the B and D outputs to the NAND gate inputs the 'tens' counter can be produced exactly as before (Figure 3.18). Try connecting other outputs instead. Can you make a 'threes' counter, or a 'twelves' counter?

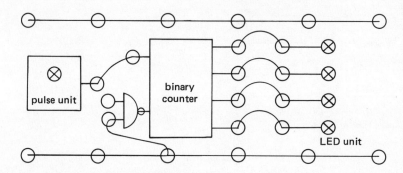

Figure 3.17 The single chip binary counter

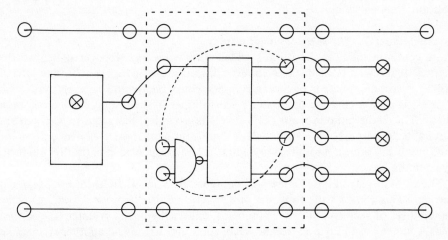

Figure 3.18 The decade counter

The 'tens' counter is so common that it too is made as a separate device (SN 7490). Its output is still a set of four binary digits which uses the binary code to count up to nine. These four-bit numbers are called **binary coded decimal (BCD)** numbers. Binary is not the easiest way of counting for humans, so to make life simpler, we need a way of converting this BCD number into its equivalent decimal number (0 to 9).

The decade display

A set of logic gates can be used to switch on any one of ten outputs (0 to 9), when the correct BCD input is fed into it. Figure 3.19 indicates how this could be done for the number 9. Inputs A and D must be HIGH. Inputs B and C must be LOW to make gate 1 and gate 2 go HIGH too. This causes gate 3 to go LOW, which 'pulls' the LED on.

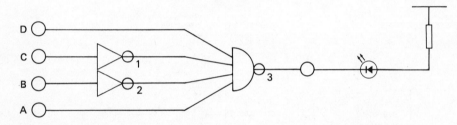

Figure 3.19 Decimal 9 decoder

The same is done for the other digits too, with each output connected to a different numbered LED. All the gates are put into a single chip with four inputs and ten outputs (SN 7441). This device was in common use a few years ago, for driving a ten-position decade display.

Investigation 3.5   The seven-segment display

More common today is the seven-segment display. It was discovered that all the decimal digits could be made up from seven lines as shown in Figure 3.20. This type of display is in common use in pocket calculators, petrol pumps and cash registers. Each segment is a light emitting diode and all the diodes in the display have a common anode. Thus if the cathode of any of the diodes is grounded, that segment will light up. A suitable decoder (SN 7447) turns a BCD number into the correct segment pattern for each number. Connect the units as in Figure 3.21 and display each of the digits in turn, by counting pulses.

The BCD display unit of Figure 3.21 contains the SN 7447 BCD to seven-segment decoder. This converts the four bits of a binary number between 0 and 9 into the required set of segments for that number. Connect the binary counter (rigged as a 'tens' counter') as in Figure 3.18 and begin counting. If you had another system like this, how could you connect it to the first sytem to count up to 99?

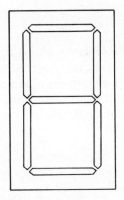

Figure 3.20 The seven-segment display

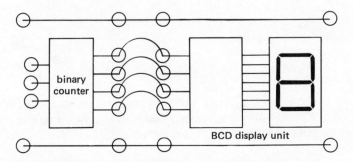

Figure 3.21 Counting with a seven-segment display

Automatic counting and timing

In Chapter 1 we looked at the astable and the monostable. The astable can be made to produce automatic pulses to drive the counter in Figure 3.21. The pulse unit has an output which produces one pulse approximately every second. Connect this output to the binary counter input to achieve automatic counting.

As you might expect the astable and monostable circuits are also available in integrated circuit form. The most useful of these is the 555-timer, which will perform both functions. A push-button switch is used to trigger the monostable. The output then goes HIGH for about one second and then goes LOW again. The length of time it remains HIGH (called its **time constant**) depends upon how long the capacitor takes to charge up. As we have already seen, this depends upon the size of the capacitor and the resistor through which it is charged. If the 555-timer is retriggered, when it reaches the end of its delay period, it produces a continuous stream of pulses like an astable. Again the period of the output pulses depends upon the capacitor and its associated resistor. *Adventures in Microelectronics* by T. Duncan shows several applications of this device.

Memory

We have already seen that a bistable can be used to remember or store a single bit of data. A whole row of eight bistables can thus be used to store the whole of an eight-bit number, with each bit stored in a different bistable (Figure 3.22). A set of eight bistables like this is called a byte. (This same word is used in microcomputing to describe how big a memory microcomputers have.)

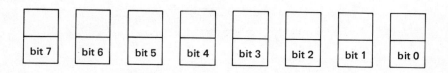

Figure 3.22 A memory device

Each bit of the byte has a different value (in the same way that the two 9s in the decimal number 959 have different values). The most significant bit (MSB) is worth 128, whereas the least significant bit is worth only 1 in decimal. The values of each bit are as follows:

Bit position	Byte	Value
7	1000 0000	128
6	0100 0000	64
5	0010 0000	32
4	0001 0000	16
3	0000 1000	8
2	0000 0100	4
1	0000 0010	2
0	0000 0001	1

Notice the funny way that computer scientists count! Instead of the first bit position (least significant bit) being called number one, it is called number nought. This can be very confusing until you get used to it (for instance, there are eight chapters in this book, numbered 0 to 7).

A microcomputer stores information in its memory, one piece in each byte. Since the information can only be a binary number from 0000 0000 to 1111 1111, it is clear that it must be coded in some way. We have already used the binary code for numbers from 0 to 15, but there are many other possible codes. A popular one is **ASCII**, which allows letters of the alphabet, the decimal digits and other keyboard characters, such as commas to be encoded. Here are a few examples:

Character	ASCII code	Decimal value
A	0100 0001	65
B	0100 0010	66
C	0100 0011	66
9	0011 1001	57
0	0011 0000	48
?	0011 1111	63
space	0010 0000	32
.	0010 1110	46

It is thus quite easy to see how a microcomputer can store text such as pages of a book or names and addresses. Each character is stored in a different byte in the computer's memory.

We have already discussed how each memory location (byte) has a unique address, so that the data it contains can be passed to a microprocessor. If the microprocessor wants to fetch the data inside byte number 1100 0111, say, it puts the address 1100 0111 onto the address bus. This opens the gates from byte number 1100 0111 and the data in this byte passes onto the data bus.

In a typical microcomputer each byte will have eight bits, so that the data bus will be eight bits wide. The address bus will be sixteen bits wide, giving a possible 65 536 different addresses.

Investigation 3.4   The SN 7489 memory unit

We can investigate the process with a very simple memory device, the SN 7489. Its address bus is only four bits wide, giving sixteen possible addresses and each data byte is also four bits wide. We can thus use the switch units and LED indicators to investigate it.

In this investigation you are acting on behalf of the microprocessor (Figure 3.23). First set the address switches to select the desired address. Then set the data switches to

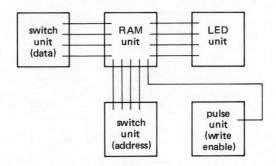

Figure 3.23   The memory unit

decide what data is to be stored in the memory. Then switch the **R/W input (read/write)** to write and press the push button switch to enable the memory. This causes the data to be written into the addressed location (that is, the byte whose address was selected). This data will remain in the memory until it is changed, or until the power is switched off. Try loading different data into different locations.

To read the data that you have stored, the R/W switch should be switched to read and the address bus should be set up to the desired address. Then, when the enable switch is pressed, the data in the addressed location will be displayed by the LEDs. This type of memory is called **read/write memory** although it is more commonly called **RAM** (which stands for **Random Access Memory**).

Now connect the binary counter to the address bus of the memory as in Figure 3.24. The addresses can now be produced one after the other (sequentially). The push button switch also provides the enable pulse at the same time. The data in any location can be seen at the four LED indicators, when the address of that location is selected. When the unit is first connected to the power supply, the locations will probably contain random numbers. So when the push button is pressed repeatedly (with R/W switched to read) the LEDs will flash at random. Now go back to the circuit of Figure 3.23 and load each location with something meaningful. Here are a few examples:

1   Load 0000 into the location at address 0000, load 0001 into the location at the address 0001, load 0010 into the location at the address 0010, and so on. This will result in binary numbers being seen on the LEDs when you return to the circuit of Figure 3.24.
2   Load 0001 into location 0000, load 0010 into location 0001, load 0100 into location 0010, load 1000 into location 0011. Then begin again with 0001 in location 0100 and so on. When this data is output in sequence it will clearly produce a shift register.
3   Load the following data into the successive locations 0000 to 1111:
    1000,1000,1000,1000,1000,1100,1100,1100
    0010,0010,0010,0010,0010,0100,0100,0100
    What does the result remind you of?

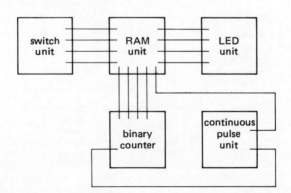

Figure 3.24   Automatic address selection

Now think up data sequences of your own and then try them out with the circuit of Figure 3.24.

The microprocessor

It can be seen that this method of storing a sequence of data is quite a powerful one. The same circuits were used to produce traffic lights, a binary counter and a shift register. This is unlike Investigation 3.2, where the circuits had to be taken apart each time to change the way they work. Thus the same microprocessor can go into a motor car, a dishwasher, a teddy bear and a microcomputer. It is only the sequence of data (the instructions) that need to be changed each time. Because the same microprocessor is used, it can be produced very cheaply in large quantities. This is why microelectronics is having such a powerful impact on the world.

Because you are not likely to have a spare microprocessor lying around, (even if you did, it would be very difficult to use on its own) we shall use the microprocessor inside a microcomputer. This is what Chapter 5 is about.

4   Analogue systems

'...and being so many different sizes in a day is very confusing.'
(Lewis Carroll, *Alice's Adventures in Wonderland*)

Introduction

This chapter deals with another aspect of microelectronics. We shall study the properties and uses of operational amplifiers and look at the analogue computer and its applications. In Chapter 5 we shall see how the same sort of problems can also be solved with digital computers. This topic cannot really be understood without a good mathematical knowledge, but analogue techniques are such an important part of microelectronics that they must be included somewhere in a school course. I have tried to avoid the traditional mathematical approach and have relied on description and analogy instead. At the end of this chapter is a section showing how analogue voltages can be converted into digital signals and vice versa. This allows digital computers to make measurements in the laboratory, a most important application of microelectronics.

Alternating voltages

Analogue systems are often concerned with alternating voltages and currents. Examples are the electric currents in a telephone wire, the signals picked up by a tape recorder head, the voltages fed into a loudspeaker and the radio waves transmitted by a broadcasting station. Such voltages vary in a regular way with time. The voltage–time graph of a typical alternating voltage is shown in Figure 4.1.

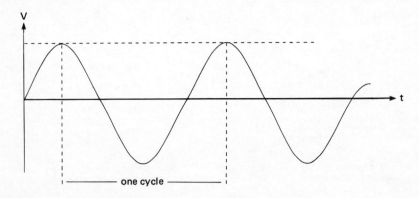

Figure 4.1   An alternating voltage

Frequency

The actual voltage changes from a peak to a trough and back to the next peak in a regular way; this is called a **cycle.** The number of cycles completed in each second is called the **frequency** of the alternating voltage. A high frequency goes through many cycles in one second; a low frequency goes through few cycles per second. Frequency is measured in hertz (Hz), which is another name for cycles per second.

In most analogue systems the frequency of the alternating voltage does not change as it goes through the system. The frequency of the output voltage is usually the same as the input voltage. There are, however, two important ways in which the input and the output voltages can be different; in **amplitude** or **phase.**

Amplitude

Since an alternating voltage is changing all the time, it is a little difficult to describe how big it is. This problem is overcome by referring to its maximum or peak voltage. Thus an alternating voltage may go from +5 V to –5 V and back to 5 V during each cycle. We could describe this as having a peak voltage of 5 V. Another name for this is **amplitude.** This gives us a way of comparing the input and output voltages of an analogue system. For example in an amplifier the output voltage would be greater than the input voltage. By dividing the peak output voltage by the peak input voltage we get a measure of the amount of amplification, called the **voltage gain** of the amplifier (Figure 4.2).

In practice this statement is not quite true. An amplifier can only amplify alternating voltages up to some maximum frequency. Above this frequency the voltage gain of the amplifier is reduced and will eventually become less than one. At this point the input voltage is greater than the output voltage; the amplifier has ceased to amplify!

Phase

It is also possible for the input and output voltages to differ in phase. **Phase** is the term used to describe whether the voltages rise and fall at exactly the same time, or whether they are out-of-step (or as we say, out-of-phase). Figure 4.3A shows the input and output voltages exactly in phase and Figure 4.3B shows them in anti-phase (exactly out-of-phase). These are the most common cases to occur.

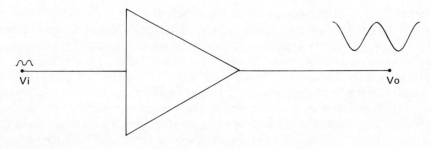

Figure 4.2   An amplifier

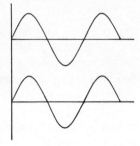 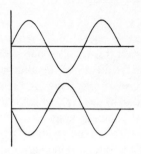

Figure 4.3   A In phase   B Out-of-phase

A simple voltmeter cannot be used to measure alternating voltages, nor can it show the phase difference between two alternating voltages. Instead we use a cathode ray oscilloscope (CRO) with two traces. This can display the waveforms of both an input and an output voltage at the same time. Their frequencies, phases and amplitudes can all be compared. The practical investigations in this chapter require such a dual-trace (or a double-beam) oscilloscope. We shall also need a way of producing alternating voltages at different frequencies and amplitudes, that is an oscillator.

The voltage divider again

We saw in Chapter 0 that the voltage divider is a linear network. The ratio of the output voltage to the input voltage is a constant; it does not depend on the frequency, the amplitude or the phase of the alternating voltages. Figure 4.3A shows how the input and output voltages are related to each other. Note that the output voltage goes up and down at the same time as the input voltage (that is, in phase with it). To compare the amplitudes of the two voltages we measure their peak voltages. The ratio of these voltages depends on the size of the two resistors. With the values quoted in Figure 4.4, we would expect this ratio to be about .25. If we kept the peak input voltage the same (say at 5 V) and changed the frequency, we would not expect this ratio to change.

Investigation 4.1   The voltage ratio of the voltage divider
Connect the oscilloscope to the voltage divider as shown in Figure 4.4, so that channel one displays the input voltage and channel two displays the output voltage. Feed a small alternating voltage from the oscillator to the input of the voltage divider network. Keep the frequency of the oscillator at 500 Hz, change the peak input voltage over the range 0 V to 5 V and measure the peak output voltage each time. In principle this is exactly the same as Investigation 1.2. The voltage characteristics of this circuit are also the same; the ratio of the input and output voltages is a constant (about .25). The graph (Figure 4.5) shows how the output voltage varies with the input voltage; a linear relationship.

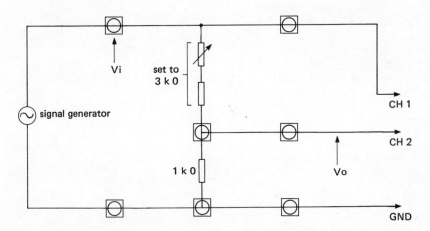

Figure 4.4 Measuring alternating voltages

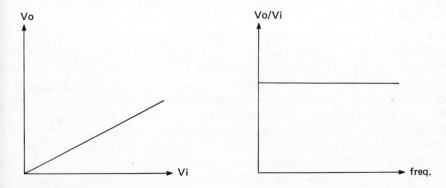

Figure 4.5 The voltage characteristics
of the voltage divider network

Figure 4.6 Frequency characteristics
of the voltage divider network

Now keep the input voltage fixed at a peak value of 3 V. Note how the output voltage changes as the frequency is increased. You should see that it does not change; it is frequency independent. The same would happen if the input voltage were 1 or 2 V. The voltage ratio of the output voltage to the input voltage can be found by measuring the amplitude of the output voltage and the amplitude of the input voltage on the CRO and dividing the one by the other. The graph (Figure 4.6) shows how this voltage ratio changes with frequency.

Note that in all these measurements the output voltage is always in-phase with the input voltage. This is unlikely to be true for the other circuits we shall be investigating.

Investigation 4.2   The low-pass filter

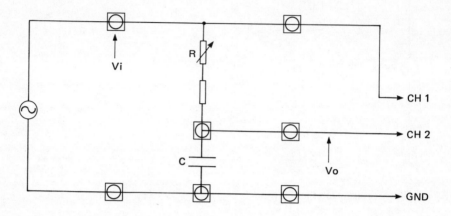

Figure 4.7   The low-pass filter

Replace the resistor R2 by a 0.1 microfarad capacitor, C. Now the characteristics will be quite different, because the capacitor has a different 'resistance' at different frequencies.

The simplest way to think about the capacitor is as a variable resistor, whose resistance changes with frequency. Actually it is more accurate to say the **impedance** of the capacitor changes with frequency. Impedance is the alternating equivalent of resistance and we reserve the word 'resistance' for proper resistors. At low frequencies the impedance is large, but as the frequency increases this impedance gets less. The size of the capacitor is measured in microfarads and this too affects its impedance. For any given frequency the impedance Z of the capacitor decreases as the capacitance C increases. Thus if the capacitor replaces R2 in the voltage divider network, we would expect it to have the following effects. If the frequency is fixed at some value, the voltage ratio should be constant, so the graph of output voltage against input voltage should be linear (Figure 4.8).

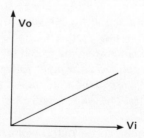

Figure 4.8   Voltage characteristics of the low-pass filter

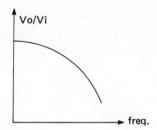

Figure 4.9 Frequency characteristics of the low-pass filter

Secondly if the input voltage is fixed and the frequency is changed, the impedance of the capacitor will decrease which is like reducing the resistance of R2 in the voltage divider. The output voltage will go down. Thus the voltage ratio of this circuit will decrease as the frequency rises. The graph showing how the voltage ratio changes with frequency is shown in Figure 4.9.

You can now see why it is called a low-pass filter. It allows the low frequencies to pass through, but the high frequencies are blocked. To observe these properties, carry out an investigation similar to that of 4.1. Measure the voltage characteristics and the frequency characteristics and plot them on a graph. At the same time you should note that the input and output voltages of the low-pass filter do not remain in-phase at all frequencies. At the lower frequencies the two voltages are in-phase but as the frequency is raised they get more and more out-of-phase.

Investigation 4.3   The high-pass filter
Change the relative positions of the capacitor and the resistor and you will produce the high-pass filter (Figure 4.10). This can be done by turning the voltage divider unit upside-down and changing over the terminals. As its name suggests, this circuit allows

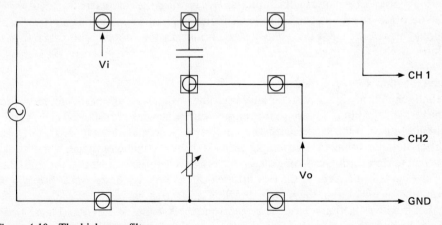

Figure 4.10   The high-pass filter

high frequencies to pass through, but not the lower frequencies. It is left to you to carry out this exercise, since it is the same as Investigation 4.2. Note in this case that the input and output voltages are now in-phase at high frequencies and get more and more out-of-phase as the frequency is reduced. Can you work out why the circuit behaves in this way?

Investigation 4.4　The Wein bridge network

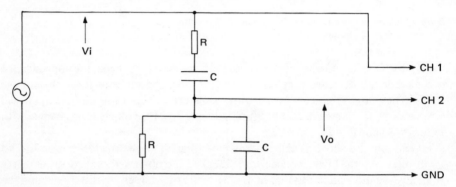

Figure 4.11　The Wein bridge network

The Wein bridge network (Figure 4.11), which is developed from the Wein bridge (used in frequency measurement) is a very important one in electronics (later we shall use it to produce an oscillator). It looks like a combination of the high-pass and the low-pass filters. Investigate it in the same way that those circuits were studied, by looking at the voltage and the frequency characteristics.

The important feature of this circuit is the phase relation between the input and output voltages. Note that there is only one frequency at which the input and the output voltages become exactly in-phase. This is called the **characteristic frequency** of the network. See if you can find the characteristic frequency of your network. You should also note that at this characteristic frequency the voltage ratio is exactly one third.

Investigation 4.5　The diode
All the circuits investigated so far have been linear; that is, at any particular frequency the ratio of the input voltage to the output voltage has been constant. The following circuits are non-linear, because the devices they contain behave differently for different input voltages. An example of this is the semiconductor diode, which allows current to flow through it in one direction only. It is helpful to think that the resistance of the diode is different in the two different directions. In the *forward* direction its resistance is low, but in the *reverse* direction it is very high.

For this investigation we use the Y-plates and the X-plates of the CRO (Figure 4.12). This allows us to plot graphs on the CRO screen. Unfortunately the X-plates may not

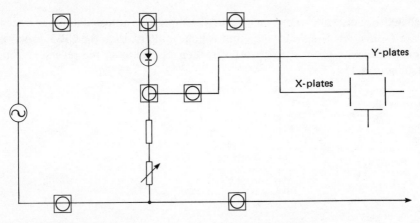

Figure 4.12 Measuring current–voltage characteristics of a diode

have any amplitude (gain) control and if too big a voltage is applied, they will saturate and give a false picture. The best way is to increase the voltage applied to the X-plates gradually until the graph is just wide enough to fill the screen. The gain of the Y-plates can then be adjusted to fill the screen in the vertical direction too.

With a non-linear device it is useful to find out how its resistance varies with the applied voltage. Again the voltage divider network is invaluable for this. The resistance of R2 in the above circuit does not change with the voltage across it, so this voltage is directly proportional to the current flowing through it. Thus the Y-plates of the CRO will display the current flowing through this resistor, which is the same as the current flowing through the diode (or any other device in its place).

The X-plates measure the voltage applied to the diode *and* resistor. But if we choose R2 to have a small resistance compared with the diode, it is a reasonable approximation to say that the X-plates measure the voltage across the diode. The above arrangement will thus display a graph of current against voltage for the device in the circuit.

The investigation is easy, once the CRO has been set up. At a frequency of about 500 Hz the input voltage is gradually raised from zero until the CRO trace just fills the

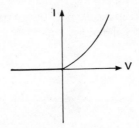

Figure 4.13 Current–voltage characteristics of the diode

screen in the X-direction. Then the gain on the Y-plates is adjusted until the trace just fills the Y-direction also. Since the input voltage is alternating, the CRO displays the current–voltage graph in the forward direction as well as in the reverse direction, giving Figure 4.13.

Rectification

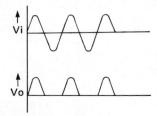

Figure 4.14   The rectifying property of the diode

A most useful application of the diode is rectification, the turning of an alternating voltage to a direct voltage. The arrangement in Figure 4.12 is used with the current through the resistor measured at the Y2-plates of the CRO. The Y1 trace now displays the input voltage and the Y2 trace displays the output voltage, which thus consists of a series of pulses in one direction only. This is rectified alternating voltage. Before it can be used in place of a battery it needs to be smoothed to get rid of the humps. A method for doing this is given in Chapter 6. This shows a circuit for the 5 V supply which is needed for the digital investigations in this book.

Investigation 4.6   The zener diode
Repeat Investigation 4.5 using a 3 V zener diode instead of the ordinary diode (Figure 4.15). You should obtain a CRO trace like the one shown in Figure 4.16.

These characteristics are just like those of the ordinary diode in the forward direction and also like them in the reverse direction up to a point. This point is called the breakdown voltage of the zener diode. A reverse voltage greater than the breakdown voltage causes the diode to start conducting again. This property is very useful for stopping a voltage from exceeding a certain value. The output from the rectifier in the previous investigation is not the steady 5 V d.c. that a power supply should be, it is made like this by a voltage regulator. Inside this voltage regulator is a zener diode, which is used to keep the output voltage constant, even though the input voltage is changing. This is how the power supply described in Chapter 6 is made.

Figure 4.15   Symbol for the zener diode

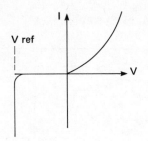

Figure 4.16 Current–voltage characteristics of the zener diode

The operational amplifier

In Chapter 1 we looked at the d.c. properties of the operational amplifier or op.amp. as we called it. To handle alternating voltages an op.amp. needed two power supplies, positive and negative. For its d.c. properties it was possible to use a single 5 V power supply only. The dual power supply can, however, be obtained from a 5 V supply with a special voltage converter (see Chapter 6). This supply is connected to the op.amp. as shown in Figure 4.17.

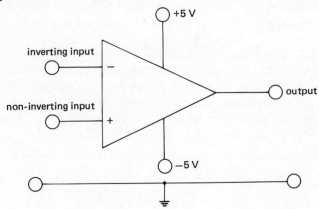

Figure 4.17 The basic operational amplifier

The two inputs to the op.amp. are called the inverting input and the non-inverting input. These names come from the fact that an input voltage applied to the inverting input becomes an output that is exactly out-of-phase with it. The same voltage applied to the non-inverting input produces an output that is exactly in-phase. The same feedback circuit used in Figure 1.24 can still be applied, so that the voltage output of this op.amp. is still given by

$$Vo = V1 / f$$

where f is the feedback factor $R2/(R1 + R2)$.

Investigation 4.7   The op.amp. as an amplifier

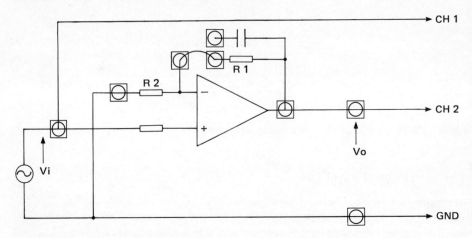

Figure 4.18   The op.amp. as an amplifier

Measure the voltage gain of the op.amp. circuit at different frequencies as shown in Figure 4.18. Note especially how the voltage gain falls off at higher frequencies.

Investigation 4.8   The Wein bridge oscillator

The simple amplifier circuit can be used with the Wein bridge network to produce a sine wave oscillator (Figure 4.19). It works as follows. The Wein bridge network produces a whole range of frequencies called **electrical noise,** which are caused by the random motion of the electrons in the wires. Let us consider one of these frequencies

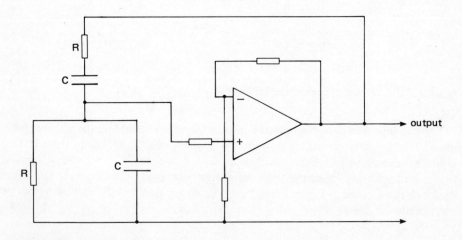

Figure 4.19   The Wein bridge oscillator

and call it a 'signal'. This signal is fed into the non-inverting input of the op.amp., and it emerges amplified and in-phase from the output of the op. amp. From there it is fed back into the Wein bridge network and emerges again to go to the non-inverting input of the op. amp. The whole process is thus repeated. But the Wein bridge network will change the phase of the signal, so that on the second time round it will be slightly out-of-phase with its previous time round. Eventually this will cause the signal to be exactly in anti-phase with itself, so it will effectively cancel itself out!

At one particular frequency which is determined by the sizes of the resistors and the capacitors, the phase of the signal does *not* change as it goes through the network. This **characteristic frequency,** as it is called, will be amplified every time round, so it will be selectively favoured and will eventually become the dominant species; the system will oscillate at the characteristic frequency.

There does have to be a careful balancing act to maintain a steady sine wave output. The amplitude must not become too great, otherwise the output will become a square wave and the output will become **digital,** simply switching on and off. On the other hand, if the gain of the amplifier is too low, the Wein bridge will take more energy out of the system than the op.amp. is putting in and the oscillations will not be maintained. A fine balance can be achieved by including two zener diodes in the feedback circuit placed back-to-back. At low voltages one or other of these diodes will be in the reverse direction and will not conduct, so they will have no effect. At higher voltages the breakdown voltage of the diodes will be reached, so they will start to conduct. This will reduce the effective value of the feedback resistor (R1), thus reducing the gain. The overall amplitude will therefore be restricted to the breakdown voltage of the zener diodes.

Finally, a practical Wein bridge amplifier needs some means of adjusting its frequency. This is achieved by making the resistors of the network into variable resistors and including a rotary switch to change the values of the capacitors.

Investigation 4.9   The op.amp. as an inverting amplifier

In the applications described above we used the op.amp. as an amplifier by providing feedback to the inverting input and by connecting the input signal to the non-inverting input. The op.amp. amplified the difference in voltage between the two inputs. It is equally possible to connect the input signal to the inverting input, provided we fix the other input at some convenient voltage. The obvious choice for this voltage is half-way between +5 V and −5 V, that is, at 0 V as in Figure 4.20.

The way the op.amp. works, has not been changed by these new arrangements, the output voltage is still given by the formula:

$$Vo = G \times (V1 - V2)$$

However, since V1 is now zero, this reduces to

$$Vo = -G \times V2$$

Unless the op.amp. is driven into saturation (+5 or −5 V), it is not possible for the point X in this circuit to be very different from 0 V, it is in fact called the **virtual earth.**

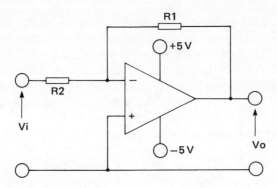

Figure 4.20 The inverting amplifier

The voltage at one end of the resistor network (R1 and R2) is Vo and at the other end it is Vi, and the voltage in th middle is zero. One side of the voltage divider is R2 and the other is R1, so it seems reasonable that the ratio R1/R2 is the same as the ratio Vo/Vi, which is true, except for the inverting effect. The correct formula is

$$Vo = -Vi \times (R1/R2)$$

or

$$Vo = -N \times Vi,$$

where N = (R1/R2).

Since we are only concentrating on the input and output voltages, it seems unnecessary to draw in the extra features of the power supply lines and the non-inverting input. We know that these have to be included each time, so we do not need to show them. This gives us a simpler diagram (Figure 4.21), which concentrates on the essential details of each individual circuit.

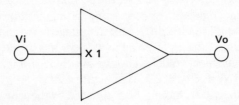

Figure 4.21 The analogue multiplier

We can now see a use for this circuit. Apart from the negative sign, which just means that the output is in anti-phase with its input, the output voltage is the input voltage multiplied by a constant. This number, called the **multiplying factor,** is determined by the values of R1 and R2 in Figure 4.20.

Investigation 4.10   The analogue multiplier

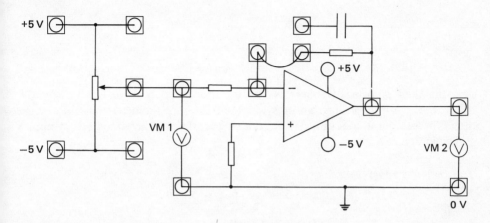

Figure 4.22   Practical connections for the analogue multiplier

Change the input voltage to −5 V, measured with the voltmeter VM1. Then measure the output voltage with VM2. Negative voltages are measured by swapping over the connections to the voltmeter. Repeat for different input voltages from −5 V to +5 V. Since we have chosen the ratio (R1/R2) to be about three, the output voltage should be three times the input voltage (apart from being in anti-phase). Is this true? Note also what happens to the output voltage when the input voltage is large. Does it saturate?

This analogue multiplier is actually a mathematical *computer*. It 'computes' by multiplying the input voltage by a constant number (provided the output voltage is kept within the limits of +5 to −5 V).

The potentiometer

The potentiometer is also a computer (Figure 4.23). It multiplies the input voltage by a constant number (although this number is always less than one). We can write the formula for the relationship between the input and output voltages of the potentiometer thus:

$$Vo = k \times Vi$$

Figure 4.23   The potentiometer as an analogue computer

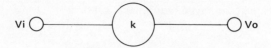

Figure 4.24   Symbol for the potentiometer in analogue computer systems

Note that there is no negative sign this time, the input and output voltages are in phase. As before, we want a diagram or symbol for the potentiometer that focuses the attention on what it does rather than on how it works. The potentiometer symbol is shown in Figure 4.24.

The analogue adder

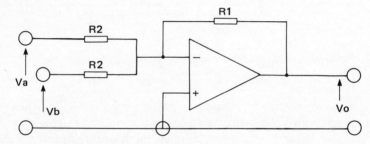

Figure 4.25   The analogue adder

Figure 4.25 shows an op.amp. with two resistors connected to the same input and with two input voltages Va and Vb. It seems obvious (and can be proved) that these two voltages are added together by the op.amp. The output voltage Vo will thus be the sum of the two input voltages (again remembering the negative sign).

$$Vo = -N \times (Va + Vb)$$

As before N is fixed by the resistors R1 and R2. The symbol for this adder is shown in Figure 4.26.

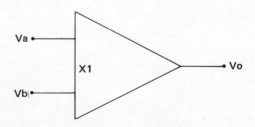

Figure 4.26   Symbol for the analogue adder

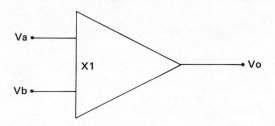

Figure 4.27 Symbol for the adder multiplier

By having different values for the R2 resistors, it is possible (and even usual) to combine the adder and the multiplier into one. Figure 4.27 shows the symbol for this **adder multiplier,** where input A is multiplied by one and input B is multiplied by five before adding them together.

The output from this circuit is

$$Vo = -(1 \times Va + 5 \times Vb)$$

Investigation 4.11   The analogue adder multiplier

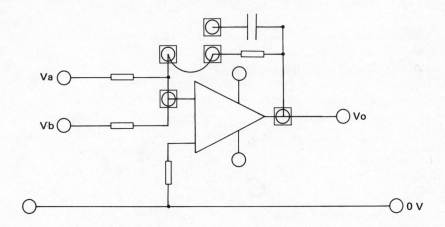

Figure 4.28 Practical connections for the analogue multiplier

The voltmeter has to measure three voltages for this investigation (Figure 4.28). Va and Vb are obtained from the + 5/−5 V supply using potentiometers to vary them. Check on the truth of the above formula for the output voltage. Does this formula still apply when Va and/or Vb are negative voltages too?

The integrator

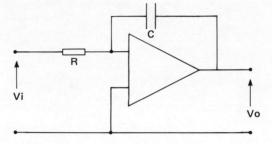

Figure 4.29 The integrator

If the feedback resistor in the multiplier is replaced by a capacitor, a very useful circuit is obtained called an **integrator** (Figure 4.29). It should be clear that the integrator will be frequency dependent, since the capacitor changes its impedance with frequency. This will affect the multiplying factor N, which will become less as the frequency increases. The system will in fact act like a low-pass filter. The integrator may also be an adder and also a multiplier, all at the same time, by choosing different values for the input resistors. Figure 4.30 shows the symbol for such an integrator and Figure 4.31 shows its practical realization.

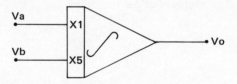

Figure 4.30 Symbol for the integrator adder multiplier

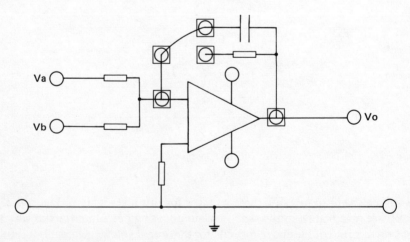

Figure 4.31 Practical connections for the integrator multiplier adder

Unfortunately it is very difficult to explain what an integrator does without advanced mathematics. We can only try to do it by using an analogy from the real world. Imagine a fly crawling up a window at a constant velocity u. (We use 'u' rather than 'v' to avoid getting confused with voltage.) After a time t the fly has moved a distance s given by

s = u x t

Suppose now that the fly is not moving with a constant speed, but moves quickly, then more slowly and then stops altogether. It is more difficult to work out how far the fly has moved. An integrator will do this calculation for us. If its input voltage represents the velocity of the fly, then the output voltage will represent the distance that the fly has moved. There has to be some point from which we measure this distance. This is the position of the fly when we start to measure the time. Similarly the integrator needs to know when to start its calculation. This is achieved with a short circuit across the capacitor, so that at the start the output voltage is zero (the fly is at the starting place). At the beginning of the calculation (the **integration**) this short circuit is removed. The output voltage will then gradually increase, which represents the movement of the fly from its starting place. It does not matter if the velocity of the fly changes, the integrator takes care of this and always shows how far the fly has gone.

Investigation 4.12 Constant velocity

Figure 4.32 shows how the integrator is made up from the op.amp. unit to **simulate** (or copy) the motion of the fly. The velocity of the fly is represented by the setting of the potentiometer. This can be anything from 5 to +5 metres per second (−5 to +5 V). You are advised to use speeds near to zero to begin with, otherwise the fly will reach the edge of the window before you get time to study it. The distance that the fly has moved

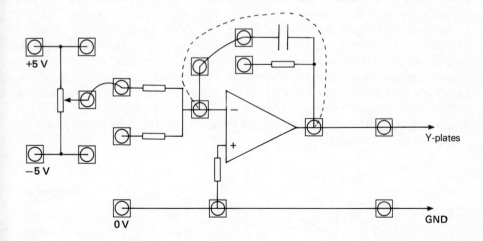

Figure 4.32 Practical connections for constant velocity

can be shown on a voltmeter, the bigger the voltage, the further it has gone. Another way is to connect the integrator output to a CRO (d.c. input) with the time-base switched off and the spot adjusted to the centre of the screen. When the short circuit across the capacitor is removed, the fly will crawl up or down the screen (depending upon whether the input voltage is negative or positive). Its speed is determined by the initial input voltage. Try this for several different settings of this velocity. You will need to bring the fly back to the start by short circuiting the capacitor each time.

The analogue computer

The system produced by combining op.amp. circuits together with potentiometers in this way is called an **analogue computer.** This is very useful for simulating the behaviour of different objects, particularly objects in complicated motions. As mentioned before, it is really necessary to know integral calculus before a full understanding of analogue computers can be obtained, we can only simulate a few simple motions otherwise. Each of the following simulations is a practical investigation also, but the practical connections are not shown each time. Only the symbolic connections are shown, and you are expected to work out for yourself what the practical connections to the op.amp. unit have to be. The best means of displaying the result in each case is the CRO. Sometimes the connections are best made to the X-plates and sometimes to the two sets of Y-plates on a dual-trace oscilloscope. This is indicated on each symbolic diagram. Where more than one integrator is used, it is necessary to remove the short circuit from both integrators at the same time. This instant represents the start of the motion.

Investigation 4.13 Free fall under gravity

If the input voltage is positive, the output voltage will be negative, representing a downward motion. A constant input voltage results in a steadily increasing distance as we saw before. However, the same system can be thought of like this. Let the input voltage represent gravity, which is a constant downward force. The output from the integrator then represents the way that the downward speed increases under the influence of this force. To put it another way, the input represents acceleration and the output represents the velocity resulting from that acceleration. If we then feed this velocity into a second integrator, the output from this will represent the distance as before (Figure 4.33). But it will now be motion under constant acceleration rather than motion under constant velocity. To ensure that the final direction of motion is downward, the initial acceleration should be downward too, that is, the first input voltage should be negative.

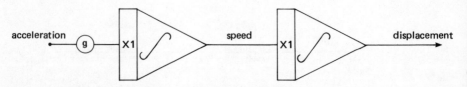

Figure 4.33   Practical details for acceleration due to gravity

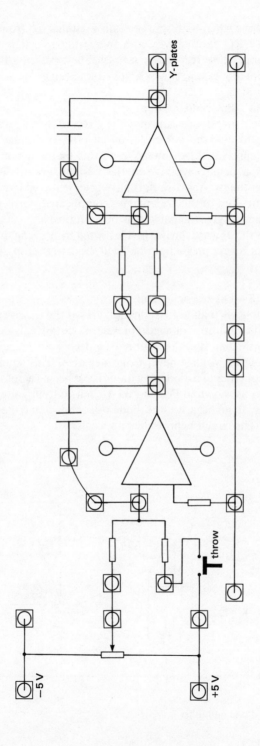

Figure 4.34 Practical details for the simulation of a projectile

The motion starts when both short circuits are removed from the two integrators. Notice that the CRO spot moves with increasing speed, it really does simulate accelerated motion. The effect can be seen even better if the CRO timebase is turned on so that the spot moves very slowly across the screen at the same time.

Investigation 4.14   Projectile motion
With our simulated gravity we can study the effect of throwing a ball into the air. To do this we want to give the system an initial positive voltage (that is, an upward acceleration to represent the throw). We do this by momentarily touching a push-button to apply a positive voltage to the first integrator. We ought to do this immediately after the two short circuits have been removed from the integrators, but the practical difficulties of this become too complicated. Instead we can just use the push-button switch to give the ball a new upward throw.

The motion of the upward thrown ball is started by pressing the push-button switch momentarily. If it is kept pressed, the ball will shoot to the top of the CRO screen and stay there.

Investigation 4.15   The bouncing ball
An odd thing about the ball in Investigation 4.14 is the way it can fall below ground level, since the final output voltage, representing distance, is negative. It is as if the person throwing the ball is at the bottom of a deep well! To simulate a real ball, we would like the output voltage never to go negative. This sounds difficult until we remember the properties of a diode. If a diode is connected across the feedback resistor R1 in a multiplier as shown in Figure 4.35, then its output voltage can never become negative. If it tries to go negative, the diode will conduct and the gain of the amplifier will fall to zero. The circuit behaves like a rectifier.

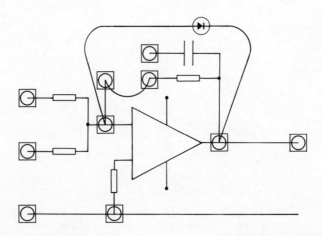

Figure 4.35   The diode multiplier

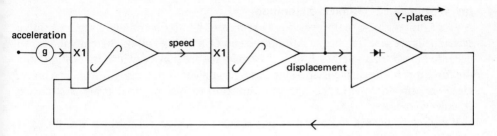

Figure 4.36 The bouncing ball

If this circuit is added to the end of our analogue computer as in Figure 4.36, it will behave as follows. The distance of the ball above ground is represented by the output voltage of the second integrator. This goes to the diode multiplier so that as long as the distance above ground is positive, the diode will be a low resistance and the output from the diode multiplier will be zero. But if the ball starts to fall below ground level, the input voltage to the diode multiplier will go negative. The diode will be reverse biased and will stop conducting so the gain of the diode multiplier will increase. The output voltage will thus go positive and is added back to the original input, which represents the force of gravity. The extra input represents a strong upward kick on the ball, so it bounces back up again.

Investigation 4.16   Friction

Our simulation is still not quite right. Firstly there is the difficulty of stopping the ball from bouncing too high every time. There ought to be some control over this. We can control the size of the acceleration due to gravity with the potentiometer, P1. A second potentiometer, P2, allows us to control the bounce too. A third potentiometer, P3, allows us to add a frictional force proportional to the speed of the ball (Figure 4.37). With these extra potentiometers it is possible to simulate a true free-fall, resulting in the **terminal velocity** being reached. Since this frictional force has to be proportional to the velocity of the ball, we use the output from the first integrator, which represents velocity.

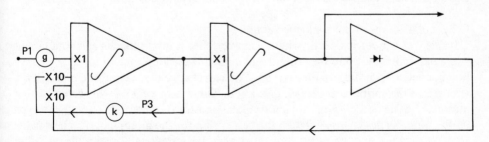

Figure 4.37 Adding a frictional force

Investigation 4.17   Simulated vibrations

A very simple change to the previous system turns it into the simulation of a vibrating system (Figure 4.38). A heavy bob on the end of a spring will oscillate up and down because of two forces acting upon it. These forces are gravity (which is constant) and the force due to the spring itself. This force gets bigger as the spring is stretched more. However, the force is in the opposite direction to the way the spring is stretched (**Hooke's law**).

We already have a voltage that represents the distance by which the spring is stretched; this is the output of the second integrator. We cannot just feed this back to the first input (which represents force or acceleration), because it is in the same direction as the way the spring has been stretched. We need to convert it from a positive to a negative voltage. This is done by using a multiplier with a gain of −1. We then have a computer to simulate the motion of the mass on the end of the spring.

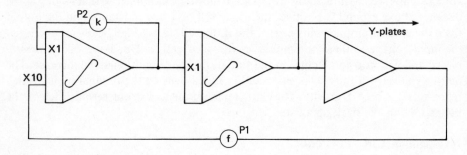

Figure 4.38   The simulated vibrator

The first potentiometer, P1, controls the force of gravity, which itself is proportional to the mass of the bob and the springiness of the spring. The second potentiometer, P2, controls the frictional forces acting on the system. Try this simulation yourself and see how each potentiometer has its own special effect. A push-button can be used to set the bob bouncing again after it has stopped.

Other applications of the analogue computer

Consider for a moment exactly what you have done. A few moments ago your circuit was a ball falling down to the ground and bouncing back up again. Now it is a heavy bob bouncing up and down on a spring. You can change the mass of the bob and the strength of the spring at the touch of a knob. Think how valuable this could be to a motor car designer. Without having to make and try out many different prototype motor cars, the designer can design the best spring for the motor car. The best value for its springiness and the best sort of shock absorber (**frictional force**) could be found much more easily.

Although the digital computer can carry out investigations of this type in an entirely different way, the use of analogue computers often gives a cheaper solution. In many cases analogue and digital computers work together in the solution of problems, a combination which gives a **hybrid computer.** To do this there have to be ways for the digital computer and the analogue system to exchange information. It is to this topic that we now turn.

Digital to analogue conversion

Microprocessors are *digital* devices that expect their data as HIGH or LOW voltage levels. Thus it is quite impossible for a microprocessor to produce *all* voltages in a given range. The best that can be done is to produce a set of voltages in discrete steps. However these steps may be sufficiently close together so as to be acceptable as a continuous range. The process is known as **digital to analogue conversion.** Figure 4.39 demonstrates how a **digital to analogue converter (DAC)** can be achieved with an op.amp.

The op.amp. is an adder multiplier and each of its eight input voltages is multiplied by a number that is proportional to the decimal value of its bit position, as follows:

least significant bit	0000 0001	1
	0000 0010	2
	0000 0100	4
	0000 1000	8
	0001 0000	16
	0010 0000	32
	0100 0000	64
most significant bit	1000 0000	128

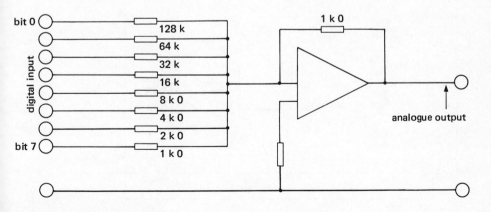

Figure 4.39   An op.amp. DAC

In practice it is difficult to obtain an accurate set of resistors for this circuit. In any case, it only works if each line has exactly the same output voltage. This is not true for most digital circuits (after all, they are only bothered about being HIGH or LOW). More reliable DACs therefore convert each line into a standard voltage set by an external or internal **reference voltage.**

A popular DAC is the ZN 425. This operates on the 'ladder' principle, using the HIGH and LOW voltages from the bits to *switch* resistors into or out of the summing amplifier circuit. Each step in the ladder, working from the **most significant bit (MSB)** towards the **least significant bit (LSB)** halves the effective voltage. Each bit at logic 1 is connected to the reference, which is usually fixed at 2.5 V, so all logic 1 bits start from the same level. The voltage of the LSB is halved a total of seven times, so that it ends up at 1/128th of the voltage from the MSB.

Investigation 4.18   The DAC unit

The ZN 425 requires eight inputs and this is a little complex. Our DAC unit (Figure 4.40) only uses the four most significant bits, which is good enough for a demonstration. The actual current output from the ZN 425 itself is rather limited, so a voltage follower is introduced to buffer the ZN 425 from anything that is connected to this output. This buffer does not amplify the voltage, its main purpose is to increase the amount of current that it will source.

Connect the four inputs of the DAC (Figure 4.40) to the four-switch unit and connect the DAC output to a 0 to 5 V voltmeter. Use this arrangement to check on the linearity of the DAC. Set the switches to each of the binary numbers 0000 to 1111 in turn and measure the DAC output voltage for each. Then plot a graph of this output voltage against its corresponding decimal number from 0 to 15. You should obtain a straight line graph that increases by about 0.25 V per bit.

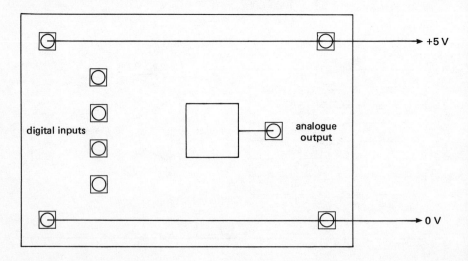

Figure 4.40   The ZN 425 DAC

In books, which are planned as sequels to this one (for example, *The BBC microcomputer in science teaching,* we shall make much more use of this device for creating voltages with different waveforms. Then we shall use all eight inputs, which will give an output of about 15 mV per bit. On a CRO this will look almost as if we are able to produce any voltage in the range 0 V to 4 V. For some purposes, though, even this is not good enough and engineers then use a twelve-bit DAC to get extra *resolution.*

Investigation 4.19 Programmed waveforms
In Chapter 3 we looked at a sixteen address, four-bit byte memory unit and noted how it could produce a sequence of binary numbers automatically. We can now feed these numbers into our DAC to produce a programmed waveform. First write the binary numbers for each of the following waveforms into the memory unit. (Note that these numbers are actually specified as decimals.) Then switch the memory unit to read and connect it to a binary counter and astable unit as described in Chapter 3 (Figure 4.41). Cycle through the numbers and observe the result from the DAC output with a CRO.

Binary address	Waveform			
	Sine	Triangular	Ramp	Square
0000	8	0	0	0
0001	11	2	1	0
0010	13	4	2	0
0011	14	6	3	0
0100	15	8	4	0
0101	14	10	5	0
0110	13	12	6	0
0111	11	14	7	0
1000	8	14	8	15
1001	5	12	9	15
1010	3	10	10	15
1011	2	8	11	15
1100	1	6	12	15
1101	2	4	13	15
1110	3	2	14	15
1111	5	0	15	15

Analogue to digital conversion

Investigation 4.20 Ramp ADC
The reverse process (turning an analogue voltage into a binary number) is more complicated. One possible way is to use the DAC in conjunction with the differential amplifier we studied in Investigation 1.17 (Figure 4.42). The voltage to be measured is connected to the non-inverting input of the op.amp. unit. The DAC output is

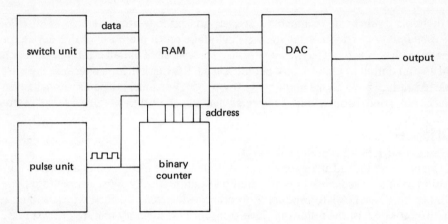

Figure 4.41 Programmed waveforms

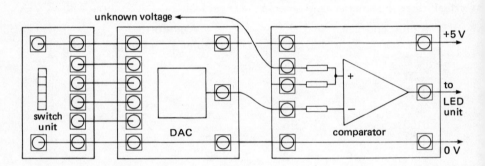

Figure 4.42 A demonstration ADC

connected to the inverting input. The op.amp. output is connected to an LED indicator.

Start with the switches at 0000 and make the unknown voltage about 2 V with the potentiometer. The DAC output will be zero and less than this unkown voltage, so the op.amp. output will be HIGH (and the LED will be on). Now increment (increase by one) the binary number by changing the switches and continue to do this until the LED goes out. This happens because the DAC output has reached the point where it just exceeds the unknown voltage. The switches thus show the binary number that is the nearest above the value of the unknown voltage; the latter has be measured. In practice this whole process is carried out automatically (Figure 4.43). Note how digital and linear devices combine to produce the total system.

Such a useful device is a clear candidate for a single chip. Many such ADCs do exist and some can convert voltages very quickly indeed. They do not, however, use this method of conversion, which has several serious faults. Firstly the ADC has to count up from zero for every conversion it undertakes. An eight-bit ADC needs 255 steps to

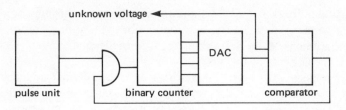

Figure 4.43 An automatic ADC

count up to its maximum, which is slow. Also, the conversion time is greater for larger voltages, because the ADC has to count further.

A more efficient method of conversion starts from the *most* significant bit and works down. If the DAC output exceeds the unknown voltage when any bit is set, then that bit is set back to zero and the next lowest bit is tried. If the DAC output is still less than the unknown voltage when a particular bit is set, then that bit is left set. At the end of the conversion, therefore, the binary equivalent of the unknown voltage is obtained. The advantage of this system is that an eight-bit ADC requires eight steps to convert any voltage. This is not only faster than the other (ramp) method, but also it always takes the same time, so that the user knows exactly when the result of the conversion is available. A powerful ADC based on this principle is the ZN 448, with the very fast conversion time of 10 microseconds. *The BBC microcomputer in science teaching* gives details of this ZN 448 device, which is easily connected to most microcomputers.

Investigation 4.20   The ADC

As with the DAC unit the ADC unit does not use all eight bits for this demonstration (Figure 4.44). It has been designed to measure 0.25 V per bit, the same as the DAC. Connect the ADC input to the potentiometer and the 0 V to 5 V voltmeter, and connect

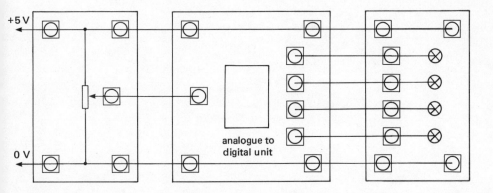

Figure 4.44 The ADC unit

the ADC digital outputs to the LED indicator unit. Increase the input voltage slowly and see what happens to the LEDs. You should observe that they are counting up in binary. Take readings on the voltmeter each time the least significant LED changes and thus test the linearity of this unit.

The potentiometer may be replaced with the voltage divider unit and different transducers may be introduced. This would give a digital light meter with the photocell and a digital thermometer with the thermistor. Nearly all digital meters convert the physical quantity being measured into a binary number in this way.

5 Microcomputer control

'The question is,' said Humpty Dumpty, 'which
is to be Master – that's all.'
(Lewis Carroll, *Through the Looking Glass*)

Interfacing a microcomputer

Most control applications use **two-state** devices. An electric light switch can be up or
down. An electromagnetic relay can be on or off. A valve can be open or closed.
Digital electronic systems are used to switch such devices on or off. Although quite
complex, a microcomputer is still only another digital system, so it is possible to use a
microcomputer to control the above devices. It can switch lamps, relays, motors and
valves on or off.

This is not a normal function of a microcomputer and it has not been designed
specifically to do this. Consequently the current needed to switch on these devices may
be larger than that provided by the microcomputer output. There has to be some
interface between the microcomputer and the device being switched, to boost the
switching current to the correct levels.

A microcomputer can also be used to detect whether any particular two-state device
is in its on or its off state. Here, the switching voltages involved may be different for
each device, so some interface must be used to change the voltage levels of the device to
the levels acceptable to the microcomputer.

In digital electronics we are only concerned with two-state devices, ones that can be
switched on or off. Generally, to switch a device on, we send a HIGH voltage to its
input. To turn it off, we send a LOW voltage. 'HIGH' and 'LOW' are obviously not
the same for different devices, here are a few examples:

Device	On	Off
light emitting diode	1.2 V	0.5 V
torch bulb	3.0 V	1.5 V
electromagnetic relay	5.0 V	2.0 V
silicon transistor	0.7 V	0.5 V
TTL integrated circuit	2.4 V	0.4 V

To remove this uncertainty about what is HIGH and what is LOW, engineers use
TTL logic levels. TTL stands for **transistor transistor logic;** it is a particular standard
used in the electronics industry. A TTL HIGH voltage is between 2.4 and 5.5 V, which,
as you can see, will switch on all the above devices. A TTL LOW voltage is between 0.4
and 0 V, which will switch all these devices off. A HIGH voltage is also called a logic
level 1 and a LOW voltage is called a logic level 0.

Connections to a microcomputer are made through its **user port.** This is described in detail in the follow-up books to this (for example, *The BBC microcomputer in science teaching*), but here we shall just use it without explaining how it works. A logic board or a two-input board should be connected to the user port and all investigations in this chapter will be done with these. The design of these boards and the method of connecting them to the user port are described in Chapter 6. In the case of the Apple, BBC, ZX 81 and ZX Spectrum microcomputers the power supply to these logic boards comes from the microcomputer itself. The PET user port does not do this and a separate 5 V power supply needs to be connected to the boards.

The two-input board

The two-input board (Figure 5.1) has two input sockets and a transistor driven LED to indicate the logic state of the output. It can be used by the microcomputer to simulate each of the standard logic gates introduced in Chapter 2. Once the board has been connected to the microcomputer in the manner discussed in the next chapter, Program 5.1 (LOGIC GATES) should be loaded and run. This program is listed in five different versions (for each of our chosen microcomputers) at the end of this chapter.

The inputs of the two-input board are labelled A and B. When the program is run it asks which logic gate is to be simulated (the choice is AND, OR, NOT, NAND, NOR, EXCLUSIVE-OR or EQUIVALENCE. After the selection is made (by pressing one of keys 1 to 7) the screen displays a diagram of the board, indicates the current logic states of the inputs and the output, displays the appropriate truth table and highlights the particular line of this truth table which is currently being implemented.

The input logic levels can be changed by connecting them to the 5 V terminals (red), which makes them go HIGH. Or they may be connected to the black 0 V terminals, which makes them go LOW. Unconnected inputs float HIGH in the normal TTL way. When the logic level of either input is changed, the display also changes accordingly.

This program has been found to give a good introduction to the principles of logic gates. It also illustrates the way that a *programmable* device, like a microcomputer, can be used to produce different Boolean functions under the control of a program.

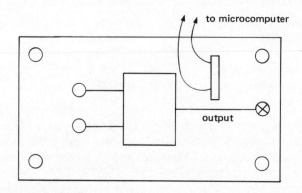

Figure 5.1 The two-input board

The logic board

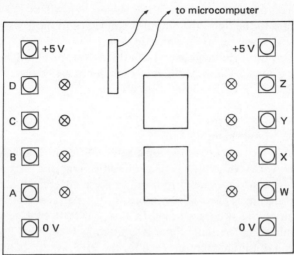

Figure 5.2   The logic board

The logic board (Figure 5.2) has four input terminals labelled A, B, C and D and four output terminals labelled W, X, Y and Z. All terminals are connected to LED indicators to show their logic state. When a terminal is HIGH, its LED is on, when a terminal is LOW, its LED is off. The LEDs connected to A, B, C and D indicate the state of the inputs. These states are determined by the voltages at the input terminals, usually from some external device like a switch. The LEDs connected to W, X, Y and Z show the output logic levels. These are the levels chosen by the microcomputer. They do not depend upon the devices connected to the output terminals.

Investigation 5.1   Logic inputs

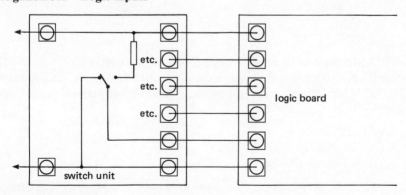

Figure 5.3   Switch inputs

133

The easiest way to create HIGH and LOW logic inputs is with switches. When a switch is to the left, its output is connected to the 0 V line, so it will be LOW, or at logic 0. When the switch is to the right, the output is connected to the 5 V line through the 1 kilohm resistor, so it will be HIGH, or at logic 1.

Connect the outputs from the four-switch unit to the logic board inputs as in Figure 5.3. Make sure that the 5 V and 0 V lines of each board are connected too. When the switches are operated, the LEDs should go on and off.

Investigation 5.2   Logic gates

In Chapter 2 we looked at hard-wired logic gates. Different Boolean functions were made by connecting NAND gates together. The advantage of a programmable system is that the *same* circuit can be used to produce these different functions, under the control of the program. This can be demonstrated with program 5.1, but the more powerful version of this program called LOGIC TUTOR enables several different gates to be simulated at the same time. It is listed as Program 5.2 in five different versions at the end of the chapter, one each for the PET, Apple, BBC, ZX 81 and ZX Spectrum microcomputers. This program use the logic board and makes each of the four outputs into different Boolean functions of the inputs. For example, in Figure 5.4, output W has been set up as the AND combination of inputs A and B. The program allows you to set up any output as a particular logical combination of any inputs. The best way of explaining it is to do this example.

When the program is RUN, it asks which Boolean function is required, thus:

BOOLEAN FUNCTION
SELECT ONE OF THESE FUNCTIONS BY TYPING ITS NUMBER
THEN PRESS <RETURN>
1   AND
2   OR
3   NOT
4   EXCLUSIVE-OR
5   EQUIVALENCE
6   NAND
7   NOR

Select the AND function by pressing key 1 followed by the RETURN key. On the ZX Spectrum the ENTER key is used and on the ZX 81 the NEW-LINE key is used instead of a RETURN key. The program will then ask which output you want to provide this function.

WHICH OUTPUT ?
ENTER ONE OF W, X, Y OR Z
THEN PRESS <RETURN>

Select output W by pressing key W followed by the RETURN key. The program now asks:

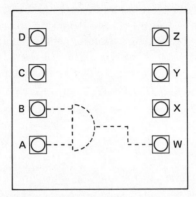

Figure 5.4   Using the logic board for Boolean functions

HOW MANY INPUTS ?
ENTER 1, 2, 3 OR 4 AND THEN PRESS <RETURN>

Select two inputs by pressing key 2 followed by RETURN. Finally the program asks:

WHICH INPUTS ?
ENTER TWO OF A, B, C OR D
THEN PRESS <RETURN>

Select inputs A and B, by typing A follwed by RETURN and then B followed by RETURN. The screen clears to display a symbol for the AND gate, indicating your chosen inputs and outputs. At the same time the logic board is set up to behave in the same way. Output W will become the AND combination of inputs A and B. The display will show the logic state of the inputs and the outputs as a 1 or as a 0.

Connect the logic board to the switches as in Figure 5.3 and then investigate this AND combination by switching inputs A and B HIGH and LOW. Note what happens to the LEDs associated with W and with A and B. First make both inputs LOW and check on the W output. Then make input B HIGH and input A LOW. Then make input A HIGH and input B LOW. Finally make both inputs HIGH. Note that the screen display also shows the logic state of these inputs and outputs (although there is a short delay after they are changed, because the program is in BASIC and is rather slow).

It is possible to summarize all the information about the AND gate with its truth table

Input A	Input B	Output
LOW	LOW	LOW
LOW	HIGH	LOW
HIGH	LOW	LOW
HIGH	HIGH	HIGH

The HIGH and LOW in this table are voltages. Note that the output from the AND gate is only HIGH if both of its inputs are HIGH. If only one or neither inputs are HIGH, then the output is LOW. The reason for calling this an AND gate is now clear. The output is HIGH only if both input A *and* input B are HIGH.

There are two other ways of writing the truth table for the AND gate, as follows:

A	B	Output	A	B	Output
0	0	0	L	L	L
0	1	0	L	H	L
1	0	0	H	L	L
1	1	1	H	H	H

The H and L stand for HIGH and LOW voltages as before, and the 1 and 0 have the same meaning: they are called logic 1 and logic 0 to avoid confusion with the numbers 0 and 1.

The NOT gate

Select the NOT function by entering key 3 when the menu is displayed. Make W the output for this function in the way described above. A NOT gate only has one input, so make this input A, by entering A as the required input.

A switch can be used to make this input HIGH or LOW and the LED can be used to see if the output is HIGH or LOW. Copy and complete this table

Input	Output (HIGH/LOW)
LOW	
HIGH	

You will notice that the output is always the exact opposite or inverse of the input, which gives this function its other name: the **INVERTER.**

The NAND gate

Now create the NAND function by selecting 6 on the menu. Set up W as the output and A and B as the inputs, exactly as for the AND function above. Two switches are needed to provide the inputs to this NAND gate, called input A and input B. The LED indicators show the logic level of these inputs and of the NAND gate output. Try different combinations of inputs A and B and note the effect on the output each time. Copy and complete this table:

Input A	Input B	Output
LOW	LOW	
LOW	HIGH	
HIGH	LOW	
HIGH	HIGH	

The OR gate

Repeat, after selecting the OR function with key 2. Copy and complete this table:

Input A	Input B	Output
LOW	LOW	
LOW	HIGH	
HIGH	LOW	
HIGH	HIGH	

The NOR gate

Repeat after selecting the NOR function with key 7. Copy and complete this table:

Input A	Input B	Output
LOW	LOW	
LOW	HIGH	
HIGH	LOW	
HIGH	HIGH	

The EXLUSIVE-OR gate

Select the EXCLUSIVE-OR gate by entering key 4 from the menu. Copy and complete this table:

Input A	Input B	Output
LOW	LOW	
LOW	HIGH	
HIGH	LOW	
HIGH	HIGH	

The EQUIVALENCE gate

Select the EQUIVALENCE gate with key 5 and continue as before.

Input A	Input B	Output
LOW	LOW	
LOW	HIGH	
HIGH	LOW	
HIGH	HIGH	

In this investigation we have looked at several different types of logic gate. Each has its own truth table. The electronic symbols for these five gates are given in Figure 2.16. These symbols are used when drawing diagrams of digital systems.

Investigation 5.3 Programmable logic

In Chapter 2 we introduced a practical example – the garage doors problem. The solution to this problem was made up with two light-operated switches, each acting as an input to an AND gate. The AND output was used to open the garage doors and the doors were closed again afterwards by a switch outside the doors. In Chapter 2 we studied how to build up this digital system using integrated circuits. It is useful now to see what difference the microprocessor makes to the design of digital systems.

If the designer of this system wanted it to behave in a different way, he or she would have to design a new circuit. It is most unlikely that extra components could just be added on to the original circuit, the whole system would have to be re-made from the beginning. This is how digital systems were built in the 1960s and 70s, from combinations of separate integrated circuits. They were all wired together in the correct way to produce the desired function. Even if the system was sold in large numbers, each one had still to be built up separately on a printed circuit board, so that the different gates could be correctly wired together.

The microprocessor changes this, because, as we have seen, the same arrangement of components can be made to do different things merely by changing the program. The same microprocessor can thus be made to do many different things, from shearing sheep and controlling a power station to making a teddy bear speak and, of course, Space Invaders. Because the same microprocessor is used in each case, a very large number of them can be produced very cheaply.

Program 5.3 called LOGIC MAKER, is a variation of LOGIC TUTOR, that allows you to create your own Boolean functions. In order to do this the required function must be entered as part of the program, so it is helpful if you know a little about programming in BASIC to start with. Begin by connecting the logic board exactly as before and then load the program called LOGIC MAKER. This can be run to produce the logic function A AND B, which will appear at gate W and on the screen the inputs and outputs of the logic board will be displayed too.

To change the function, press key E, which will end the program, leaving lines 5000 to 5100 of the program displayed on the screen. You may now create any function of your own, provided it conforms to the syntax rules of BASIC and the ways we have already described for writing out Boolean functions.

Change the function in line 5010 to any other function (and remember to press <RETURN> to enter the new function). Then type RUN <RETURN> to re-run the program and it will now execute with your new function. For example:

```
5010   LET Z = (NOT A OR B)
```

or

```
5010   LET Z = NOT (NOT A AND NOT B)
```

The input variables should be A, B, C or D, which must be upper case letters (capitals) in every case. The final outputs are W, X, Y or Z as in the previous program. One difference between this program and LOGIC TUTOR is that the symbols for the gate will not appear on the screen. It is possible to use other variables, but you will not be able to find out what values they take. For example:

```
5010   LET T = NOT A AND B
5020   LET S = NOT B AND A
5030   LET Z = T OR S
```

This example also shows that it is possible to put in more than one line for the function, provided it does not have to work backwards. That is, you cannot put:

```
5010   LET Z = NOT T
5020   LET T = NOT B OR A
```

because T does not have its correct value in line 5010 until after line 5020 has been executed. On the BBC and Spectrum microcomputers this will cause the fatal error 'Variable not found'. A few more examples are given below, but the purpose of this program is to create your own functions and then see what you have produced. Do this by stepping through the truth table with the switches and noting the outputs in each case.

```
5010   LET Z = NOT (A OR B)
5010   LET Z = NOT (NOT A AND NOT B)
5010   LET Z = NOT (A AND B)
5010   LET Z = NOT (NOT A AND NOT B)
5010   LET Z = (NOT A AND B) OR (A AND NOT B)
```

Using the logic board for control

The microcomputer can be used to sense and control its environment. To do this it needs to be connected to various inputs, such as switches, photocells, thermometers etc. and also to different outputs such as motors, relays, heaters and the like. This area is so vast that it is the subject of a different book, the sequel to this. Three versions of it are planned, one for each of the ZX 81, ZX Spectrum and BBC microcomputers. In the rest of this chapter are some of the simpler ideas taken from these books, to illustrate what can be done. It is not possible here to explain how each program works, and only the program listings are given for each of the chosen microcomputers.

Before the user port of a microcomputer can be used, it may be necessary to define some lines as inputs and others as outputs. This is done through the **data direction register.** This is usually done, in the case of the PET, Apple and BBC microcomputers, with lines 10 and 100 of the program listings.

Each input or output of the logic board is connected to a different bit of the microcomputer user port. To refer to a particular input or output, the decimal value of its bit position must be used as follows:

PET, Apple and BBC microcomputers

Logic board	Bit	Decimal value
output Z	1000 0000	128
output Y	0100 0000	64
output X	0010 0000	32
output W	0001 0000	16
input D	0000 1000	8
input C	0000 0100	4
input B	0000 0010	2
input A	0000 0001	1

ZX 81 and ZX Spectrum microcomputers

Logic board		Bit	Decimal value
input D	output Z	0000 1000	8
input C	output Y	0000 0100	4
input B	output X	0000 0010	2
input A	output W	0000 0001	1

Outputs

To switch any particular output on, its decimal value must be written into the address of the user port. This address is different for each microcomputer as follows. The principle will be described for each microcomputer separately.

PET: the user port address is 59471

POKE 59471,0 (in binary: 0000 0000) sends all outputs LOW.
POKE 59471,32 (0010 0000) sends output X HIGH and Z, Y and W LOW.
POKE 59471,112 (0111 0000) sends outputs W, X and Y HIGH and Z LOW.
POKE 59471,240 (1111 0000) sends all outputs HIGH.

Apple: the user port address is 49344

POKE 49344,0 (in binary: 0000 0000) sends all outputs LOW.
POKE 49344,32 (0010 0000) sends output X HIGH and Z, Y and W LOW.
POKE 49344,112 (0111 0000) sends outputs W, X and Y HIGH and Z LOW.
POKE 49344,240 (1111 0000) sends all outputs HIGH.

BBC microcomputer: the user port address is 65120
BBC BASIC uses the ? operator instead of POKE

?65120 = 0 (in binary: 0000 0000) sends all ouputs LOW.
?65120 = 32 (0010 0000) sends output X HIGH and Z, Y and W LOW.
?65120 = 112 (0111 0000) sends outputs W, X and Y HIGH and Z LOW.
?49344 = 240 (1111 0000) sends all outputs HIGH.

ZX Spectrum: the user port address is 95 or 63
Spectrum BASIC uses OUT instead of POKE.

OUT 63,0 (in binary: 0000 0000) sends all outputs LOW.
OUT 63,2 (0000 0010) sends output X HIGH and Z, Y and W LOW.
OUT 63,7 (0000 0111) sends outputs W, X and Y HIGH and Z LOW.
OUT 63,15 (0000 1111) sends all outputs HIGH.

ZX 81: the user port address is 22500

POKE 22500,0 (in binary: 0000 0000) sends all outputs LOW.
POKE 22500,2 (0000 0010) sends output X HIGH and Z, Y and W LOW.
POKE 22500,7 (0000 0111) sends outputs W, X and Y HIGH and Z LOW.
POKE 22500,15 (0000 1111) sends all outputs HIGH.

Inputs

The logic state of an input is found by reading the user port address. To determine which lines are HIGH and which are LOW, the decimal number obtained must be decoded to find which bits are HIGH and which are LOW using the above table. If more than one line is HIGH, the value obtained will be a combination of the corresponding numbers above. Thus if the value is 6, this means that inputs B and C are HIGH and the others are LOW. Similarly if the value is 3, this means that the inputs A and B are HIGH and the others are LOW. The statements for each microcomputer are as follows:

PET: LET N = PEEK(59471)

Apple: LET N = PEEK(49344)

BBC microcomputer: LET N = ?65120

ZX 81: LET N = PEEK 22500

ZX Spectrum: LET N = IN 63

The decimal value returned in N may be decoded to see which inputs are HIGH and which are LOW. For the programs in this chapter, we have not bothered to do this, but details are given in the sequel to this book.

Controlling the environment

Since each input can be connected to some external two-state device, such as a temperature sensor, magnetic switch, float switch, proximity switch etc., the microcomputer can be used to detect its environment and to respond to it in different ways. We thus have a way of communicating information to the microcomputer other than via the keyboard.

Using these ideas with the logic board, it is possible to simulate all of the digital electronics of Chapters 2 and 3. In fact LOGIC TUTOR has already repeated most of Chapter 2. With a microcomputer it is easy to solve standard electronics problems in logic, for example:

Design a circuit to be used in a quiz with four competitors. After the question is asked, the first competitor to press his or her switch has a light come on to signify the fact. After the first switch has been pressed no other lamp may come on, even if the first competitor then releases the switch.

One of the great advantages of microelectronics is that problems of this complexity are now extremely easy to solve, all that is needed is a BASIC program. The programs that follow exemplify these ideas. Note that the listings that follow have different versions for each of the chosen microcomputers.

Increasingly in industry, the solution of problems in electronics is becoming one of adapting a general purpose circuit to a specific application, rather than designing a special circuit each time. Traditional control technology in schools has laid emphasis upon the second of these approaches: the hardware solution. The user port of the microcomputer can be used to demonstrate the more modern software approach. The first programs described below demonstrate how to control the LEDs of the logic board. Note that in each case the electronic circuit remains the same, it is only the programs that are changed.

Investigation 5.4   Switching outputs

This investigation enables you to switch the outputs on or off in any sequence. The first example shows how any outputs can be switched on in any order for different intervals of time. For this program it is assumed that the top three LEDs on the right side of the logic board (Z, Y and X) represent the red-amber-green traffic lights. After running this program try switching on the output LEDs in a different sequence with different delays.

PET:

```
  1   REM CONTROL EXAMPLE 1 – TRAFFIC LIGHTS
 10   DDR = 59459 : REM DATA DIRECTION REGISTER
 20   PRT = 59471 : REM USER PORT
100   POKE DDR,240:REM SET UP INPUTS AND OUTPUTS
110   POKE PRT,128:REM SWITCH ON RED
120   FOR T = 1 TO 4000:NEXT T:REM LONG DELAY
130   POKE PRT,128 + 64:REM SWITCH ON RED AND AMBER
140   FOR T = 1 TO 800:NEXT T:REM SHORT DELAY
150   POKE PRT,32:REM SWITCH ON GREEN
160   FOR T = 1 TO 4000:NEXT T:REM LONG DELAY
170   POKE PRT,64 :REM SWITCH ON AMBER
180   FOR T = 1 TO 800:NEXT T:REM SHORT DELAY
200   GOTO 110:REM REPEAT SEQUENCE
```

Apple:

```
  1   REM CONTROL EXAMPLE 1 – TRAFFIC LIGHTS
 10   DDR = 49346 : REM DATA DIRECTION REGISTER
 20   PRT = 49344 : REM USER PORT
100   POKE DDR,240:REM SET UP INPUTS AND OUTPUTS
110   POKE PRT,128:REM SWITCH ON RED
120   FOR T = 1 TO 4000:NEXT T:REM LONG DELAY
130   POKE PRT,128 + 64:REM SWITCH ON RED AND AMBER
140   FOR T = 1 TO 800:NEXT T:REM SHORT DELAY
150   POKE PRT,32:REM SWITCH ON GREEN
160   FOR T = 1 TO 4000:NEXT T:REM LONG DELAY
170   POKE PRT,64 :REM SWITCH ON AMBER
180   FOR T = 1 TO 800:NEXT T:REM SHORT DELAY
200   GOTO 110:REM REPEAT SEQUENCE
```

BBC microcomputer:

```
  1   REM CONTROL EXAMPLE 1 – TRAFFIC LIGHTS
 10   DDR = 65122:REM DATA DIRECTION REGISTER
```

```
20    PRT = 65120 : REM USER PORT
100   ?DDR = 240:REM SET UP INPUTS AND OUTPUTS
110   ?PRT = 128:REM SWITCH ON RED
120   FOR T = 1 TO 8000:NEXT T:REM LONG DELAY
130   ?PRT = 128 + 64:REM SWITCH ON RED AND AMBER
140   FOR T = 1 TO 1500:NEXT T:REM SHORT DELAY
150   ?PRT = 32:REM SWITCH ON GREEN
160   FOR T = 1 TO 8000:NEXT T:REM LONG DELAY
170   ?PRT = 64 :REM SWITCH ON AMBER
180   FOR T = 1 TO 1500:NEXT T:REM SHORT DELAY
200   GOTO 110:REM REPEAT SEQUENCE
```

ZX 81:

```
1     REM CONTROL EXAMPLE 1 – TRAFFIC LIGHTS
20    REM USER PORT ADDRESS
21    LET P = 22500
100   REM SWITCH ON RED
110   POKE P,8
120   PAUSE 250
130   REM SWITCH ON RED AND AMBER
140   POKE P,12
150   PAUSE 100
160   REM SWITCH ON GREEN
170   POKE P,2
180   PAUSE 250
190   REM SWITCH ON AMBER
200   POKE P,4
210   PAUSE 100
220   REM REPEAT SEQUENCE
230   GOTO 110
```

ZX Spectrum:

```
1     REM Control example 1 – Traffic lights
10    REM Define outputs
20    LET red = 8
30    LET amber = 4
40    LET green = 2
50    LET outputs = 63
100   REM traffic lights sequence
110   OUT outputs,red
120   PAUSE 250
130   OUT outputs,red + amber
140   PAUSE 100
150   OUT outputs,green
```

```
160   PAUSE 250
170   OUT outputs,amber
180   PAUSE 100
500   GO TO 100
```

The next program switches on the LEDs in an orderly way, by adding 16 (or 1) to the number written into the user port address each time. The LEDs thus count up in binary.

PET:
```
  1   REM CONTROL EXAMPLE 2 – BINARY COUNTER
 10   DDR = 59459 : REM DATA DIRECTION REGISTER
 20   PRT = 59471 : REM USER PORT
100   POKE DDR,240:REM SET UP INPUTS AND OUTPUTS
110   FOR R = 0 TO 240 STEP 16
120   POKE PRT,R
130   FOR T = 1 TO 500:NEXT T:REM SHORT DELAY
140   NEXT R
150   GOTO 110
```

Apple:
```
  1   REM CONTROL EXAMPLE 2 – BINARY COUNTER
 10   DDR = 49346 : REM DATA DIRECTION REGISTER
 20   PRT = 49344 : REM USER PORT
100   POKE DDR,240:REM SET UP INPUTS AND OUTPUTS
110   FOR R = 0 TO 240 STEP 16
120   POKE PRT,R
130   FOR T = 1 TO 500:NEXT T:REM SHORT DELAY
140   NEXT R
150   GOTO 110
```

BBC microcomputer:
```
  1   REM CONTROL EXAMPLE 2 – BINARY COUNTER
 10   DDR = 65122:REM DATA DIRECTION REGISTER
 20   PRT = 65120 : REM USER PORT
100   ?DDR = 240:REM SET UP INPUTS AND OUTPUTS
110   FOR R = 0 TO 128 STEP 16
120   ?PRT = R
130   FOR T = 1 TO 1000:NEXT T:REM SHORT DELAY
140   NEXT R
150   GO TO 110
```

ZX 81:
```
  1   REM CONTROL EXAMPLE 2 – BINARY COUNTER
 20   LET P = 22500
100   FOR R = 0 TO 15
```

```
120   POKE P,R
130   PAUSE 50
140   NEXT R
150   GOTO 110
```

ZX Spectrum:

```
  1   REM Control example 2 – A binary counter
 20   REM Define outputs
 50   LET outputs = 63
100   REM switch lamps
110   FOR i = 0 TO 15
120   OUT outputs,i
130   PAUSE 50
140   NEXT i
500   GO TO 100
```

One common chip used in microelectronics is the shift register, which is simulated by this example. It is particularly useful for converting **serial data,** where the eight bits are sent one after another along a single pair of lines, into **parallel data,** where all eight bits are sent simultaneously along a set of eight separate lines.

PET:

```
  1   REM CONTROL EXAMPLE 3 – SHIFT REGISTER
 10   PRT = 59471:REM USER PORT
 20   DDR = 59459:DATA DIRECTION REGISTER
100   POKE DDR,240:REM SET UP INPUTS AND OUTPUTS
110   R% = 4
120   R% = R% + R%
130   IF R% > 200 THEN 110
140   POKE PRT,R%
150   FOR T = 1 TO 500:NEXT T:REM SHORT DELAY
160   GOTO 120
```

Apple:

```
  1   REM CONTROL EXAMPLE 3 – SHIFT REGISTER
 10   PRT = 49344:REM USER PORT
 20   DDR = 49346:DATA DIRECTION REGISTER
100   POKE DDR,240:REM SET UP INPUTS AND OUTPUTS
110   R% = 4
120   R% = R% + R%
130   IF R% > 200 THEN 110
140   POKE PRT,R%
150   FOR T = 1 TO 500:NEXT T:REM SHORT DELAY
160   GOTO 120
```

BBC microcomputer:

```
  1   REM CONTROL EXAMPLE 3 – SHIFT REGISTER
 10   DDR = 65122:REM DATA DIRECTION REGISTER
 20   PRT = 65120 : REM USER PORT
100   ?DDR=240:REM SET UP INPUTS AND OUTPUTS
110   R% = 4
120   R% = R% + R%
130   IF R% > 200 THEN 110
140   ?PRT=R%
150   FOR T=1 TO 500:NEXT T:REM SHORT DELAY
160   GOTO 120
```

ZX 81:

```
  1   REM CONTROL EXAMPLE 3 – SHIFT REGISTER
 10   LET P = 22500
100   POKE P,0
110   PAUSE 50
120   POKE P,1
130   PAUSE 50
140   POKE P,2
150   PAUSE 50
160   POKE P,4
170   PAUSE 50
180   POKE P,8
190   PAUSE 50
200   GOTO 100
```

ZX Spectrum:

```
  1   REM Control example 3 – A shift register
 20   REM Define outputs
 50   LET outputs = 63
100   REM switch lamps
110   OUT outputs,0
120   PAUSE 25
130   OUT outputs,1
140   PAUSE 25
150   OUT outputs,2
170   PAUSE 25
180   OUT outputs,4
190   PAUSE 25
200   OUT outputs,8
210   PAUSE 25
500   GO TO 100
```

Using these principles you should now be able to control any system you wish. For example the logic board outputs could be connected via relays to a mobile crane. One output might be connected to switch on a motor in the forward direction to lower an electromagnet. Another output could switch the power to this electromagnet to pick up a load. Another might drive the crane forwards and the fourth could drive it backwards. The distances travelled could be controlled by the length of time that the motor is switched on.

If such a system is tried out, you will discover one problem. A motor switched on for, say ten seconds, in the forward direction might cause the crane to travel say fifty centimetres. Ten seconds in the reverse direction produces a movement of say forty-five centimetres. So each sequence results in the crane ending up in a different place. What is missing is **feedback.** The microcomputer needs to know exactly where the crane has got to at any instant. This is the reason for providing the microcomputer with inputs.

Investigation 5.5   Using the inputs
The inputs to the logic board can be used to send information to the microcomputer. This program uses outputs Z, Y and X for the red, amber and green traffic lights, but adds another, connected to output W, which simulates the pedestrian wait lamp on a pelican crossing (Figure 5.5). The pedestrian request button of the crossing is simulated by momentarily closing (or opening) a switch connected to one of the inputs of the logic board. This simple arrangement allows for the pedestrian to request the traffic to stop, upon which, the traffic lights go through their sequence to red and the wait lamp then goes out to indicate that it is safe to cross. The program also shows how easy it is to flash an LED on and off.

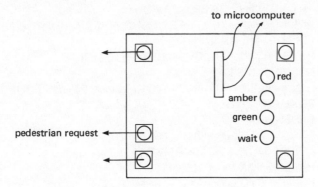

Figure 5.5   Pelican crossing

PET:
```
   1   REM CONTROL EXAMPLE 4 – PELICAN CROSSING
  10   DDR = 59459 : REM DATA DIRECTION REGISTER
```

```
 20   PRT = 59471 : REM USER PORT
100   POKE DDR,240:REM LAST FOUR LINES AS OUTPUTS,
      FIRST FOUR AS INPUTS
110   POKE PRT,32:REM GREEN TRAFFIC LIGHT
120   N = PEEK(PRT)
130   IF N = PEEK(PRT) THEN 130:REM WAIT FOR REQUEST
140   POKE PRT,48:REM GREEN TRAFFIC AND
      PEDESTRIAN WAIT LIGHTS
150   FOR T = 1 TO 2000:NEXT T :REM DELAY
160   POKE PRT,80:REM AMBER TRAFFIC AND
      PEDESTRIAN WAIT LIGHTS
170   FOR T = 1 TO 800:NEXT T :REM SHORT DELAY
180   POKE PRT,128:REM RED TRAFFIC LIGHT ONLY
190   FOR T = 1 TO 4000:NEXT T :REM DELAY
200   FOR I = 1 TO 20:REM FLASH AMBER AND
      PEDESTRIAN WAIT LIGHT
210   POKE PRT,80
220   FOR T = 1 TO 100:NEXT T
230   POKE PRT,0
240   FOR T = 1 TO 100:NEXT T
250   NEXT I
260   GOTO 110:REM RESTART SEQUENCE
```

Apple:

```
  1   REM CONTROL EXAMPLE 4 – PELICAN CROSSING
 10   DDR = 49346 : REM DATA DIRECTION REGISTER
 20   PRT = 49344 : REM USER PORT
100   POKE DDR,240:REM LAST FOUR LINES AS OUTPUTS,
      FIRST FOUR AS INPUTS
110   POKE PRT,32:REM GREEN TRAFFIC LIGHT
120   N = PEEK(PRT)
130   IF N = PEEK(PRT) THEN 130:REM WAIT FOR REQUEST
140   POKE PRT,48:REM GREEN TRAFFIC AND
      PEDESTRIAN WAIT LIGHTS
150   FOR T = 1 TO 2000:NEXT T :REM DELAY
160   POKE PRT,80:REM AMBER TRAFFIC AND
      PEDESTRIAN WAIT LIGHTS
170   FOR T = 1 TO 800:NEXT T :REM SHORT DELAY
180   POKE PRT,128:REM RED TRAFFIC LIGHT ONLY
190   FOR T = 1 TO 4000:NEXT T :REM DELAY
200   FOR I = 1 TO 20:REM FLASH AMBER AND
      PEDESTRIAN WAIT LIGHT
210   POKE PRT,80
220   FOR T = 1 TO 100:NEXT T
```

```
230   POKE PRT,0
240   FOR T = 1 TO 100:NEXT T
250   NEXT I
260   GOTO 110:REM RESTART SEQUENCE
```

BBC microcomputer:

```
  1   REM CONTROL EXAMPLE 4 – PELICAN CROSSING
 10   DDR = 65122:REM DATA DIRECTION REGISTER
 20   PRT = 65120 : REM USER PORT
100   ?DDR = 240:REM LAST FOUR LINES AS OUTPUTS,
      FIRST FOUR AS INPUTS
110   ?PRT = 32:REM GREEN TRAFFIC ON
120   N = ?PRT
130   IF N = ?PRT THEN 130:REM WAIT FOR REQUEST
140   ?PRT = 48:REM GREEN TRAFFIC AND
      PEDESTRIAN WAIT LIGHTS
150   FOR T = 1 TO 4000:NEXT T :REM DELAY
160   ?PRT = 80:REM AMBER TRAFFIC AND
      PEDESTRIAN WAIT LIGHTS
170   FOR T = 1 TO 1500:NEXT T :REM SHORT DELAY
180   ?PRT = 128:REM RED TRAFFIC LIGHT ONLY
190   FOR T = 1 TO 8000:NEXT T :REM DELAY
200   FOR I = 1 TO 20:REM FLASH AMBER AND
      PEDESTRIAN WAIT LIGHT
210   ?PRT = 0
220   FOR T = 1 TO 200:NEXT T
230   ?PRT = 80
240   FOR T = 1 TO 200:NEXT T
250   NEXT I
260   GOTO 110:REM RESTART SEQUENCE
```

ZX 81:

```
  1   REM CONTROL EXAMPLE 4 – PELICAN CROSSING
 20   LET P = 22500
100   REM SWITCH ON GREEN
110   POKE P,2
120   REM SAVE INPUT STATUS
130   LET N = PEEK P
140   REM WAIT FOR PEDESTRIAN REQUEST
150   IF N = PEEK P THEN GOTO 150
160   REM GREEN TRAFFIC AND PEDESTRIAN WAIT LIGHTS
170   POKE P,3
180   PAUSE 200
190   REM AMBER TRAFFIC AND PEDESTRIAN WAIT LIGHTS
200   POKE P,5
```

```
210   PAUSE 100
220   REM RED TRAFFIC LIGHT ONLY
230   POKE P,8
240   PAUSE 250
250   REM FLASH AMBER AND PEDESTRIAN WAIT LIGHT
260   FOR I = 1 TO 20
270   POKE P,5
280   PAUSE 20
290   POKE P,0
300   PAUSE 20
310   NEXT I
320   GOTO 100
330   REM RESTART SEQUENCE
```

ZX Spectrum:

```
  1   REM Control example 4 – Pelican crossing
 10   REM Define inputs and outputs
 20   LET red = 8
 30   LET amber = 4
 40   LET green = 2
 50   LET wait = 1
 60   LET outputs = 63
 70   LET inputs = 63
 80   LET off = 0
100   REM set lights at green and wait for pedestrian request
110   OUT outputs,green
120   PAUSE 1:LET status = IN inputs
130   PAUSE 1:IF status = IN inputs THEN GO TO 130
140   REM input status has changed
150   REM traffic lights sequence
160   OUT outputs,(green + wait)
170   PAUSE 150
180   OUT outputs,(amber + wait)
190   PAUSE 100
200   OUT outputs,red
210   PAUSE 250
220   REM flash amber
230   FOR c = 1 TO 10
240   OUT outputs,amber
250   PAUSE 20
260   OUT outputs,off
270   PAUSE 20
280   NEXT c
500   GO TO 100
```

Burglar alarm

One traditional electronic circuit is the burglar alarm. This can now be made far more versatile. The hard-wired version of Chapter 3 does not allow the owner to get out of the house without setting off the alarm. This program introduces a delay, during which the alarm will not operate. The owner has about ten seconds between switching on the system (i.e. starting the program) and the system's being active. The presence of a burglar can be simulated with a switch. The switch will have no effect for about ten seconds after the program starts.

PET:

```
  1  REM CONTROL EXAMPLE 5 – BURGLAR ALARM
 10  DDR = 59459 : REM DATA DIRECTION REGISTER
 20  PRT = 59471 : REM USER PORT
100  POKE DDR,240:REM LAST FOUR LINES AS OUTPUTS,
     FIRST FOUR AS INPUTS
105  POKE PRT,0:REM ALL LEDS OFF
110  FOR T = 1 TO 10000:NEXT T:REM DELAY
120  N = PEEK(PRT)
130  IF N = PEEK(PRT) THEN 130:REM WAIT FOR BURGLAR
140  FOR I = 1 TO 100
150  POKE PRT,240:REM ALL ALARM LIGHTS ON
160  FOR T = 1 TO 20:NEXT T :REM DELAY
170  POKE PRT,0:REM ALL LIGHTS OFF
180  FOR T = 1 TO 20:NEXT T
190  NEXT I
```

Apple:

```
  1  REM CONTROL EXAMPLE 5 – BURGLAR ALARM
 10  DDR = 49346 : REM DATA DIRECTION REGISTER
 20  PRT = 49344 : REM USER PORT
100  POKE DDR,240:REM LAST FOUR LINES AS OUTPUTS,
     FIRST FOUR AS INPUTS
105  POKE PRT,0:REM ALL LEDS OFF
110  FOR T = 1 TO 10000:NEXT T:REM DELAY
120  N = PEEK(PRT)
130  IF N = PEEK(PRT) THEN 130:REM WAIT FOR BURGLAR
140  FOR I = 1 TO 100
150  POKE PRT,240:REM ALL ALARM LIGHTS ON
160  FOR T = 1 TO 20:NEXT T :REM DELAY
170  POKE PRT,0:REM ALL LIGHTS OFF
180  FOR T = 1 TO 20:NEXT T
190  NEXT I
```

BBC microcomputer:

```
  1  REM CONTROL EXAMPLE 5 – BURGLAR ALARM
 10  DDR = 65122 : REM DATA DIRECTION REGISTER
```

```
 20   PRT = 65120 : REM USER PORT
100   ?DDR = 240:REM LAST FOUR LINES AS OUTPUTS,
      FIRST FOUR AS INPUTS
105   ?PRT = 0:REM ALL LEDS OFF
110   FOR T = 1 TO 10000:NEXT T:REM DELAY
120   N = ?PRT
130   IF N = ?PRT THEN 130:REM WAIT FOR BURGLAR
140   FOR I = 1 TO 20
150   ?PRT = 240:REM ALL ALARM LIGHTS ON
160   FOR T = 1 TO 200:NEXT T :REM DELAY
170   ?PRT = 0:REM ALL LIGHTS OFF
180   FOR T = 1 TO 200:NEXT T
190   NEXT I
```

ZX 81:

```
  1   REM CONTROL EXAMPLE 5 – BURGLAR ALARM
 20   LET P = 22500
100   REM ALL LEDS OFF
110   POKE P,0
120   REM DELAY TO ALLOW TIME TO LEAVE
130   PAUSE 500
140   REM SAVE STATUS OF INPUT
150   LET N = PEEK P
160   REM WAIT FOR BURGLAR
170   IF N = PEEK P THEN GOTO 170
180   REM FLASH ALARM LIGHTS
190   FOR I = 1 TO 100
200   POKE P,15
210   PAUSE 10
220   POKE P,0:REM ALL LIGHTS OFF
230   PAUSE 10
190   NEXT I
```

ZX Spectrum:

```
  1   REM Control example 5 – Burglar alarm
 10   REM Define inputs and outputs
 60   LET outputs = 63
 70   LET inputs = 63
 80   LET off = 0
 90   LET on = 15
 95   OUT outputs,off
100   REM delay initially
110   PAUSE 500
120   LET status = IN inputs
```

```
130    PAUSE 1:IF status = IN inputs THEN GO TO 130
140    REM Burglar is present
150    REM Alarm sequence
160    OUT outputs,on
170    PAUSE 10
180    OUT outputs,off
190    PAUSE 10
200    NEXT i
```

Investigation 5.6 Time measurement

The principle of measuring time intervals is as follows. The user port is read and stored in a memory location called status. The current state of the user port is then monitored continuously and compared with status. Normally it will be the same, but when it is different, this is because an input has been activated. The microcomputer's internal clock is then started and the new status of the user port is saved in status. When the user port again changes its status, the current contents of the microcomputer's internal clock are noted. The time interval involved can then be calculated and displayed.

Time intervals exceeding a few tenths of a second are measured quite satisfactorily in this way. This simple timer can replace the centisecond timers used in school laboratories in most instances. The usual problems over 'make to start', 'break to stop' are avoided, since the routine detects *any* change at the input. However accurate timing of short intervals is only possible using machine code routines.

PET:
The PET has a sixtieth of a second clock.

```
  1    REM CONTROL EXAMPLE 6 – A SIMPLE TIMER
 10    DDR = 59459 : REM DATA DIRECTION REGISTER
 20    PRT = 59471 : REM USER PORT
100    POKE DDR,240:REM LAST FOUR LINES AS OUTPUTS,
       FIRST FOUR AS INPUTS
110    N = PEEK(PRT)
120    IF N = PEEK(PRT) THEN 120
130    N = PEEK(PRT):REM INPUT HAS CHANGED
140    T = TI:REM START CLOCK
150    IF N = PEEK(PRT) THEN 150
160    REM INPUT HAS CHANGED AGAIN
170    PRINT "ELAPSED TIME = ";(TI–T)/60;" SECONDS"
```

Apple:
The Apple has no internal clock and simple timing methods are not possible. More advanced methods are discussed in *Microcomputers in Science Teaching*.

BBC microcomputer:

The BBC microcomputer has a centisecond timer.

```
1   REM CONTROL EXAMPLE 6 – A SIMPLE TIMER
10  DDR = 49346 : REM DATA DIRECTION REGISTER
20  PRT = 49344 : REM USER PORT
100 ?DDR,240:REM LAST FOUR LINES AS OUTPUTS,
    FIRST FOUR AS INPUTS
110 N = ?PRT
120 IF N = ?PRT THEN 120
130 N = ?PRT:REM INPUT HAS CHANGED
140 TIME = 0:REM START CLOCK
150 IF N = ?PRT THEN 150
160 REM INPUT HAS CHANGED AGAIN
170 PRINT "ELAPSED TIME = "; TIME/100;" SECONDS"
```

ZX 81:

The ZX 81 has a fiftieth of a second clock.

```
1   REM CONTROL EXAMPLE 6 – A SIMPLE TIMER
20  LET P = 22500
100 SAVE INPUT STATUS
110 LET N = PEEK P
120 REM WAIT FOR INPUT STATUS TO CHANGE
130 IF N = PEEK P THEN GOTO 130
140 REM INPUT HAS CHANGED
150 LET N = PEEK P
160 REM START CLOCK
170 POKE 16436,255
180 POKE 16437,255
190 IF N = PEEK PRT THEN GOTO 190
200 REM INPUT HAS CHANGED AGAIN
210 LET T = 65536 – 256*PEEK 16437 – PEEK 16436
220 PRINT "ELAPSED TIME = ";T/50;" SECONDS"
```

ZX Spectrum:

The ZX Spectrum has a fiftieth of a second clock.

```
1   REM Control example 6 – A simple timer
10  REM Define inputs
20  LET inputs = 63
30  PAUSE 1:LET status = IN inputs
100 REM wait for input status to change
110 PAUSE 1:IF status = IN inputs THEN GOTO 110
120 PAUSE 1:LET status = IN inputs
130 REM reset clock
140 POKE 23672,0
```

```
150   POKE 23673,0
160   POKE 23674,0
170   REM wait for input status to change again
180   PAUSE 1:IF status = IN inputs THEN GOTO 180
190   REM read clock
200   LET time1 = 65536*PEEK(23674) + 256*PEEK(23673) + PEEK(23672)
210   LET time2 = 65536*PEEK(23674) + 256*PEEK(23673) + PEEK(23672)
220   IF time1 > time2 THEN LET time2 = time1
230   PRINT "Time taken = ";time2/50;" seconds"
```

Investigation 5.7   Counting

The next example shows how the microcomputer can be used to count closures of a switch. In Chapter 3 we used a bistable to prevent contact bounce, but now we can overcome this problem with a software solution. The program senses a switch closure, waits for a while, and then checks to make sure that the switch is still closed. If not, then no count is made. If the switch is still closed, the program records the count and then waits until the switch is released again.

PET:

```
  1   REM CONTROL EXAMPLE 7 – AN INPUT COUNTER
 10   DDR = 59459 : REM DATA DIRECTION REGISTER
 20   PRT = 59471 : REM USER PORT
100   POKE DDR,240:REM LAST FOUR LINES AS OUTPUTS,
      FIRST FOUR AS INPUTS
110   N = PEEK(PRT):REM INITIALIZE SWITCH STATUS
120   LET C = 0 : REM INITIALIZE COUNTER
130   IF N = PEEK(PRT) THEN 130
140   REM INPUT HAS CHANGED
150   FOR T = 1 TO 10:NEXT T:REM DELAY TO DEBOUNCE SWITCH
160   IF N = PEEK(PRT) THEN 130:REM CHANGE IS NOT VALID
170   C = C + 1:REM CHANGE IS GENUINE
180   PRINT "CURRENT COUNT = "; C
190   IF N <> PEEK(PRT) THEN 190:REM WAIT FOR
      SWITCH TO BE RELEASED
200   GOTO 130
```

Apple:

```
  1   REM CONTROL EXAMPLE 7 – AN INPUT COUNTER
 10   DDR = 49346 : REM DATA DIRECTION REGISTER
 20   PRT = 49344 : REM USER PORT
100   POKE DDR,240:REM LAST FOUR LINES AS OUTPUTS,
      FIRST FOUR AS INPUTS
110   N = PEEK(PRT):REM INITIALIZE SWITCH STATUS
120   LET C = 0 : REM INITIALIZE COUNTER
130   IF N = PEEK(PRT) THEN 130
```

```
140   REM INPUT HAS CHANGED
150   FOR T = 1 TO 10:NEXT T:REM DELAY TO DEBOUNCE SWITCH
160   IF N = PEEK(PRT) THEN 130:REM CHANGE IS NOT VALID
170   C = C + 1:REM CHANGE IS GENUINE
180   PRINT "CURRENT COUNT = "; C
190   IF N <> PEEK(PRT) THEN 190:REM WAIT FOR
        SWITCH TO BE RELEASED
200   GOTO 130
```

BBC microcomputer:

```
  1   REM CONTROL EXAMPLE 7 – AN INPUT COUNTER
 10   DDR = 65122 : REM DATA DIRECTION REGISTER
 20   PRT = 65120 : REM USER PORT
100   ?DDR = 240:REM LAST FOUR LINES AS OUTPUTS,
        FIRST FOUR AS INPUTS
110   N = ?PRT:REM INITIALIZE SWITCH STATUS
120   LET C = 0 : REM INITIALIZE COUNTER
130   IF N = ?PRT THEN 130
140   REM INPUT HAS CHANGED
150   FOR T = 1 TO 100:NEXT T:REM DELAY TO DEBOUNCE SWITCH
160   IF N = ?PRT THEN 130:REM CHANGE IS NOT VALID
170   C = C + 1:REM CHANGE IS GENUINE
180   PRINT "CURRENT COUNT = "; C
190   IF N <> ?PRT THEN 190:REM WAIT FOR
        SWITCH TO BE RELEASED
200   GOTO 130
```

ZX 81:

```
  1   REM CONTROL EXAMPLE 7 – AN INPUT COUNTER
 20   LET P = 22500
100   REM INITIALIZE SWITCH STATUS
110   LET N = PEEK PRT
120   REM INITIALIZE COUNTER
130   LET C = 0
140   IF N = PEEK P THEN GOTO 140
150   REM INPUT HAS CHANGED
160   REM DELAY TO DEBOUNCE SWITCH
170   PAUSE 5
180   IF N = PEEK P THEN GOTO 140
190   REM CHANGE IS NOT VALID
200   REM CHANGE IS GENUINE, INCREMENT CLOCK
210   C = C + 1
220   PRINT "CURRENT COUNT = "; C
230   REM WAIT FOR SWITCH TO BE RELEASED
```

```
240   IF N <> PEEK P THEN GOTO 240
250   GOTO 140
```

ZX Spectrum:

```
  1   REM Control example 7 – An input counter
 10   REM Initialize
 20   LET inputs = 63
 30   PAUSE 1:LET status = IN inputs
 40   LET count = 0
100   REM wait for input status to change
110   PAUSE 1:IF status = IN inputs THEN GOTO 110
120   PAUSE 2:REM Delay to debounce switch
130   IF status = IN inputs THEN GOTO 110:REM invalid switch closure
140   LET count = count + 1:REM Switch closure is genuine
150   PRINT AT 10,2;"Current count = ";count
160   REM wait for switch to be released
180   PAUSE 1:IF status <> IN inputs THEN GOTO 180
190   GO TO 100
```

Investigation 5.8   Digital to analogue conversion

We noted in Chapter 4 how the digital output from a binary counter can produce analogue voltages using a digital-to-analogue converter (DAC). The DAC unit can be connected to the logic board for the same purpose (Figure 5.6). The binary number to be converted is written into the user port address and the analogue voltage is produced at the output of the DAC a few microseconds later.

To investigate this application connect a 0 to 5 V voltmeter between the output terminal of the DAC and ground. Then connect the inputs of the DAC unit to the four outputs of the logic board. Run the program CONTROL EXAMPLE 2 – BINARY

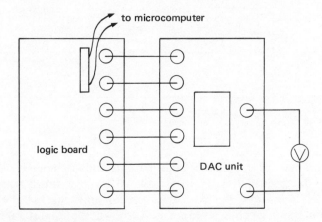

Figure 5.6   Voltage production

COUNTER to produce a ramp voltage. The period of this oscillation is about 12 seconds. Almost any waveform is possible, by writing different numbers into the user port, particularly for a sinusoidal voltage.

Investigation 5.9   Analogue to digital conversion

In Chapter 4 we saw how an analogue to digital converter converts a voltage in the range 0 to 4 V into a binary number from 0000 to 1111, with an accuracy of one in sixteen. There we looked at the ramp method of conversion using the binary counter but this is even easier when the DAC is connected to the user port of the microcomputer (Figure 5.7).

The method consists in feeding binary numbers in succession to a DAC and comparing its output voltage with the unknown voltage being measured. When the two voltages are the same, the binary number currently in the DAC is the digital equivalent of the required voltage. The comparison is done with a differential amplifier, the output of which is connected to an input of the logic board. If the unknown voltage is greater than the DAC output, the differential amplifier will send a HIGH level to the input. As soon as the DAC output becomes greater than the unknown voltage, the input will go LOW.

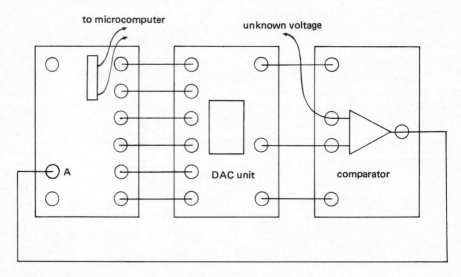

Figure 5.7   Ramp ADC

The microcomputer starts counting from zero and sends each number in turn to the DAC (this was discussed above). The DAC voltage thus rises slowly from 0 V. After each number has been sent to the DAC, the microcomputer checks if the input status has changed and if not, it continues to count. As soon as the input status changes, the microcomputer stops counting and displays the number that it has currently reached.

The routine to run this ramp ADC is as follows. Note that with the PET, Apple and BBC microcomputers the output status is read at the same time as the input status, so it has to be subtracted from the reading to get the true input status.

PET:
```
  1   REM CONTROL EXAMPLE 8 – RAMP ADC
 10   DDR = 59459 : REM DATA DIRECTION REGISTER
 20   PRT = 59471 : REM USER PORT
 60   POKE DDR,240: REM CONFIGURE INPUTS AND OUTPUTS
 70   POKE PRT,0
 80   LET N = PEEK(PRT):REM INITIALIZE INPUT STATUS
 90   V = 0
100   REM RAMP THE OUTPUT VOLTAGE
110   FOR I = 0 TO 240 STEP 16
120   POKE PRT,I
130   IF N <> PEEK(PRT) –I THEN V = I:I = 240
140   NEXT I
150   PRINT "THE VOLTAGE IS ";
160   IF V = 0 THEN PRINT "OUT OF RANGE":END
170   PRINT V/100
```

Apple:
```
  1   REM CONTROL EXAMPLE 8 – RAMP ADC
 10   DDR = 49346 : REM DATA DIRECTION REGISTER
 20   PRT = 49344 : REM USER PORT
 60   POKE DDR,240: REM CONFIGURE INPUTS AND OUTPUTS
 70   POKE PRT,0
 80   LET N = PEEK(PRT):REM INITIALIZE INPUT STATUS
 90   V = 0
100   REM RAMP THE OUTPUT VOLTAGE
110   FOR I = 0 TO 240 STEP 16
120   POKE PRT,I
130   IF N <> PEEK(PRT) –I THEN V = I:I = 240
140   NEXT I
150   PRINT "THE VOLTAGE IS ";
160   IF V = 0 THEN PRINT "OUT OF RANGE":END
170   PRINT V/100
```

BBC microcomputer:
```
  1   REM CONTROL EXAMPLE 8 – RAMP ADC
 10   DDR = 65122 : REM DATA DIRECTION REGISTER
 20   PRT = 65120 : REM USER PORT
 60   ?DDR = 240: REM CONFIGURE INPUTS AND OUTPUTS
 70   ?PRT = 0
```

```
 80   LET N = ?PRT:REM INITIALIZE INPUT STATUS
 90   LET V = 0
100   REM RAMP THE OUTPUT VOLTAGE
110   FOR I = 0 TO 240 STEP 16
120   ?PRT=I
130   IF N <> (?PRT) −I THEN V=I:I=240
140   NEXT I
150   PRINT "THE VOLTAGE IS ";
160   IF V=0 THEN PRINT "OUT OF RANGE":END
170   PRINT V/100
```

ZX 81:

```
  1   REM CONTROL EXAMPLE 8 − RAMP ADC
 20   LET P = 22500
 30   POKE P,0
100   REM INITIALIZE INPUT STATUS
110   LET N = PEEK(PRT)
120   LET V = 0
130   REM RAMP THE OUTPUT VOLTAGE
140   FOR I = 0 TO 15
150   POKE P,I
160   IF N <> PEEK P THEN LET V=I
170   IF V = I THEN LET I = 15
180   NEXT I
190   PRINT "THE VOLTAGE IS ";
200   IF V=0 THEN PRINT "OUT OF RANGE"
210   IF V<>0 THEN PRINT V/10
```

ZX Spectrum:

```
  1   REM Control example 8 − Ramp ADC
 20   REM Initialize
 40   LET inputs = 63
 50   LET outputs = 63
 60   OUT outputs,0
 70   LET V = 0
 80   PAUSE 1:LET status = IN inputs: REM Initialize input status
100   REM ramp voltage
110   FOR i = 0 TO 15
120   OUT outputs,i
130   PAUSE 1:IF status <> IN inputs THEN LET V = i:LET i = 15
140   NEXT i
150   PRINT AT 10,2;"The voltage is "
160   IF V = 0 THEN PRINT AT 10,17;"out of range": STOP
170   PRINT AT 10,17;V*0.16
```

6   Practical details

'It's a plan of my own invention.
You may try it if you like.'
(Lewis Carroll, *Through the Looking Glass*)

Construction of the electronic units used in the investigations

As far as possible use has been made of equipment available commercially. Two manufacturers to date make most of the units used in the investigations in this book, Griffin and George Ltd and Unilab Ltd. Some teachers will not have sufficient funds to purchase this equipment, but have willing helpers who can construct it from the basic components. Provided that labour is not costed, this is clearly the cheapest way to do it. With these teachers in mind the following diagrams describe the layout of the components and point-to-point wiring diagrams. The best way is certainly to have one board for each circuit, but that is very expensive. What I have proposed is a compromise between expense and ease of understanding.

One possible way of mounting components is on Protoboard (also known as El-socket or Bimboard) (Plate 1). The components are pushed into sockets in a matrix and connections between them made with wires. My own investigations indicate that only very able pupils actually understand this method, for the majority the exercise is more like a jig-saw puzzle.

Most components can be obtained from RS Components Ltd and Verospeed Components. Both companies are useful to schools since they sell most components individually or in small packs. The price to be paid for this extra packaging is usually acceptable, but if large quantities are being obtained then other suppliers are sometimes cheaper (e.g. Farnell Ltd).

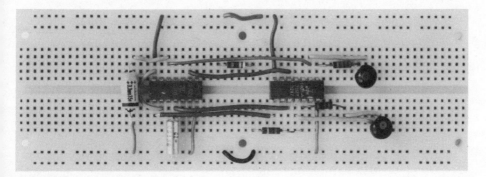

Plate 1   El-socket breadboard

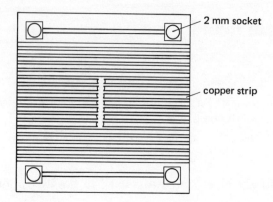

Figure 6.1   Using Stripboard

Circuits should be constructed on Veroboard or Stripboard. This has holes on a 0.1 inch matrix connected together with copper strip. Do not make these boards too small, about 100 mm long by 95 mm wide is ideal. This is 34-hole wide stripboard (RS Components stock no. 433-826). Alternatively, Verospeed Components stock a wider range of boards. The copper tracks of these boards run parallel to one another and join up all the holes in one line. Components like resistors can be used to link two such lines, for example, from the 5 V power line to a HIGH input terminal. Some components, for example integrated circuit sockets, require some of the Stripboard lines to be cut (Figure 6.1). This should be done with a cutting tool or a drill before the sockets are soldered into place.

This is a convenient point to mention the new terminology for resistors used in this book:

1 M 0 represents a 1 Megohm resistor
22 K represents a 22 kilohms resistor
4 K 7 represents a 4.7 kilohms resistor
560 R represents a 560 ohms resistor
8 R 2 represents an 8.2 ohms resistor

Sockets for connections to other boards should be the 2 mm type, which can be soldered onto the Stripboard. The RS Components type is not recommended since it only has side entry and students can rip them off the board by pulling the plugs out carelessly. Better are the top entry type from Verospeed Components (order code 63-1934 to 63-1941 depending on the colour). The cost of stackable 2 mm plugs is great, but they do save on the number of sockets to be provided on each board. Single 2 mm plugs are available from RS Components (444-472 etc.) or Verospeed Components (63-1862 etc.). My only source of stackable plugs so far is Unilab Ltd.

Integrated circuits should be mounted in 14-, 16- or 18-pin sockets (RS 401-790, 401-829 and 402-204). This does unfortunately increase the overall cost, but integrated circuits can be destroyed and it is almost impossible to remove one that has been soldered into a board without also damaging the board. The ICs required for each board are described later. Each has 14-, 16- or 18-pins arranged as two parallel rows. Once the appropriate socket has been soldered into place and the rest of the board completed, the integrated circuit can be pushed into the socket. Care should be taken over this, most ICs have their legs too far apart to go into the socket and they need to be gently squeezed together first. Do not use too much force either, if the IC won't go in easily, then investigate why. It is very, very easy to bend over a leg with excessive force (which won't always be obvious).

Care also needs to be taken to insert the ICs the right way round. It is worthwhile marking the socket to show which is to be pin 1. This pin is usually marked on the IC itself with a small indentation just beside pin 1. Wrong insertion usually means a 'blown' chip when the power is applied, this is an unnecessary expense. The other pins are numbered in succession; Figure 6.2 shows the pins of a 16-pin device as viewed from the top. Remember that when the board is turned over the pins are in different relative positions. This is a fruitful source of mistakes when constructing the board. All diagrams in this book assume that the pins are being viewed from above (and soldered from beneath).

Resistors, capacitors, diodes and transistors can be soldered directly onto the board. Usually it isn't too difficult to unsolder them again if necessary. Do not push the leads of these components completely through the hole. Leave about 3 mm above the board

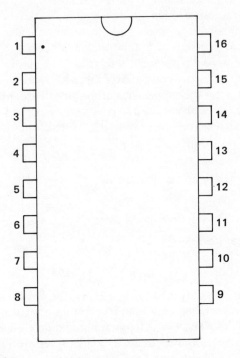

Figure 6.2   16-pin device

to facilitate later removal. Any excess wire on the soldered side should be removed with side-cutters. Wire should be the solid-core type for connections between holes on the board and stranded for connections to other boards. The latter are best stripped, twisted and tinned (covered with a thin film of solder) to allow easier insertion into the holes. The best wire is ribbon cable, since it allows different colours to be used. The resistor colour code can then be used to identify data lines or address lines more easily.

Tools
An electric soldering iron is essential, it is quite impossible to do good printed circuit board work with a plumber's iron heated by a bunsen flame! Ideally, the small 12 V irons should be obtained, but failing this an 18 W soldering iron with its bit filed almost to a point can be used (RS Components 542-920). The 25 W type with a 6 mm bit tend to be too big, causing adjacent copper strips to be soldered together. If this does happen the excess solder should be sucked up with a desoldering tool (RS Components 547-391) or absorbed with desoldering braid (RS 554-608). The thinner solder (22 s.w.g.) is best (RS 555-235) but the other is quite satisfactory if used carefully (RS 554-917).

After soldering resistors and wires into place any excess of lead will need to be cut off. Small side cutters are best for this (RS 544-370) but pliers should not be used. It is quite easy to damage the copper strips by vigorously waggling a wire back and forth to break it off. Nor is it usually possible to use the cutting part of pliers, since they cannot cut off the excess wire short enough.

Pliers are useful for bending resistors and wires. They can also be used for stripping plastic covered wire. Wire strippers do this too, but not usually as effectively, the wire strippers always seem to be too big and merely stretch the plastic or too small and nick the wire. There is usually better control over this with a pair of pliers.

A cutter is needed to cut the copper strip of the Stripboard, but I usually use a drill for this. Very thin drills are also needed to enlarge the holes in the Stripboard to take some components, particularly potentiometers, switches and the 2 mm sockets.

The electronic units used in this book

The pulse unit
For this unit (Figure 6.3) a double throw switch is essential.

Cheap slide switch: RS 339-673
Push-button switch: RS 337-942
Hall effect switch (already debounced): RS 337-295

In Figure 6.3 and in both the Unilab (Plate 2) and the Griffin and George (Plate 3) versions, the pulse unit produces single and/or continuous pulses. Continuous pulses are produced with a NAND astable circuit at approximately 1 Hz. Single pulses are produced with a bistable debounce circuit. The Griffin version has one output which is switch selected, while the Unilab version has a separate output for each.

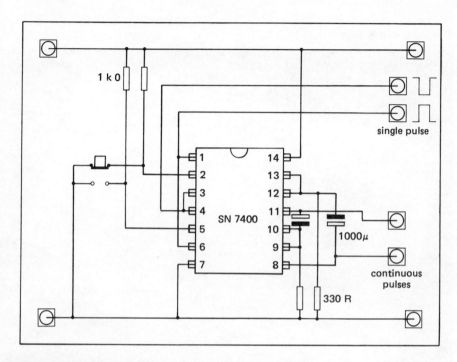

Figure 6.3 Pulse unit

Plate 2 Pulse unit

Plate 3 Pulse unit

165

The four-switch unit

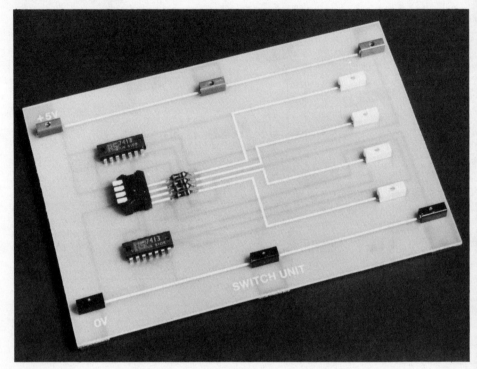

Plate 4   Four-switch unit

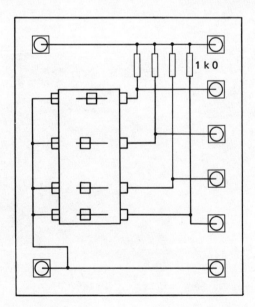

Figure 6.4
Four switch unit

The slide-type **DIL (dual in-line)** four-switch set (RS 337-548) is difficult to use (a ball-point pen helps). Easier to handle is the lever-type (RS 335-817) (Plate 4). Four separate switches (RS 339-673) are best of all. The switches should be orientated so that left or up gives the LOW output and right or down gives the HIGH output. The latter is achieved with 1 kilohm pull-up resistors (Figure 6.4).

The NAND gate unit

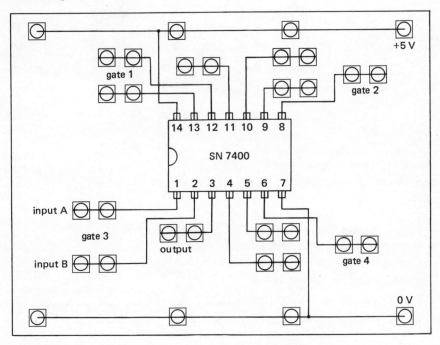

Figure 6.5   NAND gate unit

The SN 7400 device (RS 305-490) contains all four NAND gates needed for this unit (Figure 6.5). The commercial versions also show the NAND gate symbols, which is a great advantage. The Griffin version (Plate 6) shows the older (and internationally accepted symbol) while the Unilab version (Plate 5) is more up-to-date in this respect. A more important difference is that the Unilab version has single terminals only, which means that stackable plugs have to be used for some applications. The Griffin version provides sockets in pairs so that stackable plugs may not be needed. Note that the Unilab version has built-in LED indicators, which are useful for showing the logic state of each output, without having extra leads to confuse the issue. Finally, note how the Griffin boards all have in-built protection against connecting the 5 V power supply the wrong way round. This may be more valuable than the fact that the Unilab boards will accept a range of power supply voltages from 5 to 15 V.

167

Plate 5 NAND gate unit

Plate 6 NAND gate unit

All this illustrates the problems in making direct comparisons between the boards offered by the different manufacturers. It is rarely easy for a teacher to make a wise choice.

The binary counter unit

The binary counter unit (Figure 6.6) requires the SN 7493 binary counter (RS 306-443). The Griffin version (Plate 7) is very similar to this.

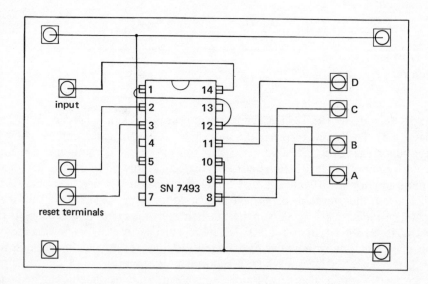

Figure 6.6 Binary counter unit

Plate 7   Binary counter

The transistor unit

The Unilab transitor unit (Plate 8) is more sophisticated than my own, since it also contains its own voltage divider. In the DIY version the LED (RS 586-475) must be connected the right way round, the flat edge on the LED is the cathode, which goes to the collector of the transistor. The other lead should be connected to the 5 V line in series with a protective resistor (Figure 6.7). The BC 109 transistor (RS 293-549) can be soldered directly onto the board. The small tag on the case of the transistor identifies the emitter, thereafter the legs follow in sequence (Figure 6.8).

Plate 8   Transistor unit

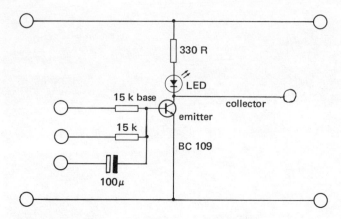

Figure 6.7 Transistor unit

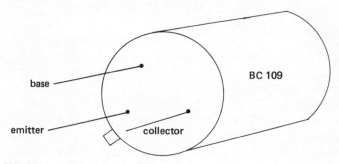

Figure 6.8 BC 109 transistor

The LED indicator unit

The left-most photograph of Plate 9 shows the Griffin LED indicator board. This is particularly useful for the traffic lights experiment, since it contains red, amber and green LEDs. In my own four-LED unit (Figure 6.9) the LEDs are driven by

Plate 9 Additional units

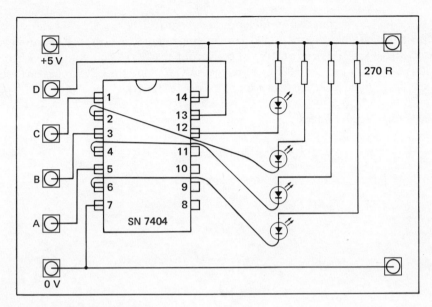

Figure 6.9   LED indicator unit

INVERTERs as described in Chapter 2 with their cathodes connected to the SN 7404 outputs (RS 305-529). The 270 ohms resistors are essential for limiting the current and can be obtained as a single package (RS 140-029).

The bistable unit

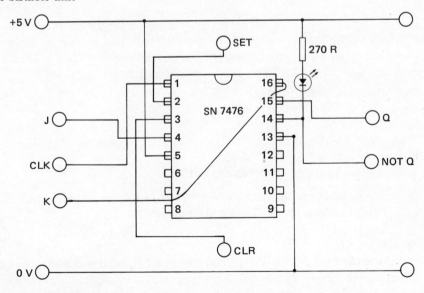

Figure 6.10   Bistable unit

171

It is possible to mount two bistables on one board, since the SN 7476 devices does contain two bistables. This can lead to a cluttered board so it is best just to use one such device (RS 306-421) (Figure 6.10). By connecting the NOT Q output to the LED, the latter comes on when the NOT Q output goes LOW. Thus the LED comes on to show when the bistable is on (i.e. when the Q output is HIGH).

The voltage divider board

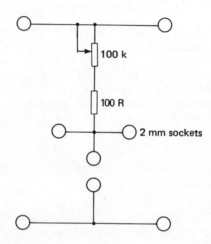

Figure 6.11   Voltage divider board

It should be possible to mount the 100 kilohms variable resistor directly on the board. The PCB type (RS 184-388) is most satisfactory but for this the holes in the Stripboard will need to be enlarged slightly to take the legs of the variable resistor (Figure 6.11). Transducers that may be mounted in this unit are as follows:

1000 μF capacitor (RS 103-525)
4 K 7 resistor
Diode IN 4001 (RS 261-148)
Zener diode 3 V (RS 282-022)
Light dependent resistor (RS 305-620)
Bead type thermistor (RS 151-142 or 151-158)

Both the LDR and thermistor should be mounted on stripboard for protection. All should be provided with flexible leads and 2 mm plugs.

The potentiometer
A low resistance of around 100 ohms is best (Figure 6.12), but this cannot then be used as a variable resistor too. If leads with 2 mm plugs are soldered onto the potentiometer terminals, then the latter does not need to be mounted on a board. In this case a

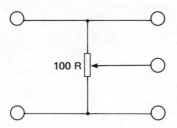

Figure 6.12 Potentiometer

substantial potentiometer is needed (RS 173-029). Commercial mounted potentiometers are available from the Nuffield range of electronic units (Plate 23).

The single rail op.amp. unit

The LM 324 device (RS 307-884) contains four op.amps. It is better not to use them all, or the board becomes too cluttered. Figure 6.13 shows one possible arrangement.

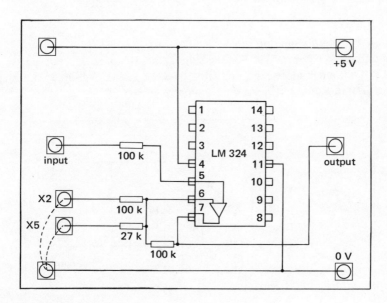

Figure 6.13 Single rail op.amp. unit

The transducer op.amp. unit

A similar arrangement is used for the op.amp. switch (Figure 6.14), which is used in conjunction with the voltage divider.

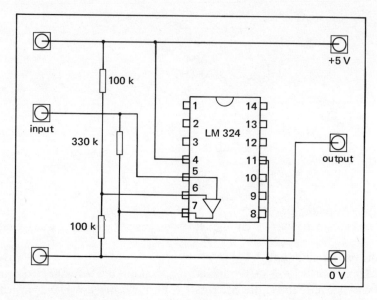

Figure 6.14 Op.amp. switch unit

The dual power supply op.amp. unit

The ubiquitous 741 device (RS 305-311) is satisfactory (Figure 6.15), but the 531 device is faster and not much more expensive (RS 305-872). The Unilab op.amp. unit (Plate 10) is useful in containing its own potentiometer.

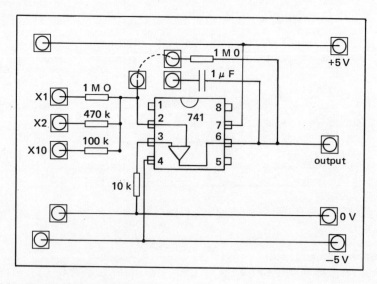

Figure 6.15 Dual rail op.amp. unit

Plate 10   Op.amp. unit

The 5 V power supply

With the vast numbers of 12 V a.c. supplies in most schools, it is not worth getting a separate transformer for this. The 5 V supply can be obtained directly from this 12 V a.c. supply. The Griffin version (Plate 11) contains protection against short-circuiting. (See also Plate 23 for a self-contained 5 V supply.) The DIY version needs a rectifier capable of delivering at least 1 A, hence the 2 A PCB units from RS Components Ltd are ideal (RS 261-592). The regulator circuit is the 7805 type (RS 305-888), which cuts out automatically if overloaded. A diode (RS 261-148) may be included to prevent

Plate 11   5 V power supply unit (PSU)

175

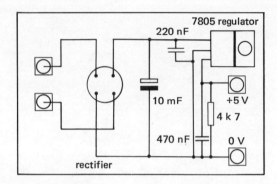

Figure 6.16 5 V power supply

damage if the power supply is connected to other units the wrong way round. The small capacitors are necessary to cut out high frequency ripple (Figure 6.16).

10 mF capacitor (RS 102-409)
470 nF capacitor (RS 113-926)
220 nF capacitor (RS 113-910)

A simple + 15/−15 V power supply
One simple way to make a dual power supply for op.amps is to use a 5 V to dual 15 V voltage converter (RS 591-304). However, this can be damaged if short-circuited (Figure 6.17). The 5 V can be obtained from the 5 V digital supply described above.

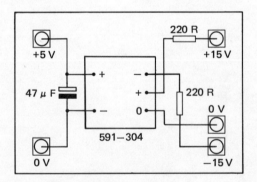

Figure 6.17 Simple + 15/−15 V power supply

A dual + 15/−15 V power supply
If more power is needed to drive several boards this can be obtained from a 15 V a.c. supply using the circuit in Figure 6.18 and a fixed dual power supply chip (RS 305-636). RS Components Ltd produce a special printed circuit board for this power

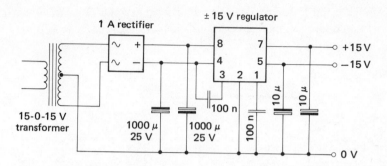

Figure 6.18   Dual + 15/−15 V power supply

supply unit (434-087) and all the other components needed to make it (RS Data sheet 2040, March 1983). If required, the board also accepts a transformer for use with the 240 V mains.

A dual +5/−5 V power supply

It is possible to produce a simple −5 V supply by inverting a + 5 V input (Figure 6.19). The power output from the −5 V line is limited but there is usually enough to drive a few op.amps. Note that the 741 device is unhappy at such low voltages, but the LM 324 device (which uses less power anyway) is ideally suited to this very cheap system.

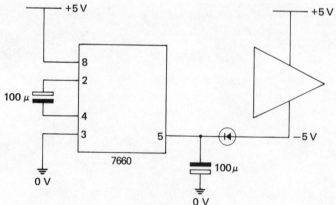

Figure 6.19   Dual + 5/−5 V power supply

The DAC unit

This is based on the ZN 425E device (RS 306-904). The op.amp. buffer is an ordinary LM 324 (RS 307-884). Only four of the DAC inputs are used (the most significant bits) (Figure 6.20). Ferranti Ltd delight in confusing everyone by labelling the most

177

significant bit as 'bit 1' down to the least significant as 'bit 8'. Beware of this initiative test. Griffin and George make a version of this (top-right of Plate 12).

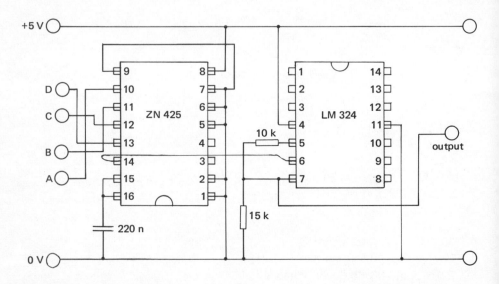

Figure 6.20 The DAC unit

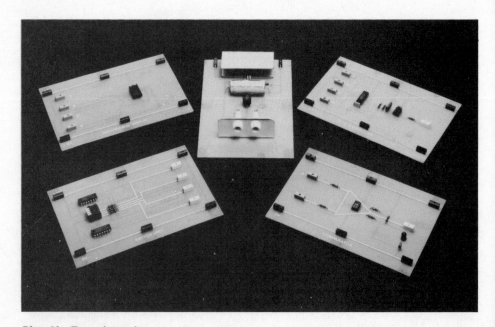

Plate 12 Extension units

The logic board

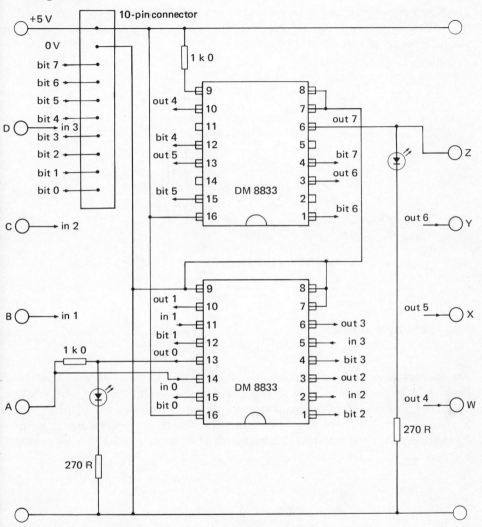

Figure 6.21 Logic board

The logic board used so extensively in Chapter 5 requires two DS 8833 quad-line transceivers (not available from RS Components but from Farnell Ltd) (Figure 6.21). Each output driver is used to drive an LED indicator. The inputs of the four transceivers used for the output terminal are not used, so they are disabled. Fuller details of this board are given in *The BBC microcomputer in science teaching*. The connector to the microcomputer user port is different for each microcomputer. This is described later.

179

The two-input board

The logic board was found to be difficult to use with beginners so the simpler two-input board was devised (Figure 6.22). The connector to the microcomputer user port is exactly the same as for the logic board.

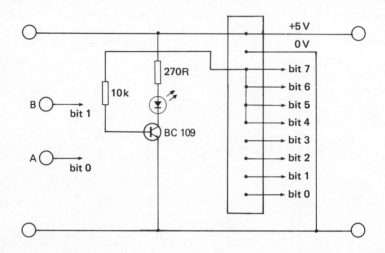

Figure 6.22   Two-input board

The memory unit

Figure 6.23 shows one way of producing a memory unit. This requires the SN 7489 device not available from RS Components but it can be obtained from Farnell Ltd. This device inverts the data, so that a separate SN 7404 device must be used either to invert the inputs or the outputs. Unilab have a useful version of this (Plate 13), which contains its own LEDs for monitoring inputs and outputs.

Plate 13   16-word memory unit

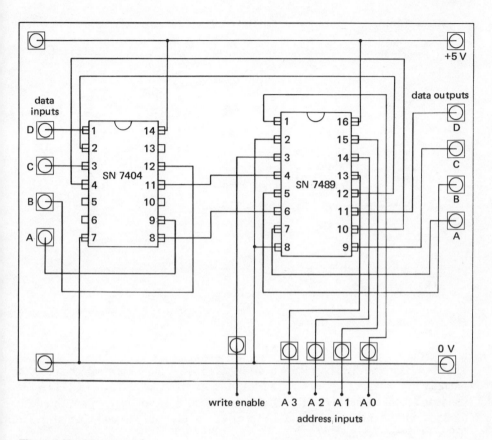

Figure 6.23 Memory unit

The seven-segment display

Plate 14 Seven-segment display unit

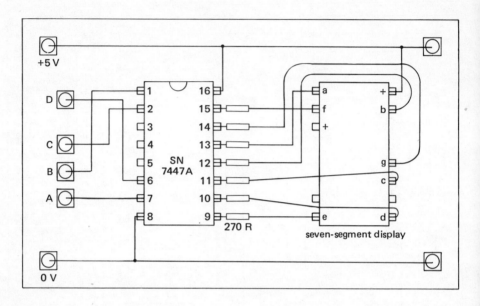

Figure 6.24   Seven-segment display

The seven-segment display (Figure 6.24) contains the display itself, which should be the red common-anode type (RS 586-526). It is driven (inversely) by a BCD to seven-segment decoder SN 7447A (RS 305-406). Protective 270 ohms resistors should be used to limit the current as with all LEDs driven in this way. The commercial version (Plate 14) is very similar.

The ADC unit
A design for this unit is not given since it is quite complicated and a four-bit unit is not worth making. Griffin and George have a suitable unit available for the investigations

Plate 15   ADC-DAC unit

of Chapter 4. The Unilab version (Plate 15) is an eight-bit unit and contains both the ADC and the DAC. The sequel books (e.g. *The BBC microcomputer in science teaching*) give several designs for fast eight-bit DACs and ADCs.

The relay units
Relays should be such that pupils can see the contacts open and close. The miniature type (RS 349-181) can be operated from the 5 V supply and can be mounted directly on Stripboard. Two pole, changeover contacts are needed to demonstrate the latching and astable connections. The Griffin and George relay unit (Plate 16) is ideal because it has both normally open and normally closed contacts. Plate 23 shows the Unilab version of this relay in action.

Plate 16   Relay unit

Connections to the user port of the BBC microcomputer
Connection to the BBC microcomputer user port is via a 20-way cable. Each end of this cable requires a 20-way cable mounting socket (RS 467-289). The other end of this should go to a PCB mounting plug (RS 467-346), which may be soldered directly onto the Stripboard. One side of this plug will be the input/output and control lines from the user port, these should be soldered onto ten adjacent copper strips as in Figure 6.21. The other side will be the 5 V and 0 V lines. They may be passed through holes in the Stripboard from which the copper has been cut away. Connections from one of the 0 V pins and one of the 5 V pins should then be taken to the 0 V and 5 V lines of the logic board respectively. The pin connections to the user port are shown in Figure 6.25. This configuration assumes that you have lifted up the front of the BBC

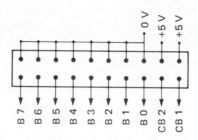

Figure 6.25   BBC user port pin connections

microcomputer and are looking underneath at the socket directly from the front. Further details on the use of this port are given in *The BBC microcomputer in science teaching*.

The Apple II user port

Figure 6.26 shows one way of fitting a user port to the Apple. It can be constructed on double-sided edge-plug stripboard (RS Components 434-122) suitably cut down to size, or alternatively, mounted on an Apple hobby card (Plate 17) (Verospeed Components order code 10-22859F). Only the B-Port lines are shown, but the A-Port

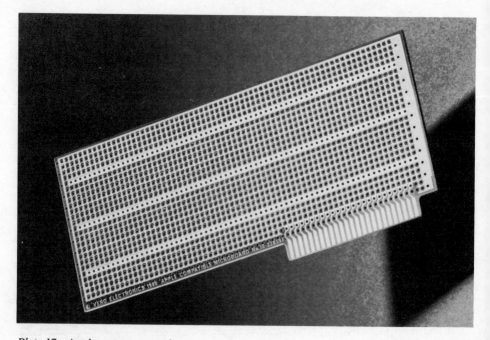

Plate 17   Apple connector card

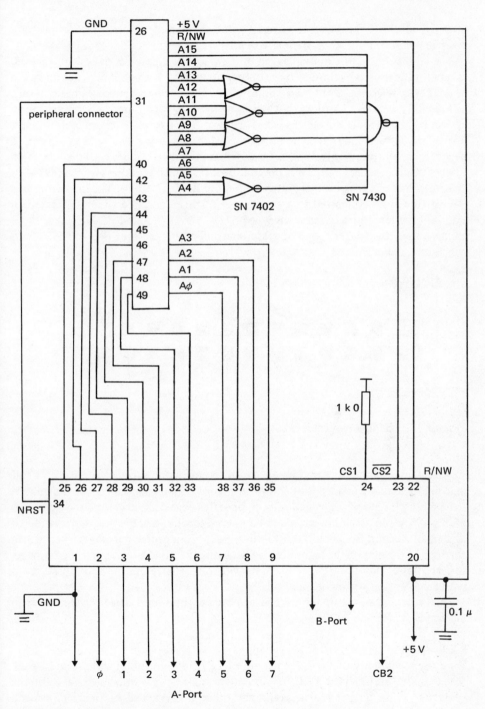

Figure 6.26 The Apple user port

lines and all the control lines are available too. Further details on this user port are given in *Microcomputers in Science Teaching*.

The Apple user port can be plugged into any of the Apple peripheral connectors, except for those used by the disk drive or the colour card, because it does not make use of the **device select** signals at each connector. This would be a better way to do it, but, as I couldn't get the VIA to work when using these signals, I made a separate gating system from the address lines instead. The lower four address lines are used to select one of the sixteen internal registers of the VIA. The other twelve lines operate a decoder, the output of which goes LOW when these twelve lines contain 1100 0000 1100 (C0C in hexadecimal). Thus the user port responds to addresses from 49344 to 49359. In this book we are only interested in the B-Port (49344). The lines from this B-Port should be connected to a small piece of Stripboard, to which is soldered a standard Molex 10-way socket (RS 467-677). The 0 V and 5 V lines should be connected to this socket too. The logic board contains ten pins (RS 467-582) onto which this socket is fixed.

The PET user port

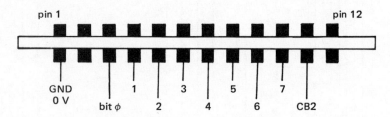

Figure 6.27 PET user port connections

The PET user port is the middle of the three edge connectors at the back of this machine. It has the connections shown in Figure 6.27. A special socket is available from most PET suppliers, which will clip onto this edge connector, and the eight lines of the A-Port plus a 0 V line should be connected to wires that are themselves soldered to a small piece of Stripboard. Onto this is soldered a Molex ten-way socket, which connects to the pins on the logic board. The tenth pin is used by other microcomputers to carry power, but the PET does not provide this. Hence this pin is not used and a separate 5 V supply provided instead.

Further applications of the PET user port can be found in *Microcomputers in Science Teaching*.

ZX Spectrum

With the availability of the Interspec interface (Plate 18) (obtainable as the I-pack from Griffin and George Ltd) it is pointless making any other interface for the Spectrum. The Interspec provides (amongst other things) and eight-bit input port and an eight-bit output port together with 5 V and 0 V lines. These should be connected to a

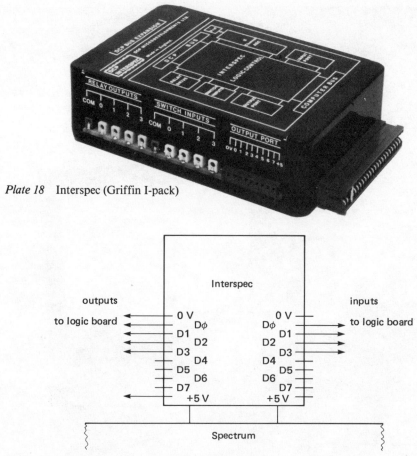

Plate 18 Interspec (Griffin I-pack)

Figure 6.28 Interspec connections to the logic board

standard Molex ten-way socket (RS 467-677), which connects via a ribbon cable to the Molex pins on the logic board or the two-input board. The connection to the input and output ports are themselves made with the same Molex ten-way pins (RS 467-582), although only the lower four input lines and the lower four output lines are needed. Alternatively, connect the logic board to the relay outputs and switch inputs directly.

Fuller details on the use of the Interspec can be found in *The ZX Spectrum in science teaching* and in the I-pack experimenter's manual from Griffin and George Ltd.

ZX 81
With the availability of the 4K RAM and I/O pack from Griffin and George Ltd (Plate 19) it is pointless making any other interface for the ZX 81. The 4K RAM and I/O provides an eight-bit input port and an eight-bit output port together with 5 V and 0 V lines. These should be connected to a 10-way ribbon cable via standard Molex 10-way

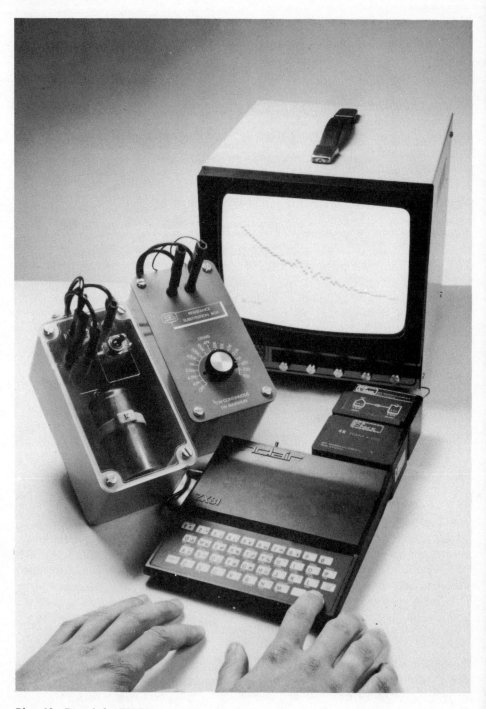

Plate 19   P-pack for ZX 81

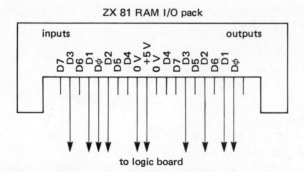

Figure 6.29   RAM-I/O Pack connections to the logic board

sockets (RS 467-677), which connect to the Molex pins on the 4K RAM Pack. The other end of this cable is connected to the Molex pins on the logic board or the two-input board via another Molex socket. In both cases the sockets are best soldered onto small pieces of Stripboard and the wires soldered onto the Stripboard too. The alternative method of using crimp connectors is less satisfactory, since, when, the wires break off, they are more difficult to reconnect. Note that only the lower four input lines and the lower four output lines are needed (Figure 6.29). Fuller details on the use of these ZX 81 interfaces will eventually be found in *The ZX 81 in science teaching*.

7   Where next?

'Would you tell me , please, which way I ought to
walk from here?'
'That depends a good deal on where you want to get
to,' said the Cat.
(Lewis Carroll, *Alice's Adventures in Wonderland*)

Electronic teaching equipment

In this book I have sought to demonstrate a method of introducing the main concepts of modern digital and linear electronics. I do not, however, wish to imply that my approach is the only one possible. There always has to be a compromise between cost and effectiveness and schools with more money or less money must find their own position in this spectrum. When using an AVO meter the operator must know the difference between volts and amps. For teaching purposes it is better to use separate voltmeters and ammeters. It is the same when teaching the concepts of microelectronics. Ideally there would be one item of equipment to illustrate each different concept. In practice this is too costly and there is a great desire to have one piece of equipment that does everything. What I have proposed is a compromise, but other teachers may see things differently.

Manufacturers of school equipment do their best to supply the whole range. The units that I described in Chapter 6 are not the only ones available, for example you can get triple-input NAND gates, monostables, shift registers and many other units. Plate 20 shows the ultimate in versatility, a single board that does everything! You just insert

Plate 20   Blank IC unit

Plate 21   The tutorkit range

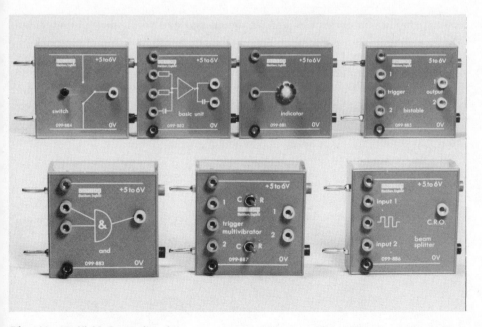

Plate 22   Nuffield electronic units

whichever IC is currently being investigated. You must then consult the manufacturer's data sheet to find out the function of each socket. Clearly this is no way to teach beginners, but it is ideal for those who have the initial concepts and are now exploring other ICs.

Nearer to the middle of this spectrum are the Tutorkits (Plate 21). These allow everything to be done at a very low cost with just a few units. Leads are included in the kit and these can be an expensive item with some other equipment. To give an idea of the savings, the LT2 Logic Tutor will allow almost all of the investigations in Chapters 2 and 3 of this book to be carried out and its current cost is less than twenty pounds. The LT1 combinational logic tutor allows Boolean logic to be thoroughly investigated and the OP1 unit is the cheapest op.amp. tutor on the market.

Schools that already have the equipment (Plate 22) for the 'Electronics and Reactive Circuit' unit of *Nuffield Advanced Physics* will find that it is still possible to do most modern microelectronics with it (a tribute to its designer G.E. Foxcroft). All the basic concepts of input, output, logic, astable, bistable and monostable are contained within that course. Plate 23 shows extensions that can be added to the basic range to extend its applicability.

Some teachers like the universal breadboard system mentioned in Chapter 6. As I said there, I find that few students understand what they are doing when using these breadboards and I think they are unsuited to beginners. They do have a place in motivating beginners, because it is relatively easy for them to make exciting circuits that work, even if they do dot understand why they work. T. Duncan has pioneered the use of these breadboards with his Adventure series (Plate 24). For those who like this approach, I can also recommend equipment like the Digi Designer, which takes some of the difficulties out of providing input signals and monitoring their outputs (Plate 25).

There are also several other ways of producing individual units, like those described in Chapter 6. Locktronics is an ideal way of introducing transistor circuits, since the components fit together onto a board in exactly the same way as the circuit diagram. Integrated circuits fit this system less well, but several interesting variants have been produced to allow the Locktronics board to accept op.amps and ICs such as

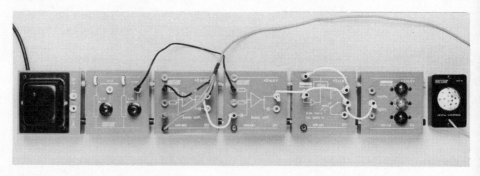

Plate 23   Nuffield extension units

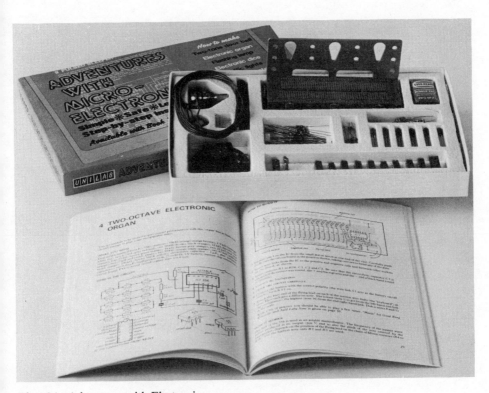

Plate 24   Adventures with Electronics

Plate 25   Digi Designer

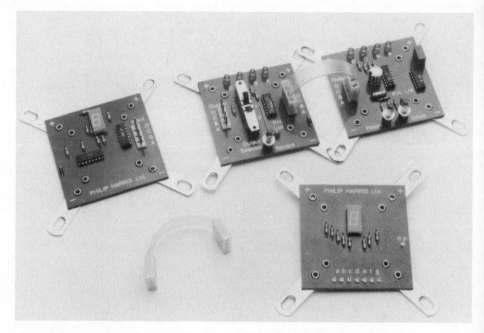

Plate 26   Harris electronic units

Rocktronics (designed by Ken Dunn at Richard Taunton College in Southampton). The Worcester Circuit Board is an excellent starting point for electrical circuits and Philip Harris Ltd have extended this system to cover just about all of basic electronics, op.amps and ICs too (Plate 26).

Even this does not begin to exhaust the number and type of electronic teaching equipment available. Almost every new course develops its own equipment. My list of known courses in microelectronics currently exceeds twenty and I am sure that many others exist too. A teacher who wishes to begin teaching microelectronics would be well advised to contact the local MEP regional information centre, most of which have someone in charge of electronics and control technology.

Electronics or microelectronics?

A recurring theme throughout this book is that microelectronics begins with programmable devices. Some would even claim that it doesn't even begin till you start programming a microprocessor. I certainly think that electronics pretending to be microelectronics is a dangerous half truth and that a way of teaching about programmable devices must be found somehow. In Chapter 5 I described some ways of doing this and I now wish to look at other possibilities. If the title of this book is to be justified, it is essential to ask how schools might be introduced to the microprocessor and its applications.

Microprocessor development kits

The first microprocessor I used was the National Semiconductor SC/MP kit. This had only 247 bytes of available memory and was programmed entirely in hexadecimal (a sort of binary coding). It had no tape or disk storage, so that every program had to be entered afresh each time. A single programming error could cause the whole system to stop working (called a **crash**) and since the program memory was not protected, there was no guarantee that the program had not been corrupted. It had to be carefully checked byte by byte before beginning again.

Since then I have used the Rockwell AIM 65, the Midwich Nanocomputer and the Acorn System 1. These are all admirable for writing and correcting machine code programs. The Nanocomputer, in particular, comes with a complete manual of instructions for writing programs and for interfacing the microprocessor to the outside world. It is unfortunately rather expensive. At the time of writing cheaper systems are available, such as the Microprofessor (Plate 27), which do the same as the others but at a lower cost. Mention must also be made of the Open University course on Microprocessors, which is an excellent introduction and uses a relatively simple tutor, the PT501 Microcomputer. Another system is the Menta, which allows programs to be written in mnemonics rather than in machine code itself. There is no doubt that budding microelectronics engineers learn much from using such systems.

General experience is that such microprocessor systems are not easy to use and beginners find themselves lost very quickly. Accordingly, several equipment manufacturers have developed simpler microprocessor tutors, that can be used with absolute beginners. These divide into two classes.

Plate 27 Microprofessor

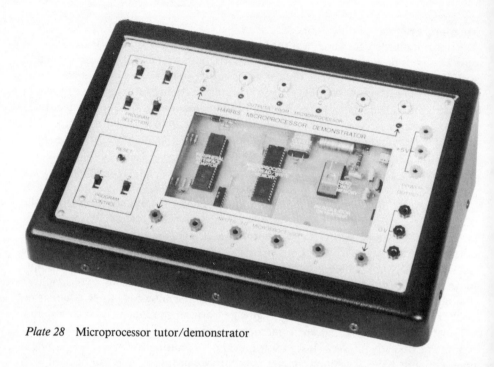

Plate 28   Microprocessor tutor/demonstrator

First are systems that demonstrate the applications of microprocessors rather then the techniques of programming them. The best example of this type is the Philip Harris Microprocessor Tutor/Demonstrator (Plate 28), which has a large number of programs already built-in. These include simulations of a lift, traffic lights and a digital thermometer. For teachers with limited time to devote to the study of microprocessors, this is an excellent piece of equipment.

The second group allows students to write their own programs. One of the problems with such programmable systems is that they quickly become too complex for beginners. One way of overcoming this is to use a simpler subset of instructions coded in binary. Switches are used to enter each binary instruction. With eight-bit instructions this soon becomes too tedious, so most of these systems work with four-bit instructions. The Welwyn Microprocessor Tutor is of this type and it has four-bit data lines as well. Although the instruction codes are non-standard, the operations they perform are quite normal and the equipment works in a fairly conventional way.

The Unilab One-bit Microprocessor (Plate 29) uses a commercial Motorola chip, which was designed specifically for control applications. This has single-bit data lines and effectively four-bit instructions. This simplicity may itself lead to difficulties and some ingenuity is needed to perform even trivial applications. The mode of working of this chip is peculiar to itself, for example, the normal branch and jump instructions are carried out in a different way from most other microprocessors. The greatest advantage of the Unilab system is the way it links so closely with digital electronics. A whole range of boards is available for forging this link (Plate 30).

Plate 29   One-bit microprocessor

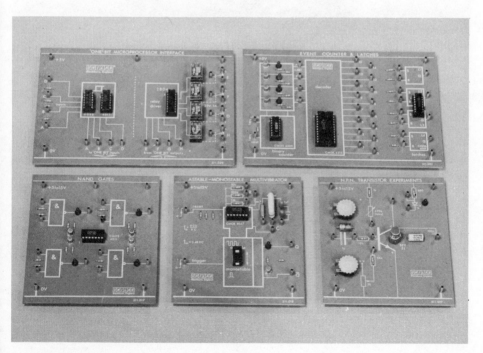

Plate 30   One-bit microprocessor link units etc.

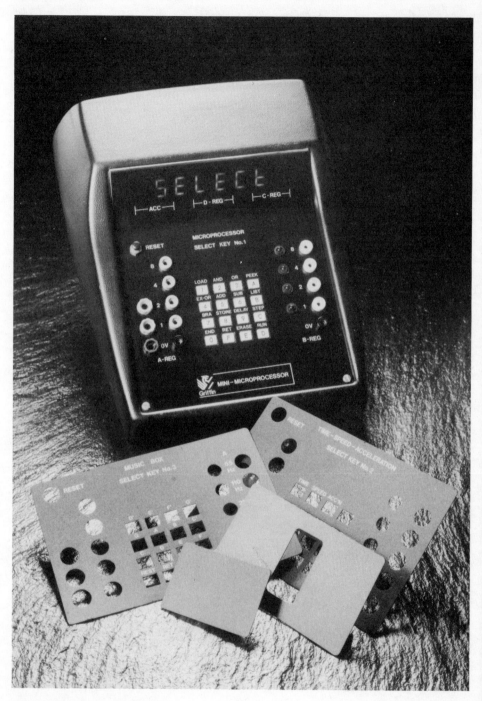

Plate 31 Mini-microprocessor

I shall now, however, reveal my prejudices. During my investigations into the best ways of introducing microprocessors to average ability students, I found that equipment based upon the Motorola one-bit microprocessor or requiring switches for entering the instructions was too complicated. I also rejected systems, which could not be programmed by the pupils themeselves, as not fulfilling my main requirement. This dissatisfaction with existing equipment led to my developing a microprocessor tutor specifically for schools. This is now marketed by Griffin & George as the Mini-microprocessor (Plate 31). Because of my particular interest in this equipment, readers will note my bias towards it, but it was intended to overcome most of the problems encountered above. It was decided that the Mini-micro should be both programmable and contain resident programs to demonstrate the power of microprocessors. Bearing in mind that schools have to consider costs very closely, it was decided to make one of the resident programs a time-speed-acceleration computer. This allows physics teachers or their students to measure the time between events easily and accurately. If these events are a card on a trolley passing in front of a photocell, then the speed and acceleration of the trolley would be computed too. The power of the microprocessor is seen because the Mini-micro can measure two such times independently; a boon when it comes to measuring two speeds at the same time (e.g. conservation of momentum experiments).

In its programmable mode the Mini-micro acts like a real microprocessor. It has input and output terminals for receiving and sending external four-bit data to switches and lamps. Thus it can be programmed to run a set of traffic lights or a pedestrian crossing. Programming is done with simple coded words (called mnemonics in microprocessor terminology) and using decimal rather than hexadecimal or binary numbers. For example, a burglar alarm program is written as follows:

```
1   LDA   A     (Look at the input)
2   Br0   1     (If the input is zero, go back to the start)
3   LDA   1     (The input is not zero, sound the alarm)
4   STA   B     (Switch the output on)
5   LDA   0
6   STA   B     (Switch the output off)
7   Br    3     (Repeat from step 3)
```

In order to make the equipment as simple as possible, the number of instructions has been limited to the essential ones. Each instruction is entered as a single keystroke from the keyboard. The number of programming steps is also restricted but is adequate for the majority of programs that students will want to write. An important design feature was to ensure that students wishing to go further have nothing to unlearn. When they get too ambitious for the Mini-micro, students can easily transfer to a more powerful microprocessor system. Finally, the Mini-micro comes with a complete set of student's and teacher's instructions, specifically written for independent learning. The system can be used by teachers who do not themselves have enough time to become experts.

Some teachers prefer to go further than just programming the microprocessor, they try to get their students to develop stand-alone dedicated systems. I certainly think that there is a place for this activity in a specialist course. The Microprofessor has an add-on unit to allow programs to be burned into EPROM and, compared with other development systems, is relatively inexpensive. My own approach is to use a microcomputer for developing programs, which may then be transferred to an EPROM. We shall return to this point later.

Microcomputers

Students wishing to become more expert at programming a microprocessor will require a more advanced system. One possibility is equipment such as the Microprofessor or the Menta. I personally do not see a place for such full-blown microprocessor systems in schools. For the average school a microprocessor has a more limited range of applications than a microcomputer. The latter can be made to do all that the former can do, so I recommend using a microcomputer, even for work which is more suited to a microprocessor. In order to do this, some form of interface is required. Also, it is necessary to get behind the microcomputer's operating system and start talking to the microprocessor directly. A machine code monitor or, better still, an assembler is essential.

The microprocessor is the heart (or perhaps it should be brain) of any microcomputer. The microprocessor in the BBC microcomputer is the Rockwell 6502, while the ZX Spectrum contains the Zilog Z80A. Note that the word 'microprocessor' refers only to one of the chips inside the microcomputer, even if it is the one which does

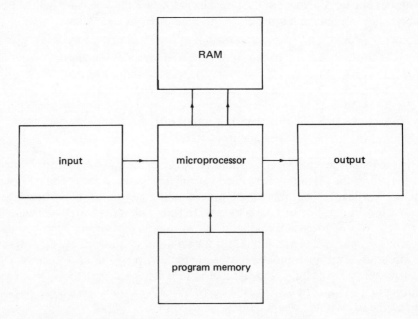

Figure 7.1   The microcomputer as a system

all the work. People should not use this word in place of the word 'microcomputer'. Figure 7.1 is a simple picture of the way that a microcomputer works.

For most purposes the input to the microcomputer is via its keyboard. The ouput is via the television screen or monitor (in computer jargon this is a **VDU** or **visual display unit).**

The program executed by the microprocessor is of two kinds, the resident program and the user-program. The same 6502 microprocessor is used in the Apple, the PET, the VIC and the Atom as well as in the BBC microcomputer. These machines all behave in different ways because they have different operating systems, which tell the microprocessor how to read the keyboard, where to print characters on the screen etc.

Programming

A microcomputer programmer can write different application programs for the microcomputer to execute. For example, one program can be written to draw pictures on the video screen, another can search through a list of numbers for the smallest value. This user-program will not remain in the machine after it has been switched off (it is said to be volatile). Every time that the microcomputer is switched on, a new user-program must be placed in its program memory. This can, of course, be entered from the keyboard or loaded from disk or cassette tape. To allow the microcomputer to store different programs, the memory for user-programs is alterable. It is called **RAM** (which stands for **random access memory**). The properties of RAM were discussed in Investigation 3.4.

To make it easier to produce such programs, they are often written in the language called BASIC. The microprocessor does not understand BASIC, it is a digital device and only 'understands' digital signals. Information can only be sent to the microprocessor as a set of HIGH and LOW voltage levels. The 6502 microprocessor has eight lines for this information and it reads all eight lines at once. From our point of view these eight lines can be considered to be a binary number. (Note, however, that the microprocessor does not understand binary any more than it understands BASIC.) With eight lines there are 256 possible binary numbers (in the range 0000 0000 to 1111 1111) and any information received by the microprocessor must be one of these numbers. Each bit of this binary number is either a 0 or a 1. To make it easier for us, we usually convert these binary numbers into decimals.

The whole set of eight bits is called a **byte.** One measure of the power of a computer is the number of bytes of information that it can store. The BBC microcomputer Model A can store about 16 000 bytes and the Model B about 32 000. It might seem that having only eight bits to a byte is very limiting, if we can only give the microprocessor 256 different pieces of information. However there are only seventy keys on a typewriter keyboard, yet how many different books can be written? It is clearly the sequence of the instructions given to the microprocessor that is important.

Machine language

Investigation 3.4 demonstrated the principles of a programmable device: switching traffic lights on in a sequence which had previously been entered and stored in the

RAM. One way of programming a microprocessor would be to give it sequences of binary numbers via eight switches. A separate switch could be used to tell the microprocessor when the next coded instruction was ready. This is obviously very slow and many mistakes might be made. (It was the way that the early computers were programmed.)

A better way would be to write all the binary numbers into the memory beforehand. The microprocessor could then fetch each one in turn and execute it. It would be better still if we could type in these numbers from the keyboard. This is the purpose of a machine language monitor. (The word 'monitor' here has no connection with the television monitor, that is a different use of the same word.) The early microcomputers like the PET and Apple 1 possessed these monitors as standard and it was great fun to enter and run machine code programs with them.

The monitor allows machine code routines to be more easily entered, run and corrected. A wrong instruction in a BASIC program will not be accepted by the microcomputer and will generate an error message. Machine code programs simply crash. The screen goes black or blank and the keyboard may lose control. Either way the program has probably been lost and it will need to be reloaded. A monitor eases some of these problems. It allows breakpoints to be inserted into the program, so that it will run up to the breakpoint and then stop (which is very useful for locating an error). It allows chunks of machine code to be moved around from one place to another in the memory and the contents of memory or the status of the different microprocessor internal registers to be displayed. A very useful feature is a warm restart, which allows control to be regained after a crash without losing the program.

The more modern machines have dispensed with such monitors, but it is possible to buy them for the ZX 81, ZX Spectrum and BBC microcomputers as separate programs. As a means of entering machine code programs, however, they are now superceded by more powerful methods.

Assembly language

Using a machine language monitor is slow, laborious and very prone to mistakes. An assembler allows the programmer to type in instructions for the microprocessor in a special assembly language. For example, the instruction to the microprocessor to return from a subroutine is 0110 0000 in binary and RTS in assembly language. The latter is obviously easier to remember. Programmming the Griffin and George Mini-micro is rather like writing an assembly language program. The BBC microcomputer is unique amongst cheaper computers in having an assembler as part of its operating system.

Other microcomputers generally have assemblers that are loaded as required. There are many of these and some guidance is useful for selecting the best sort. Ideally an assembler will also contain an editor, which allows program lines to be written and changed in much the same way as with BASIC. Lines of assembler mnemonics are usually numbered for reference, so that extra lines can be inserted or redundant ones removed. An editor allows the display of any line or lines, a search for a particular character or word and its replacement if necessary. The closer the editor gets to being a text editor the better. Additionally, an editor might allow the user to DELETE, COPY and RENUMBER lines and provide automatic line numbering too.

The job of the assembler is to compile the program, that is, to turn the mnemonics into binary code for the microprocessor. The better assemblers keep the code in a buffer from where it can be **relocated** (put somewhere else) or saved on tape or disk. Syntax errors are usually reported during or after the compilation. Unlike BASIC, assembly language syntax errors are fatal. The assembler will not just compile the bits of the program that are correct; it must all be correct beforehand.

Finally, before a microcomputer is suited for use as a microprocessor development system, it needs a **disassembler.** This takes machine code and turns it back into assembly language mnemonics. It is very useful for finding out if a program has been compiled in the way intended and also for unpicking someone else's code, particularly that of the microcomputer's operating system. The more you know about this, the better programs you can write.

BASIC

Even assembly language is not simple, so high-level languages have been developed. BASIC is one of these. The BASIC instruction to return from a subroutine is RETURN, which is even easier to remember. The microcomputer needs a special program, called the BASIC interpreter, to turn BASIC statements into the binary numbers needed by the microprocessor. This interpreter also contains error-checking, so that errors in programming produce messages for the programmer. BASIC is so very easy (by comparison with the other methods) that only a fanatic would use assembly language unnecessarily. For certain purposes, however, such as rapid measurements, assembly language programs are necessary.

BASIC is an ideal language for beginners to microelectronics (whatever its failings for the education of computer programmers). Its structure is very similar to assembly language so that students brought up on BASIC find the transition quite easy. It is an ideal language for controllling and sensing the environment, since it allows the direct addressing of inputs and outputs. Finally, it is easy to learn. Students can have programs running within minutes of starting to learn programming, an advantage shared by only a few other languages.

Dedicated systems

Most microprocessors spend their time doing one set of tasks only. It is only the few that find their way into personal or school microcomputers, that are given different tasks from day to day at the whim of the programmer. The microprocessor inside a calculator has been pre-programmed to carry out calculations only. It will not be asked to play tunes or measure time intervals or temperatures etc. The microprocessor in a supermarket checkout will not be asked to play Space Invaders as well. The microprocessors in these systems are said to be **dedicated** to their one function. The programs that run these dedicated systems are usually frozen in ROM, because there is no need to change them once they have been written and debugged.

ROM is produced by a silicon-chip manufacturer exactly as requested by the purchaser. The program is placed in the ROM by a process called **mask programming**. Once the program has been produced in this way, it is not possible to alter it later. The program remains in the ROM even if the power supply to the equipment is later switched off. When this ROM is coupled to a microprocessor, the latter will only carry out the program in the ROM.

The making of the masks for a ROM is very expensive and it is not done unless thousands are required. In the development stage, therefore, before the bugs (mistakes) have been removed, a different form of ROM is used, called **programmable ROM**. One version of this is especially useful in schools; it is called **EPROM** or **electrically programmable ROM.** This allows programs to be burned in, just as with ROM, but it is also possible to erase this program and burn in a different one, if the first is found to contain bugs. The equipment needed to burn a program into an EPROM is not too expensive (fifty pounds or so for an add-on unit to the BBC microcomputer) but it is probably not worth the average user getting such equipment. Local polytechnics and colleges of further education usually possess it and are willing to let visitors make use of it under supervision.

EPROM enables programs to be stored permanently, so that the dedicated system always has its program directly available. To get a program into the EPROM, the program is usually entered into an EPROM burner and checked. Then a freshly erased EPROM is placed in one socket and the burn commences. It takes one or two minutes for this process, after which the EPROM can be installed in the dedicated system. An EPROM can be erased again (for example, if a mistake has been made or if a better version has been developed) by exposing it to the correct dose of ultra-violet radiation. Any establishment with an EPROM burner will probably possess such a UV eraser too.

As well as its program a dedicated system will need some means of collecting data and giving information back to the user. In a microcomputer this is the typewriter keyboard and video display. In a control system this could be a sensor and a few switches for input and an elecromagnetic relay as an output (for example, the system to open the garage doors automatically upon the arrival of a motor car). In both cases some sort of input/output chip will also be needed.

The system will also need a microprocessor and some RAM for storing variable data. The amount of RAM depends upon the system, a garage-doors system may only need to remember a few bytes, whereas a programmable electronic organ may need thousands. Finally, a dedicated system will need its program stored in ROM or EPROM. For schools I like the approach of P. Nicholls (East Midlands MEP electronics coordinator), who has developed an inexpensive three-chip microcomputer/microprocessor system. This allows students to write, test and debug (correct) programs that may then be burned into an EPROM and the final system allowed to run independently.

Commercially, small dedicated systems may be developed around multi-purpose chips, such as the RRIOT (which contains ROM, RAM, input and output (I/O) lines and a timer). The user's program is burned into the ROM when it is manufactured. This is combined with a microprocessor to give a two-chip system. The ultimate is a single chip containing the RAM, ROM and I/O and the microprocessor as well. Such a chip is called a single-chip computer. These reductions in chip count give an obvious saving in cost, since the inter-connections between the different parts of the system have already been made. All that is needed is a small printed circuit board to take the remaining components and a socket for the single-chip microcomputer and the complete system is ready.

I have made several stand-alone systems (for example, the Mini-micro). I actually wrote the programs for this system using an Apple II microcomputer. The address and data lines from an Apple connector socket were connected to my system. The program was written in.the Apple's memory and when it had been debugged, the hexadecimal codes were copied out by hand. The circuit was constructed on stripboard and connected to the keyboard, display and input/output sockets. The program codes were taken to Glasgow University and typed into their EPROM burner. The EPROM was then plugged into the final system. To my utter astonishment it worked! I have been hooked on dedicated systems ever since.

There is no reason why the same arrangement I developed for the Apple would not work with any other microcomputer. However, a much better way to do such development work is with an **emulator.** This is a small board that fits the microcomputer and terminates in a twenty-four pin plug. This plug is pin-compatible with the EPROM and it is fitted into the EPROM socket of the dedicated system. A suitable program in the microcomputer turns it and the emulation board into a simulated EPROM. The routines to run the dedicated system can then be written and the system can be run to try them out. Debugging is possible and when the program has been fully developed, it can be burned into an EPROM. This can then be plugged into the stand-alone system.

At the time of writing a great deal of work is being done on systems like this. I expect that before long a complete emulation and EPROM-burning facility will be available for coupling to microcomputers. These will make the development of a dedicated system a perfectly feasible project for fifth and sixth year students. Several skeleton microcomputer systems are already available commercially, which allow dedicated systems to be built with the minimum of cost. One such is the 6502 based Cubit board from Control Universal Ltd, another is the Wireless World Picotutor, both of which allow the finished circuit to be used in real situations. In addition, single chip computers with EPROM on board are now readily available. With a suitable connection to a microcomputer the programs for this may be developed in assembly language and the EPROM burned in the usual way. The device may then be plugged into its final system. Whatever the method I am sure that building something like this would be the high point in any pupil's school experience. There is something particularly satisfying about inventing and producing your very own computer; it is real microelectronics.

Conclusion

I am convinced that the way forward for teaching microelectronics in schools is via an upgraded microcomputer in the manner described above. This has the added advantage of giving the teacher a microcomputer even when its use as a microprocessor demonstrator has ended. For this purpose I am preparing a series of books as sequels to this one, providing details of how to interface microcomputers to the outside world and giving a gentle introduction to machine code programming through the use of a microprocessor simulation program. The first of these, written with the PET and Apple microcomputers in mind, is already published under the title *Microcomputers in Science Teaching* and further versions of this for the other popular school microcomputers are in preparation. (The microprocessor simulation programs are available separately for the PET and Apple microcomputers; they were developed after their book was printed.) So far the following titles are planned: *The BBC microcomputer in science teaching, The ZX 81 in science teaching, The ZX Spectrum in science teaching.*

This brings us right up to the present in microelectronic technology, since it is the use of dedicated systems that is so profoundly affecting our lives. They are found in washing machines, sewing machines, knitting machines, motor cars, supermarket check-out points, video games and electric train sets. They control robots in factories, word processing equipment in the office and automatic stock delivery and despatch in the warehouse. What else they will do in the future is speculation, but I think it is safe to bet, that those who can understand and program microelectronic systems, are more likely to be employed than those who cannot.

Useful addresses

Electronic components

Farnell Electronic Components Ltd
Canal Road
Leeds LS2 2TU

RS Components Ltd
13-17 Epworth Street
London EC2P 2HA

Verospeed Components
Stansted Road
Boyatt Wood
Eastleigh
Hants SO5 4ZY

Periodicals and magazines

Electronic Systems News
Schools Liaison Service
Institution of Electrical Engineers
Station House
Nightingale Road
Hitchin
Herts SG5 1RJ

Electronics and Computing
Electronics Today
Practical Electronics
Wireless World

Courses in microelectronics

Examinable

A level Electronic Systems
O level Electronics
(Associated Examining Board)

Alternative Ordinary Electronics
(Joint Matriculation Board
Examinations Council)

OA level Electricity and Electronics
(Oxford Delegacy of Local
Examinations)

Non-examinable

Electronics and Microelectronics
A radio/radiovision series
BBC Publications
School Orders Section
144-152 Bermondsey Street
London SE1 3HT

Microelectronics for All
(using the Mini-microprocessor)
Griffin and George Ltd
Ealing Road
Wembley HA0 1HJ

Microelectronics for All
CLEAPSE
Brunel University
Uxbridge UB8 3PH

Microelectronics: Practical Approaches
for Schools and Colleges
BP Educational Service
Britannic House
Moor Lane
London EC2Y 9BU

Electronics
Op.Amp. Applications
Technology Microprocessor Control
National Centre for School Technology
Trent Polytechnic
Burton Street
Nottingham NG1 4BU

Starting Microelectronics
Middlesex Science & Technology
Education Centre
Middlesex Polytechnic
Trent Park
Cockfosters Road
Barnet
Herts EN4 0PT

Elementary Electronics
Cambion Electronic Products Division
Midland Ross Corporation
Cambion Works
Castleton
nr Sheffield S30 2WR

Overhead transparencies

Series 1. Combinational logic
Series 2. Sequential logic
Series 3. Digital arithmetic
Pennant
456 High Street
Cheltenham
Gloucestershire
Logic tutors

Breadboarding

Digilab
Educational Electronics
30 Lake Street
Leighton Buzzard
Beds LU7 8RX

Digi Designer
B. Hepworth and Co. Ltd
Kidderminster

E & L Instruments Ltd
Whitegate Industrial Estate
Whitegate Road
Wrexham LL13 8UG

Microprocessor tutors

MENTA: Microelectronic Mnemonic
Teaching Aid
Dataman Designs
Lombard House
Cornwall Road
Dorchester
Dorset CT1 1RX

Exploded View Computer
Microelectronics Education Program
Electronics and Control Domain
Cheviot House
Coach House Campus
Newcastle NE7 7XA

Microprofessor
Mini-microprocessor
Griffin and George Ltd
Ealing Road
Wembley HA0 1HJ

Microprocessor Demonstrator/Tutor
Philip Harris Ltd
Lynn Lane
Shenstone WS14 0EE

Microprocessor Tutor
Irwin Desman Ltd
294 Purley Way
Croydon CR9 4QL

Logic Tutors

STEM Logic Board
STEM Walton Unit
65 Walton Lane
Liverpool L4 4HG

LT1 Combinational Logic Tutor
LT2 Sequential Logic Tutor
OP AMP Tutor
PB1 IC Patchboard

Tutorkit Products
Llay Industrial Estate
Wrexham
Clwyd LL1 0TU

Electronic modules
Griffin and George Ltd
Ealing Road
Wembley HA0 1HJ

Alpha/Blue Chip Range
Unilab Ltd
Clarendon Road
Blackburn BB1 9TA

Westminster Logic Modules
Philip Harris Ltd
Lynn Lane
Shenstone WS14 0EE

Locktronics
A M Lock
Neville Street
Middleton Road
Oldham
Lancs

Control Application Modules
Griffin and George Ltd
Ealing Road
Wembley HA0 1HJ

Feedback Instruments Ltd
Park Road
Crowborough
Sussex TN6 2QR

Bibliography

This list is not comprehensive, but is a selection of books I have found the most useful.

Technical

TEC Series on Microelectronics, 1982, Hutchinson
A series of six books aimed at the further education sector and providing an excellent foundation for further study.

Optoelectronics, A. Chappell, 1976, Texas Instruments Publications

Project books

Elementary Electronics, M. Sladdin, 1983, Hodder and Stoughton

Electronic Projects in the Home, Electronic Projects in Music, CMOS Digital Projects, Integrated Circuit Projects, etc., Marston and others, 1974 onwards, Newnes Technical Books
A whole series of books giving practical circuits and some explanations.

Adventures with Electronics, Adventures with Microelectronics, T. Duncan, 1980-82, John Murray

Op.Amp. Applications, M. Plant, NCST, Trent Polytechnic

For beginners

Beginner's Guide to Integrated Circuits, I.R. Sinclair, 1980, Newnes Technical Books

Electronics, Science at Work series, Addison Wesley

Program listings

PET program listings

Program 1   LOGIC GATES

```
1 REM LOGIC GATES - PROGRAM 1
10 AO%=0:BO%=0:REM PREVIOUS DATA FROM USER PORT
20 DIM A%(4):REM INPUT DATA FROM USER PORT
30 S%=0:REM SELECTION NUMBER FROM MENU
40 R=15:REM POSITION IN TRUTH TABLE
60 SR=32768:LN=40:REM SCREENTOP AND ROW CONSTANTS
70 PRT=59471:REM USER PORT
80 POKE 59459,240:REM BITS 0 TO 3 AS INPUTS, BITS 4 TO 7 AS
OUTPUTS
100 PRINT"▓               LOGIC GATES"
110 PRINT"▓SELECT DESIRED GATE BY ENTERING ONE"
115 R=15:REM RESET TABLE POINTER
116 AO%=2:REM RESET INPUT STATUS
120 PRINT"▓OF THE FOLLOWING NUMBERS"
121 PRINT"▓     1   A AND B"
122 PRINT"▓     2   A OR B"
123 PRINT"▓     3   NOT A"
124 PRINT"▓     4   (A AND NOT B) OR (NOT A AND B)"
125 PRINT"▓     5   (NOT A AND NOT B) OR (A AND B)"
126 PRINT"▓     6   NOT (A AND B)"
127 PRINT"▓     7   NOT (A OR B)"
130 PRINT"▓ THEN PRESS <RETURN>"
140 INPUT"▓    *▓▓▓▓";S$
150 S%=VAL(S$):IF S%<1 OR S%>7 THEN140
200 REM *******************************
300 REM DRAW TRUTH TABLE
310 REM *******************************
320 PRINT"▓▓▓▓▓▓▓▓▓▓"
330 PRINT"        ┌───────────────────────┐ "
340 PRINT"        | A | B | OUTPUT |"
350 PRINT"        ├───────────────────────┤ "
360 PRINT"        | 0 | 0 |        |"
370 PRINT"        |   |   |        |"
380 PRINT"        | 0 | 1 |        |"
390 PRINT"        |   |   |        |"
400 PRINT"        | 1 | 0 |        |"
410 PRINT"        |   |   |        |"
420 PRINT"        | 1 | 1 |        |"
430 PRINT"        └───────────────────────┘ "
460 REM *******************************
470 REM DISPLAY FUNCTIONS & TERMINALS*
480 REM *******************************
500 PRINT"▓"
510 GOSUB 1000:REM DISPLAY BOX
530 ON S% GOSUB 1100,1200,1300,1400,1500,1600,1700
540 PRINT"▓▓▓▓▓▓▓▓▓▓▓▓▓▓▓▓";P$;"▓▓▓▓▓▓▓▓▓▓( ) OUTPUT"
```

211

```
590 REM DISPLAY INPUTS
600 IF S%=3 THEN GOSUB 5000
605 IF S%<>3 THEN GOSUB 5100
620 PRINT"███████████████████████'C' FOR A DIFFERENT GATE,'E'
TO END";
630 GET A$
640 IF A$="C" THEN 100
650 IF A$="E" THEN END
660 REM GET INPUT DATA
680 A%=PEEK(PRT)AND 1
690 B%=(PEEK(PRT)AND 2)/2
700 IF A%=AO% AND B%=BO% THEN 630
710 AO%=A%:BO%=B%
720 REM
730 REM CHANGE INPUT VALUES ON SCREEN
740 IF S%=3 THEN 790
750 POKE 32851,B%+48
760 POKE 32931,A%+48
770 GOTO 800
790 POKE 32891,A%+48
800 REM CALCULATE OUTPUT DATA
810 ON S% GOSUB 3100,3200,3300,3400,3500,3600,3700
820 REM SEND OUTPUT TO USER PORT
830 POKE PRT,16*VO%
840 POKE 32918,VO%+48
850 REM DISPLAY LINE OF TRUTH TABLE
860 PRINT"█"
870 FOR I=1 TO R:PRINT:NEXT
880 PRINT"       ████████████   ██████       "
890 LET R=11+4*A%+2*B%
900 PRINT"█"
910 FOR I=1 TO R:PRINT:NEXT
920 PRINT"   █     ███████████████";VO%;"██████       "
930 GOTO 630
1000 REM BOX DISPLAY
1010 PRINT"████████████┌─────────────┐            "
1020 PRINT"████████████            │            "
1030 PRINT"████████████            ├───────────"
1040 PRINT"████████████            │            "
1050 PRINT"████████████└─────────────┘            "
1060 RETURN
1100 P$="  AND  ":RETURN
1200 P$="  OR   ":RETURN
1300 P$="  NOT  ":RETURN
1400 P$="EX-OR  ":RETURN
1500 P$="EQUIV. ":RETURN
1600 P$=" NAND  ":RETURN
1700 P$="  NOR  ":RETURN
3000 REM DETERMINE OUTPUTS FOR EACH FUNCTION
3100 REM AND FUNCTION
3110 VO%=A% AND B%
3120 RETURN
3200 REM OR FUNCTION
3210 VO%=A% OR B%
3220 RETURN
3300 REM NOT FUNCTION
3310 VO%=NOT A% AND 1
3320 RETURN
```

```
3400 REM EXCLUSIVE-OR FUNCTION
3410 VO%=1
3420 IF A%=B% THEN VO%=0
3430 RETURN
3500 REM EQUIVALENCE FUNCTION
3510 VO%=0
3520 IF A%=B% THEN VO%=1
3530 RETURN
3600 REM NAND FUNCTION
3610 VO%=1 AND NOT(A% AND B%)
3620 RETURN
3700 REM NOR FUNCTION
3710 VO%=1 AND NOT(A% OR B%)
3720 RETURN
5000 REM APPEND THE INPUTS
5010 REM ONE INPUT
5020 PRINT"] A( )————————"
5030 RETURN
5100 REM TWO INPUTS
5110 PRINT"I B( )————————"
5120 PRINT"N A( )————————"
5130 RETURN
READY.
```

Program 2   LOGIC TUTOR

```
1 REM LOGIC TUTOR - PROGRAM 2
10 DIM T$(4,4):REM FUNCTION VARIABLES; IN THE ORDER (INPUT,
OUTPUT)
20 DIM A%(4):REM INPUT DATA FROM USER PORT
30 DIM VI%(4):REM VALUES FOR INPUT DATA
40 DIM F%(4):REM MENU VALUE OF FUNCTION
50 N=0:M=0:REM INPUT AND OUTPUT REFERENCE NUMBERS
60 SR=32768:LN=40:REM SCREENTOP AND ROW CONSTANTS
70 PRT=59471:REM USER PORT
80 POKE 59459,240:REM BITS 0 TO 3 AS INPUTS, BITS 4 TO 7 AS
OUTPUTS
90 FOR M=1TO4:F%(M)=0:NEXT M
100 PRINT"]                BOOLEAN FUNCTIONS"
110 PRINT"NSELECT DESIRED FUNCTION BY ENTERING ONE"
120 PRINT"NOF THE FOLLOWING NUMBERS"
121 PRINT"N    1    AND"
122 PRINT"N    2    OR"
123 PRINT"N    3    NOT"
124 PRINT"N    4    EXCLUSIVE-OR"
125 PRINT"N    5    EQUIVALENCE"
126 PRINT"N    6    NAND"
127 PRINT"N    7    NOR"
130 PRINT"N THEN PRESS <RETURN>"
140 INPUT"N    *NNNN";S$
150 S%=VAL(S$):IF S%<1 OR S%>7 THEN140
151 PRINT"NNNNNNNYOUR SELECTION IS    ";
152 IF S%=1THENPRINT" AND"
153 IF S%=2THENPRINT" OR "
154 IF S%=3THENPRINT" NOT"
155 IF S%=4THENPRINT" EXCLUSIVE-OR"
156 IF S%=5THENPRINT" EQUIVALENCE"
157 IF S%=6THENPRINT" NAND"
```

```
158 IF S%=7THENPRINT" NOR"
160 PRINT"█WHICH OUTPUT FOR THIS FUNCTION ?"
170 PRINT"█ENTER ONE OF W, X, Y OR Z AND"
180 PRINT"█THEN PRESS <RETURN>"
190 INPUT"█    *████";O$
200 IF O$<>"W" AND O$<>"X" AND O$<>"Y" AND O$<>"Z" THEN190
210 IF O$="W" THEN M=4
220 IF O$="X" THEN M=3
230 IF O$="Y" THEN M=2
240 IF O$="Z" THEN M=1
245 F%(M)=S%
246 IF S%=4 OR S%=5 THEN 280
250 IF S%<>3 THEN 290
260 PRINT"███THE 'NOT' FUNCTION ONLY HAS ONE INPUT"
270 I%(M)=1:GOTO 340
280 PRINT"██THIS FUNCTION HAS TWO INPUTS"
285 I%(M)=2:GOTO 350
290 PRINT"███HOW MANY INPUTS ?"
300 PRINT"█ENTER 1, 2, 3 OR 4 THEN PRESS <RETURN>"
310 INPUT"█    *████";I$
320 I%(M)=VAL(I$)
330 IF I%(M)<1 OR I%(M)>4 THEN 310
340 IF I%(M)=1 THEN PRINT"███WHICH INPUT ?":GOTO 360
345 PRINT"█"
350 PRINT"█WHICH INPUTS ?"
360 PRINT"█ENTER A, B, C OR D FOR EACH REQUEST."
370 PRINT"█IT IS POSSIBLE TO USE ONE INPUT MORE"
380 PRINT"█THAN ONCE, PROVIDED YOU HAVE ASKED"
390 PRINT"█FOR ENOUGH INPUTS."
400 FOR N=1 TO 4:T$(N,M)="":NEXT
410 FOR N=1 TO I%(M)
420 INPUT"█    *████";I$
430 IF I$<>"A" AND I$<>"B" AND I$ <>"C" AND I$ <>"D" THEN 420
440 T$(N,M)=I$
450 NEXT N
460 REM ********************************
470 REM DISPLAY FUNCTIONS & TERMINALS*
480 REM ********************************
490 PRINT"█";
500 FOR M=1 TO 4
501 PRINT"█";
502 IF M=1 THEN 505
503 FOR C=1 TO 6*(M-1):PRINT:NEXT C
505 IF F%(M)=0 THEN 610
510 GOSUB 1000:REM DISPLAY FUNCTION
530 ON F%(M) GOSUB 1100,1200,1300,1400,1500,1600,1700
540 PRINT"██████████████████";P$;"██████████( ) ";CHR$(91-M)
590 REM DISPLAY INPUTS
600 ON I%(M) GOSUB 5000,5100,5200,5300
610 NEXT M
620 PRINT"████████████████████████████████PRESS 'F' FOR MORE FUNCTIONS,
'E' TO END";
630 GET A$
640 IF A$="F" THEN 100
650 IF A$="E" THEN END
660 REM GET INPUT DATA
670 FOR N=1 TO 4
680 A%(N)=0
```

```
690 IF PEEK(PRT)AND 2↑(N-1) THEN A%(N)=1
700 NEXT N
710 REM
720 REM
730 REM CHANGE INPUT VALUES ON SCREEN
740 FOR PN=0 TO 22
750 SC=SR+PN*LN
760 J=PEEK(SC)
770 IF J>4 THEN 790
780 POKE (SC+3),A%(J)+48
790 NEXT PN
800 REM CALCULATE OUTPUT DATA
810 FOR M=1 TO 4
820 IF F%(M)=0 THEN980
850 FOR N=1 TO I%(M)
860 IF T$(N,M)="A"THEN VI%(N)=A%(1)
870 IF T$(N,M)="B"THEN VI%(N)=A%(2)
880 IF T$(N,M)="C"THEN VI%(N)=A%(3)
890 IF T$(N,M)="D"THEN VI%(N)=A%(4)
900 NEXT N
910 ON F%(M) GOSUB 3100,3200,3300,3400,3500,3600,3700
920 REM SEND OUTPUT TO USER PORT
930 H=(2↑(8-M))
940 POKE PRT,PEEK(PRT) AND (255-H)
950 K%= H*VO%
960 POKE PRT,PEEK(PRT) OR K%
970 IF PEEK(32637+240*M)<>32 THEN          POKE 32638+240*M,
(48+VO%)
980 NEXT M
990 GOTO 630
1000 REM BOX DISPLAY
1010 PRINT"▓▓▓▓▓▓▓▓▓▓▓▓▓┌─────────────┐              "
1020 PRINT"▓▓▓▓▓▓▓▓▓▓▓▓▓│             │              "
1030 PRINT"▓▓▓▓▓▓▓▓▓▓▓▓▓│        ├───────────┤"
1040 PRINT"▓▓▓▓▓▓▓▓▓▓▓▓▓│             │              "
1050 PRINT"▓▓▓▓▓▓▓▓▓▓▓▓▓└─────────────┘              "
1060 RETURN
1100 P$="  AND  ":RETURN
1200 P$="  OR   ":RETURN
1300 P$="  NOT  ":RETURN
1400 P$="EX-OR  ":RETURN
1500 P$="EQUIV. ":RETURN
1600 P$=" NAND  ":RETURN
1700 P$=" NOR   ":RETURN
3000 REM DETERMINE OUTPUTS FOR EACH FUNCTION
3100 REM AND FUNCTION
3110 VO%=1
3120 FOR N=1 TO I%(M)
3130 VO%=VO% AND VI%(N)
3140 NEXT N
3150 RETURN
3200 REM OR FUNCTION
3210 VO%=0
3220 FOR N=1 TO I%(M)
3230 VO%=VO% OR VI%(N)
3240 NEXT N
3250 RETURN
3300 REM NOT FUNCTION
```

```
3310 VO%=0
3320 IF VI%(1)=0 THEN VO%=1
3330 RETURN
3400 REM EXCLUSIVE-OR FUNCTION
3410 VO%=1
3420 IF VI%(1)=VI%(2) THEN VO%=0
3430 RETURN
3500 REM EQUIVALENCE FUNCTION
3510 VO%=0
3520 IF VI%(1)=VI%(2) THEN VO%=1
3530 RETURN
3600 REM NAND FUNCTION
3610 VO%=1
3620 FOR N=1 TO I%(M)
3630 VO%=VO% AND VI%(N)
3640 NEXT N
3650 IF VO%=0 THEN VO%=1:RETURN
3660 IF VO%=1 THEN VO%=0:RETURN
3700 REM NOR FUNCTION
3710 VO%=0
3720 FOR N=1 TO I%(M)
3730 VO%=VO% OR VI%(N)
3740 NEXT N
3750 IF VO%=0 THEN VO%=1:RETURN
3760 IF VO%=1 THEN VO%=0:RETURN
5000 REM APPEND THE INPUTS
5010 REM ONE INPUT
5020 PRINT"⬛";T$(1,M);" ( )————"
5030 RETURN
5100 REM TWO INPUTS
5110 PRINT"⬛⬛";T$(1,M);" ( )————"
5120 PRINT"⬛";T$(2,M);" ( )————"
5130 RETURN
5200 REM THREE INPUTS
5210 PRINT"⬛⬛⬛";T$(1,M);" ( )————"
5220 PRINT"⬛";T$(2,M);" ( )————"
5230 PRINT"⬛";T$(3,M);" ( )————"
5240 RETURN
5300 REM FOUR INPUTS
5310 PRINT"⬛⬛⬛";T$(1,M);" ( )————"
5320 PRINT T$(2,M);" ( )————"
5330 PRINT"⬛";T$(3,M);" ( )————"
5340 PRINT T$(4,M);" ( )————"
5350 RETURN
READY.
```

Program 3   LOGIC MAKER

```
1 REM LOGIC MAKER - PROGRAM 3
50 PRT = 59471
60 POKE 59459,240:REM BITS 0 TO 3 AS INPUTS, 4 TO 7 AS OUTPUTS
70 DD=33019:DC=33139:DB=33259:DA=33379
80 DZ=33038:DY=33158:DX=33278:DW=33398
100 PRINT"⬛          BOOLEAN FUNCTIONS"
110 PRINT"⬛SELECT DESIRED FUNCTION BY QUITTING"
120 PRINT"⬛THIS PROGRAM AND CHANGING LINES"
130 PRINT"⬛5010 TO 5100 OF THE PROGRAM."
```

```
140 PRINT"█IF YOU HAVE NOT CHANGED THIS,"
150 PRINT"█THEN THE FUNCTION IS 'A AND B'"
160 PRINT"█WHICH APPEARS AT OUTPUT 'Z'."
200 PRINT"████PRESS 'C' TO PRODUCE THE FUNCTION."
210 PRINT"█PRESS 'E' TO EXIT THE PROGRAM."
220 GET A$:IF A$<>"E" AND A$<>"C" THEN 220
230 PRINT"████        INPUTS              OUTPUTS
240 PRINT"██        D ( )                Z ( )"
250 PRINT"██        C ( )                Y ( )"
260 PRINT"██        B ( )                X ( )"
270 PRINT"██        A ( )                W ( )"
280 PRINT"████PRESS 'E' TO EXIT THE PROGRAM."
400 IF A$="E" THEN PRINT"█████":LIST 5000-5100
450 GET A$
500 REM GET INPUTS FROM USER PORT
510 A=0:B=0:C=0:D=0
520 IF PEEK(PRT)AND 1 THEN A=1
530 IF PEEK(PRT)AND 2 THEN B=1
540 IF PEEK(PRT)AND 4 THEN C=1
550 IF PEEK(PRT)AND 8 THEN D=1
560 REM DISPLAY INPUTS
570 POKE DD,D+48
580 POKE DC,C+48
590 POKE DB,B+48
600 POKE DA,A+48
650 REM CALCULATE FUNCTION
660 GOSUB 5000
700 REM CHANGE OUTPUTS
710 IF (Z AND 1) THEN POKE PRT,PEEK(PRT) OR 128
720 IF (NOT Z AND 1) THEN POKE PRT,PEEK(PRT) AND 127
730 IF (Y AND 1) THEN POKE PRT,PEEK(PRT) OR 64
740 IF (NOT Y AND 1) THEN POKE PRT,PEEK(PRT) AND 191
750 IF (X AND 1) THEN POKE PRT,PEEK(PRT) OR 32
760 IF (NOT X AND 1) THEN POKE PRT,PEEK(PRT) AND 223
770 IF (W AND 1) THEN POKE PRT,PEEK(PRT) OR 16
780 IF (NOT W AND 1) THEN POKE PRT,PEEK(PRT) AND 239
800 REM DISPLAY OUTPUTS
810 IF (Z AND 1) THEN POKE PRT,PEEK(PRT) OR 128:POKE DZ,49
820 IF (NOT Z AND 1) THEN POKE PRT,PEEK(PRT) AND 127:POKE DZ,48
830 IF (Y AND 1) THEN POKE PRT,PEEK(PRT) OR 64:POKE DY,49
840 IF (NOT Y AND 1) THEN POKE PRT,PEEK(PRT) AND 191:POKE DY,48
850 IF (X AND 1) THEN POKE PRT,PEEK(PRT) OR 32:POKE DX,49
860 IF (NOT X AND 1) THEN POKE PRT,PEEK(PRT) AND 223 :POKE DX,48
870 IF (W AND 1) THEN POKE PRT,PEEK(PRT) OR 16 :POKE DW,49
880 IF (NOT W AND 1) THEN POKE PRT,PEEK(PRT) AND 239:POKE DW,48
890 GOTO 400
5000 REM BOOLEAN FUNCTIONS
5010 Z = A AND B
5020 Y=0
5030 X=0
5040 W=A OR B
6000 RETURN
READY.
```

Apple program listings

Program 1 LOGIC GATES

```
10   REM  LOGIC GATES
20 A% = 0:B% = 0: REM   INPUT LOGIC LEVELS
40 S% = 0: REM   MENU VALUE OF FUNCTION
60   DIM D$(7): REM   NAMES OF FUNCTIONS
70 PRT = 49344: REM  USER PORT ADDRESS
80   POKE 49346,240: REM  BITS 0 TO 3 AS INPUTS, 4 TO 7 AS OUTPUTS
100  HOME : PRINT "         LOGIC GATES"
110  PRINT : PRINT "SELECT DESIRED FUNCTION BY ENTERING ONE"
120  PRINT : PRINT "OF THE FOLLOWING NUMBERS."
130  D$(1) = "AND"
140  D$(2) = "OR"
150  D$(3) = "NOT"
160  D$(4) = "EXCLUSIVE-OR"
170  D$(5) = "EQUIVALENCE"
180  D$(6) = "NAND"
190  D$(7) = "NOR"
195  FOR I = 1 TO 7: HTAB 5: PRINT : PRINT I,D$(I): NEXT I
200  PRINT : PRINT "THEN PRESS <RETURN> ";: INPUT S$
210  S% = VAL (S$): IF S% < 1 OR S% > 7 THEN 200
220  D$(4) = "EX-OR"
230  D$(5) = "EQUIV"
1000  REM ******************************
1010  REM  DISPLAY FUNCTIONS AND TERMINALS
1020  REM ******************************
1030  HOME
1060  PRINT "            LOGIC GATES"
1070  PRINT
1080  GOSUB 10000: REM  DISPLAY FUNCTION
1090  PRINT
1100  GOSUB 4000: REM   DISPLAY TRUTH TABLE
1110  VTAB 5
1120  HTAB 15: PRINT D$(S%);: HTAB 24: PRINT "-----( )
1150  LET OL% = 1: REM  RESET TABLE POINTER
1200  REM  DISPLAY INPUTS
1210  VTAB 3
1220  IF S% = 3 THEN  GOSUB 5000
```

```
1230   IF S% ( ) 3 THEN   GOSUB 5100
1350   VTAB 23: PRINT "PRESS 'C' TO CHANGE OR (ESC) TO END"
1360   IF  PEEK (49152) ) 127 THEN 2000
1370   REM   GET INPUT DATA
1390 A% = 0:B% = 0
1400 PP =  PEEK (PRT)
1410   IF PP ) 127 THEN PP = PP - 128
1420   IF PP ) 63 THEN PP = PP - 64
1430   IF PP ) 31 THEN PP = PP - 32
1440   IF PP ) 15 THEN PP = PP - 16
1450   IF PP ) 7 THEN PP = PP - 8
1460   IF PP ) 3 THEN PP = PP - 4
1470   IF PP ) 1 THEN PP = PP - 2:B% = 1
1480 A% = PP
1490   IF S% = 3 THEN 1550
1495   IF OL% = 4 * A% + 2 * B% + 13 THEN 1360
1500   REM   CHANGE SCREEN VALUES
1510   VTAB 4: PRINT "B";: HTAB 4: PRINT B%
1520   VTAB 6: PRINT "A";: HTAB 4: PRINT A%
1530   GOTO 1800
1540   REM   ONE INPUT ONLY
1550   VTAB 5: PRINT "A";: HTAB 4: PRINT A%
1700   REM   CALCULATE OUTPUT DATA
1800   ON S% GOSUB 3100,3200,3300,3400,3500,3600,3700
1810   REM   SEND DATA TO USER PORT
1820   POKE PRT,16 * VO%
1850   REM   CHANGE SCREEN OUTPUT VALUES
1860   VTAB 5: HTAB 30: PRINT VO%
1880   VTAB OL%
1890   PRINT "    ";: HTAB 24: PRINT " ";: HTAB 26: PRINT "    "
1900   LET OL% = 4 * A% + 2 * B% + 13
1910   VTAB OL%
1920   INVERSE : PRINT "    ";: HTAB 24: NORMAL : PRINT VO%;: INVERSE : HTAB
       26: PRINT "    ": NORMAL
1950   GOTO 1360
2000   REM   KEY PRESSED
2010 QZ =  PEEK (49168): REM   CLEAR KEY
2020   IF  PEEK (49152) = 27 THEN   STOP
2030   IF  PEEK (49152) = 67 THEN 100
```

```
2040    GOTO 1360
3000    REM   DETERMINE VALUE OF FUNCTIONS
3100    REM   AND FUNCTION
3110    VO% = A% AND B%
3140    RETURN
3200    REM   OR FUNCTION
3210    VO% = A% OR B%
3240    RETURN
3300    REM   NOT FUNCTION
3310    VO% = 0
3320    IF A% = 0 THEN VO% = 1
3330    RETURN
3400    REM   EXCLUSIVE-OR FUNCTION
3410    VO% = 1
3420    IF A% = B% THEN VO% = 0
3430    RETURN
3500    REM   EQUIVALENCE  FUNCTION
3310    VO% = 0
3520    IF A% = B% THEN VO% = 1
3530    RETURN
3600    REM   NAND FUNCTION
3610    VO% =   NOT (A% AND B%)
3650    RETURN
3700    REM   NOR FUNCTION
3710    VO% =   NOT (A% OR B%)
3750    RETURN
4000    REM   TRUTH TABLE
4010    PRINT "           TRUTH TABLE"
4020    PRINT : PRINT "     A       B       OUTPUT"
4030    PRINT : PRINT "     0       0 "
4040    PRINT : PRINT "     0       1 "
4050    PRINT : PRINT "     1       0 "
4060    PRINT : PRINT "     1       1 "
4070    RETURN
5000    REM   APPEND ONE INPUT
5005    PRINT : PRINT
5010    PRINT "  ( )------"
5020    RETURN
5100    REM   APPEND TWO INPUTS
```

```
5105   PRINT
5110   PRINT "  ( )------"
5115   PRINT
5120   PRINT "  ( )------"
5150   RETURN
10000   REM  BOX
10010   INVERSE
10020   HTAB 12: PRINT "             "
10030   HTAB 12: PRINT "             "
10040   HTAB 12: PRINT "             "
10050   HTAB 12: PRINT "             "
10060   HTAB 12: PRINT "             "
10070   NORMAL
10080   RETURN
```

Program 2   LOGIC TUTOR

```
10   DIM T$(4,4): REM  FUNCTION VARIABLES IN THE ORDER (INPUT,OUTPUT)
20   DIM A%(4): REM  INPUT DATA FROM USER PORT
30   DIM VI%(4): REM  VALUES FOR INPUT DATA
40   DIM F%(4): REM  MENU VALUE OF FUNCTION
50   N = 0:M = 0: REM  INPUT AND OUTPUT REFERENCE NUMBERS
60   DIM D$(7): REM   NAMES OF FUNCTIONS
70   PRT = 49344: REM  USER PORT ADDRESS
80   POKE 49346,240: REM  BITS 0 TO 3 AS INPUTS, 4 TO 7 AS OUTPUTS
90   FOR I = 1 TO 4:F%(I) = 0: NEXT I
100   HOME : PRINT "        BOOLEAN FUNCTIONS"
110   PRINT : PRINT "SELECT DESIRED FUNCTION BY ENTERING ONE"
120   PRINT : PRINT "OF THE FOLLOWING NUMBERS."
130   D$(1) = "AND"
140   D$(2) = "OR"
150   D$(3) = "NOT"
160   D$(4) = "EXCLUSIVE-OR"
170   D$(5) = "EQUIVALENCE"
180   D$(6) = "NAND"
190   D$(7) = "NOR"
195   FOR I = 1 TO 7: HTAB 5: PRINT : PRINT I,D$(I): NEXT I
200   PRINT : PRINT "THEN PRESS <RETURN> ";: INPUT S$
210   S% =  VAL (S$): IF S% < 1 OR S% > 7 THEN 200
220   HOME : VTAB 5: PRINT "YOUR SELECTION IS '";D$(S%);"'"
```

```
230   PRINT : PRINT : PRINT "WHICH OUTPUT SHOULD HAVE THIS FUNCTION ?"
240   PRINT : PRINT "SELECT ONE OF W, X, Y OR Z AND"
250   PRINT : PRINT "THEN PRESS <RETURN>.";: INPUT O$
260   IF O$ = "W" THEN M = 4
270   IF O$ = "X" THEN M = 3
280   IF O$ = "Y" THEN M = 2
290   IF O$ = "Z" THEN M = 1
300   IF M = 0 THEN 240
310   F%(M) = S%
320   IF S% = 4 OR S% = 5 THEN 360
330   IF S% < > 3 THEN 380
340   HOME : VTAB 3: PRINT "THE 'NOT' FUNCTION HAS ONLY ONE INPUT"
350   I%(M) = 1: GOTO 500
360   HOME : VTAB 3: PRINT "THIS FUNCTION HAS ONLY TWO INPUTS"
370   I%(M) = 2: GOTO 510
380   HOME : VTAB 3: PRINT "THIS FUNCTION HAS TWO OR MORE INPUTS"
390   PRINT : PRINT : PRINT "HOW MANY INPUTS DO YOU REQUIRE "
400   PRINT : PRINT "ENTER 2, 3 OR 4, THEN PRESS <RETURN>"
410   PRINT : INPUT I$
420   I%(M) =  VAL (I$)
430   IF I%(M) < 2 OR I%(M) > 4 THEN 400
450   HOME : VTAB 3
500   IF I%(M) = 1 THEN  PRINT : PRINT "WHICH INPUT ?": GOTO 550
510   PRINT : PRINT "WHICH INPUTS ?": GOTO 550
520   PRINT : PRINT "IT IS POSSIBLE TO USE ONE INPUT MORE"
530   PRINT : PRINT "THAN ONCE, PROVIDED YOU HAVE ASKED"
540   PRINT : PRINT "FOR ENOUGH INPUTS."
550   PRINT : PRINT : PRINT "ENTER A, B, C OR D FOR EACH REQUEST"
555   PRINT : PRINT "AND PRESS <RETURN> AFTER EACH ONE."
560   FOR N = 1 TO 4:T$(N,M) = "": NEXT N
570   FOR N = 1 TO I%(M)
580   PRINT : INPUT I$
590   IF I$ < > "A" AND I$ < > "B" AND I$ < > "C" AND I$ < > "D" THEN  PRINT
      : PRINT "ENTER A, B, C OR D FOR EACH REQUEST": GOTO 580
600   T$(N,M) = I$
610   NEXT N
1000  REM ******************************
1010  REM  DISPLAY FUNCTIONS AND TERMINALS
1020  REM ******************************
```

```
1030  HOME
1040  FOR M = 1 TO 4
1050 PS = 6 * (M - 1) + 1
1060  VTAB PS
1070  IF F%(M) = 0 THEN 1300
1080  GOSUB 10000: REM  DISPLAY FUNCTION
1090  P$ =  LEFT$ (D$(F%(M)),5)
1100  IF F%(M) = 4 THEN P$ = "EX-OR"
1110 PQ = PS + 2: VTAB PQ
1120  HTAB 15: PRINT P$;: HTAB 24: PRINT "-----( ) "; CHR$ (219 - M)
1200  REM  DISPLAY INPUTS
1210  VTAB PS
1220  ON I%(M) GOSUB 5000,5100,5200,5300
1300  NEXT M
1350  VTAB 24: PRINT "PRESS `F' FOR MORE OR <ESC> TO END";
1360  IF  PEEK (49152) > 127 THEN 2000
1370  REM  GET INPUT DATA
1390 A%(1) = 0:A%(2) = 0:A%(3) = 0:A%(4) = 0
1400 PP =  PEEK (PRT)
1410  IF PP > 127 THEN PP = PP - 128
1420  IF PP > 63 THEN PP = PP - 64
1430  IF PP > 31 THEN PP = PP - 32
1440  IF PP > 15 THEN PP = PP - 16
1450  IF PP > 7 THEN PP = PP - 8:A%(4) = 1
1460  IF PP > 3 THEN PP = PP - 4:A%(3) = 1
1470  IF PP > 1 THEN PP = PP - 2:A%(2) = 1
1480 A%(1) = PP
1500  REM  CHANGE SCREEN VALUES
1510  FOR R = 1024 TO 2000 STEP 128
1520  FOR RR = 0 TO 80 STEP 40
1530 QR = R + RR
1540 J =  PEEK (QR)
1550  IF J = 160 THEN 1600
1560  IF J = 193 THEN  POKE (QR + 3),A%(1) + 176
1570  IF J = 194 THEN  POKE (QR + 3),A%(2) + 176
1580  IF J = 195 THEN  POKE (QR + 3),A%(3) + 176
1590  IF J = 196 THEN  POKE (QR + 3),A%(4) + 176
1600  NEXT RR
1610  NEXT R
```

```
1700   REM   CALCULATE OUTPUT DATA
1705 T = 0
1710   FOR M = 1 TO 4
1720   IF F%(M) = 0 THEN 1880
1730   FOR N = 1 TO I%(M)
1740   IF T$(N,M) = "A" THEN VI%(N) = A%(1)
1750   IF T$(N,M) = "B" THEN VI%(N) = A%(2)
1760   IF T$(N,M) = "C" THEN VI%(N) = A%(3)
1770   IF T$(N,M) = "D" THEN VI%(N) = A%(4)
1780   NEXT N
1800   ON F%(M) GOSUB 3100,3200,3300,3400,3500,3600,3700
1810   REM   SEND DATA TO USER PORT
1820 T = T + (2 ^ (8 - M) * VO%)
1850   REM   CHANGE SCREEN OUTPUT VALUES
1860 PT = 3 + 6 * (M - 1)
1870   VTAB PT: HTAB 30: PRINT VO%
1880   NEXT M
1890   POKE PRT,T
1900   GOTO 1360
2000   REM   KEY PRESSED
2010 QZ = PEEK (49168): REM   CLEAR KEY
2020   IF   PEEK (49152) = 27 THEN   STOP
2030   IF   PEEK (49152) = 70 THEN 100
2040   GOTO 1360
3000   REM   DETERMINE VALUE OF FUNCTIONS
3100   REM   AND FUNCTION
3105 VO% = 1
3110   FOR N = 1 TO I%(M)
3120 VO% = VO% AND VI%(N)
3130   NEXT N
3140   RETURN
3200   REM   OR FUNCTION
3205 VO% = 0
3210   FOR N = 1 TO I%(M)
3220 VO% = VO% OR VI%(N)
3230   NEXT N
3240   RETURN
3300   REM   NOT FUNCTION
3310 VO% = 0
```

```
3320   IF  VI%(1)  =  0  THEN  VO%  =  1
3330   RETURN
3400   REM   EXCLUSIVE-OR  FUNCTION
3410   VO%  =  1
3420   IF  VI%(1)  =  VI%(2)  THEN  VO%  =  0
3430   RETURN
3500   REM   EQUIVALENCE   FUNCTION
3510   VO%  =  0
3520   IF  VI%(1)  =  VI%(2)  THEN  VO%  =  1
3530   RETURN
3600   REM   NAND  FUNCTION
3605   VO%  =  1
3610   FOR  N  =  1  TO  I%(M)
3620   VO%  =  VO%  AND  VI%(N)
3630   NEXT  N
3640   VO%  =   NOT  (VO%)
3650   RETURN
3700   REM   NOR  FUNCTION
3705   VO%  =  0
3710   FOR  N  =  1  TO  I%(M)
3720   VO%  =  VO%  OR  VI%(N)
3730   NEXT  N
3740   VO%  =   NOT  (VO%)
3750   RETURN
5000   REM   APPEND  ONE  INPUT
5005   PRINT : PRINT
5010   PRINT ;T$(1,M);"  (  )------"
5020   RETURN
5100   REM   APPEND  TWO  INPUTS
5105   PRINT
5110   PRINT ;T$(1,M);"  (  )------"
5115   PRINT
5120   PRINT ;T$(2,M);"  (  )------"
5150   RETURN
5200   REM   APPEND  THREE  INPUTS
5210   PRINT ;T$(1,M);"  (  )------"
5215   PRINT
5220   PRINT ;T$(2,M);"  (  )------"
5225   PRINT
```

```
5230   PRINT ;T$(3,M);" ( )------"
5250   RETURN
5300   REM  APPEND FOUR INPUTS
5310   PRINT ;T$(1,M);" ( )------"
5320   PRINT ;T$(2,M);" ( )------"
5325   PRINT
5330   PRINT ;T$(3,M);" ( )------"
5340   PRINT ;T$(4,M);" ( )------"
5350   RETURN
10000  REM  BOX
10010  INVERSE
10020  HTAB 12: PRINT "              "
10030  HTAB 12: PRINT "              "
10040  HTAB 12: PRINT "              "
10050  HTAB 12: PRINT "              "
10060  HTAB 12: PRINT "              "
10070  NORMAL
10080  RETURN
```

Program 3   LOGIC MAKER

```
100   REM SWITCH OFF ALL OUTPUTS
110   POKE 49344,0
120   POKE 49346,240: REM  BITS 4 TO 7 AS OUTPUTS
200   HOME
230   PRINT "SELECT THE REQUIRED FUNCTION BY"
240   PRINT : PRINT "LEAVING THE PROGRAM (WITH THE SPACE BAR)"
250   PRINT "AND CHANGING LINES 5000 TO 5100."
270   PRINT : PRINT "THIS TURNS THE BOARD OUTPUTS INTO"
280   PRINT : PRINT "DIFFERENT FUNCTIONS OF THE INPUTS."
290   PRINT : PRINT "TO BEGIN WITH, THE FOLLOWING FUNCTIONS"
300   PRINT : PRINT "HAVE BEEN SET UP."
310   PRINT : PRINT "Z IS  D ";: INVERSE : PRINT "AND";: NORMAL : PRINT " C
      "
311   PRINT : PRINT "Y IS  D ";: INVERSE : PRINT "OR";: NORMAL : PRINT " C"
312   PRINT : PRINT "X IS ";: INVERSE : PRINT "NOT";: NORMAL : PRINT "(B ";
      : INVERSE : PRINT "AND";: NORMAL : PRINT " A)"
313   PRINT : PRINT "W IS ";: INVERSE : PRINT "NOT";: NORMAL : PRINT "(B ";
      : INVERSE : PRINT "OR";: NORMAL : PRINT " A)"
```

```
330    PRINT : PRINT "PRESS SPACE FOR THE SYMBOLIC DIAGRAM."
340    GET A$
350    IF A$ < > " " THEN 340
1000   REM  DRAW BLOCKS ON TEXT SCREEN
1010   HOME
1100   INVERSE : VTAB 1: HTAB 15: PRINT "          "
1110   VTAB 2: HTAB 12: PRINT "      "
1115   VTAB 2: HTAB 21: PRINT " "
1120   VTAB 3: HTAB 21: PRINT "      "
1125   VTAB 3: HTAB 15: PRINT " "
1130   VTAB 4: HTAB 12: PRINT "      "
1135   VTAB 4: HTAB 21: PRINT " "
1140   VTAB 5: HTAB 15: PRINT "          "
1150   VTAB 7: HTAB 15: PRINT "          "
1160   VTAB 8: HTAB 12: PRINT "      "
1165   VTAB 8: HTAB 21: PRINT " "
1170   VTAB 9: HTAB 21: PRINT "      "
1175   VTAB 9: HTAB 15: PRINT " "
1180   VTAB 10: HTAB 12: PRINT "      "
1185   VTAB 10: HTAB 21: PRINT " "
1190   VTAB 11: HTAB 15: PRINT "          "
1200   VTAB 13: HTAB 15: PRINT "          "
1210   VTAB 14: HTAB 12: PRINT "      "
1215   VTAB 14: HTAB 21: PRINT " "
1220   VTAB 15: HTAB 21: PRINT "      "
1225   VTAB 15: HTAB 15: PRINT " "
1230   VTAB 16: HTAB 12: PRINT "      "
1235   VTAB 16: HTAB 21: PRINT " "
1240   VTAB 17: HTAB 15: PRINT "          "
1250   VTAB 19: HTAB 15: PRINT "          "
1260   VTAB 20: HTAB 12: PRINT "      "
1265   VTAB 20: HTAB 21: PRINT " "
1270   VTAB 21: HTAB 21: PRINT "      "
1275   VTAB 21: HTAB 15: PRINT " "
1280   VTAB 22: HTAB 12: PRINT "      "
1285   VTAB 22: HTAB 21: PRINT " "
1290   VTAB 23: HTAB 15: PRINT "          "
2000   NORMAL
2010   VTAB 2: HTAB 7: PRINT "( ) D"
```

```
2020    VTAB 3: HTAB 27: PRINT "Z ( )"
2030    VTAB 4: HTAB 7: PRINT "( ) C"
2040    VTAB 8: HTAB 7: PRINT "( ) D"
2050    VTAB 9: HTAB 27: PRINT "Y ( )"
2060    VTAB 10: HTAB 7: PRINT "( ) C"
2070    VTAB 14: HTAB 7: PRINT "( ) B"
2080    VTAB 15: HTAB 27: PRINT "X ( )"
2090    VTAB 16: HTAB 7: PRINT "( ) A"
2100    VTAB 20: HTAB 7: PRINT "( ) B"
2110    VTAB 21: HTAB 27: PRINT "W ( )"
2120    VTAB 22: HTAB 7: PRINT "( ) A"
2150    VTAB 24
2200    PRINT "PRESS SPACE TO CHANGE FUNCTIONS";
4000    GOSUB 10000: REM  GET INPUTS
4005    IF  PEEK (49152) > 127 THEN 9000
5000    REM ***********************
5020    REM *   CHANGE LINES 5100+ *
5030    REM *                      *
5040    REM * TO DESIRED FUNCTION *
5050    REM *                      *
5060    REM * THEN GOTO 1000(RET) *
5080    REM ***********************
5100 Z = C AND D
5120 Y = C OR D
5140 X =  NOT (A AND B)
5160 W =  NOT (A OR B)
6000    REM  CHANGE LED DISPLAY
6010    GOSUB 11000
7000    REM  CHANGE DISPLAYED VALUES
7010    VTAB 2: HTAB 8: PRINT D
7020    VTAB 3: HTAB 30: PRINT Z
7030    VTAB 4: HTAB 8: PRINT C
7040    VTAB 8: HTAB 8: PRINT D
7050    VTAB 9: HTAB 30: PRINT Y
7060    VTAB 10: HTAB 8: PRINT C
7110    VTAB 14: HTAB 8: PRINT B
7120    VTAB 15: HTAB 30: PRINT X
7130    VTAB 16: HTAB 8: PRINT A
7140    VTAB 20: HTAB 8: PRINT B
```

```
7150    VTAB 21: HTAB 30: PRINT W
7160    VTAB 22: HTAB 8: PRINT A
8000    GOTO 4000
9000    REM  CHANGE FUNCTION
9005    NORMAL
9010    HOME
9020    LIST 5000,5200
9030    VTAB 21: PRINT "ENTER NEW FUNCTION(S) AND THEN GOTO"
9040    PRINT : PRINT "LINE 1000 TO RE-RUN THE PROGRAM."
9050    VTAB 23: STOP
10000   REM  GET INPUTS
10010   Q =  PEEK (49344)
10020   IF Q > 127 THEN Q = Q - 128
10030   IF Q > 63 THEN Q = Q - 64
10040   IF Q > 31 THEN Q = Q - 32
10050   IF Q > 15 THEN Q = Q - 16
10060   D = 0: IF Q > 7 THEN Q = Q - 8:D = 1
10070   C = 0: IF Q > 3 THEN Q = Q - 4:C = 1
10080   B = 0: IF Q > 1 THEN Q = Q - 2:B = 1
10090   A = Q
10100   RETURN
11000   REM  CHANGE OUTPUTS
11010   Q = 128 * Z + 64 * Y + 32 * X + 16 * W
11020   POKE 49344,Q
11030   RETURN
11140   VTAB 5: HTAB 15: PRINT "          "
```

BBC microcomputer program listings

Program 1   LOGIC GATES

```
  1 MODE 7
 10 REM LOGIC GATES
 20 PRT=&FE60:REM USER PORT
 25 DDR=&FE62:REM DATA DIRECTION REGISTER
 80 SR=&7C00:REM SCREEN VALUE
 90 ?DDR=240:REM BITS 0 TO 3 ARE INPUTS, BITS 4 TO 7 ARE OUTPUTS
100 REM
110 CLS
120 PRINT TAB(12,0);"LOGIC GATES"
121 PRINT TAB(0,2);"SELECT DESIRED GATE BY PRESSING ONE"
122 PRINT TAB(0,4);"OF THE FOLLOWING NUMBERS."
123 PRINT TAB(6,6);"1      AND"
124 PRINT TAB(6,8);"2      OR"
125 PRINT TAB(6,10);"3      NOT"
126 PRINT TAB(6,12);"4      EXCLUSIVE-OR"
127 PRINT TAB(6,14);"5      EQUIVALENCE"
128 PRINT TAB(6,16);"6      NAND"
129 PRINT TAB(6,18);"7      NOR"
140 LET S$=GET$
145 S%=VAL(S$)
150 IF S%<1 OR S%>7 THEN 140
151 PRINT TAB(0,20);"YOUR SELECTION IS"
152 IF S%=1 THEN PRINT TAB(20,20);"AND"
153 IF S%=2 THEN PRINT TAB(20,20);"OR"
154 IF S%=3 THEN PRINT TAB(20,20);"NOT"
155 IF S%=4 THEN PRINT TAB(20,20);"EXCLUSIVE-OR"
156 IF S%=5 THEN PRINT TAB(20,20);"EQUIVALENCE"
157 IF S%=6 THEN PRINT TAB(20,20);"NAND"
158 IF S%=7 THEN PRINT TAB(20,20);"NOR"
160 PRINT :PRINT"Press RETURN to confirm"
165 PRINT :PRINT"or press SPACE to try again.";
170 IF GET$<>CHR$(13) THEN 110
250 IF S%<>3 THEN 490
260 CLS:PRINT TAB(0,2);"THE 'NOT' FUNCTION HAS ONE INPUT."
270 PRINT:PRINT"WHICH INPUT?  PRESS A OR B"
420 I$=GET$
430 IF I$<>"A" AND I$<>"B" THEN 420
460 REM ***********************
470 REM DISPLAY FUNCTION AND TERMINALS
480 REM ***********************
490 LET row=15:LET status=1000:REM Initialize flags
500 CLS
510 GOSUB 1000:REM DISPLAY FUNCTION
520PRINT TAB(10,0);"LOGIC GATES"
530 ON S% GOSUB 1100,1200,1300,1400,1500,1600,1700
540 PRINT TAB(13,4);P$
550 PRINT TAB(30,4);"( ) OUTPUT"
560 REM DISPLAY TRUTH TABLE
570 GOSUB 4000
590 REM DISPLAY INPUTS
600 IF S%=3 THEN GOSUB 5000 ELSE GOSUB 5100
620 PRINT TAB(0,22);"Press F for different gate, or E to end."
630 A$=INKEY$(0)
640 IF A$="F" THEN 110
```

```
 650 IF A$="E" THEN CLS:END
 660 REM GET DATA
 670 LET A%=?PRT AND 1
 680 LET B%=(?PRT AND 2)DIV 2
 690 IF status=2*B%+4*A% THEN 630
 700 REM CHANGE SCREEN VALUES ETC.
 710 LET status=2*B%+4*A%
 720
 730 REM CHANGE INPUT VALUES ON SCREEN
 740 IF S%=3 THEN 800:REM ONE INPUT
 750 PRINT TAB(2,3);B%
 760 PRINT TAB(2,5);A%
 770 GOTO 830
 780
 800 REM ONE INPUT
 810 IF I$="A" THEN PRINT TAB(2,4);A%
 820 IF I$="B" THEN PRINT TAB(2,4);B%
 830 REM DISPLAY CURRENT LINE
 840 PRINT TAB(3,row);"     "
 850 PRINT TAB(28,row);"     "
 855 PRINT TAB(21,row);" "
 860 LET row=12+2*B%+4*A%
 870 PRINT TAB(3,row);"]]]]]"
 880 PRINT TAB(28,row);"[[[[["
 900 REM CALCULATE OUTPUT DATA
 910 ON S% GOSUB 3100,3200,3300,3400,3500,3600,3700
 920 REM SEND OUTPUT TO USER PORT
 930  ?PRT= 16*VO%
 940 REM SEND LOGIC LEVEL TO SCREEN
 950 PRINT TAB(31,4);VO%
 960 IF VO%=1 THEN PRINT TAB(21,row);"I"
 970 IF VO%=0 THEN PRINT TAB(21,row);"O"
 990 GOTO 630
1000 REM BOX DISPLAY
1010 PRINT TAB(11,2);CHR$(151);CHR$(55);CHR$(96);CHR$(96);CHR$(96);CHR$(96);
CHR$(96);CHR$(96);CHR$(107);CHR$(135)
1020 PRINT TAB(11,3);CHR$(151);CHR$(53);"       ";CHR$(106);CHR$(135)
1030 PRINT TAB(11,4);CHR$(151);CHR$(53);"       ";CHR$(106);CHR$(44);CHR$(44);
CHR$(44);CHR$(44);CHR$(44);CHR$(44);CHR$(44);CHR$(44);CHR$(135)
1040PRINT TAB(11,5);CHR$(151);CHR$(53);"       ";CHR$(106);CHR$(135)
1050PRINT TAB(11,6);CHR$(151);CHR$(117);CHR$(112);CHR$(112);CHR$(112);CHR$
(112);CHR$(112);CHR$(112);CHR$(122);CHR$(135)
1060 RETURN
1100 P$="  AND":RETURN
1200 P$="   OR":RETURN
1300 P$="  NOT":RETURN
1400 P$="EX OR":RETURN
1500 P$="EQUIV":RETURN
1600 P$=" NAND":RETURN
1700 P$="  NOR":RETURN
3000 REM DETERMINE OUTPUTS FOR EACH FUNCTION
3100 REM AND FUNCTION
3110 VO%=A% AND B%
3150 RETURN
3200 REM OR FUNCTION
3210 VO%=A% OR B%
3250 RETURN
3300 REM NOT FUNCTION
```

```
3310 IF S%=3 AND I$="A" THEN VO%=(NOT A%) AND 1
3320 IF S%=3 AND I$="B" THEN VO%=(NOT B%) AND 1
3330 RETURN
3400 REM EXCLUSIVE-OR FUNCTION
3410 VO%=((A% AND NOT B%) OR (NOT A% AND B%)) AND 1
3430 RETURN
3500 REM EQUIVALENCE FUNCTION
3510 VO%=((A% AND B%) OR (NOT A% AND NOT B%)) AND 1
3530 RETURN
3600 REM NAND FUNCTION
3610 VO%=NOT(A% AND B%) AND 1
3620 RETURN
3700 REM NOR FUNCTION
3710 VO%=NOT(A% OR B%) AND 1
3760 RETURN
4000 REM DRAW TRUTH TABLE
4010 PRINT TAB(8,8);CHR$(151);CHR$(55);CHR$(96);CHR$(96);CHR$(96);CHR$(55);
CHR$(96);CHR$(96);CHR$(96);CHR$(55);CHR$(96);CHR$(96);CHR$(96);CHR$(96);CHR$
(96);CHR$(96);CHR$(96);CHR$(96);CHR$(235)
4020 PRINT TAB(8,9);CHR$(151);CHR$(53);CHR$(32);CHR$(193);CHR$(32);CHR$(53);
CHR$(32);CHR$(194);CHR$(32);CHR$(53);CHR$(32);CHR$(207);CHR$(213);CHR$(212);
CHR$(208);CHR$(213);CHR$(212);CHR$(32);CHR$(234)
4030 PRINT TAB(8,10);CHR$(151);CHR$(117);CHR$(240);CHR$(240);CHR$(240);CHR$
(117);CHR$(240);CHR$(240);CHR$(240);CHR$(117);CHR$(240);CHR$(240);CHR$(240);
CHR$(240);CHR$(240);CHR$(240);CHR$(240);CHR$(250)
4040 PRINT TAB(8,11);CHR$(151);CHR$(53);CHR$(32);CHR$(32);CHR$(32);CHR$(53);
CHR$(32);CHR$(32);CHR$(32);CHR$(53);CHR$(32);CHR$(32);CHR$(32);CHR$(32);CHR$
(32);CHR$(32);CHR$(32);CHR$(32);CHR$(106)
4050 PRINT TAB(8,12);CHR$(151);CHR$(53);CHR$(32);CHR$(207);CHR$(32);CHR$(53);
CHR$(32);CHR$(207);CHR$(32);CHR$(53);CHR$(32);CHR$(32);CHR$(32);CHR$(32);CHR$
(32);CHR$(32);CHR$(32);CHR$(32);CHR$(234)
4060 PRINT TAB(8,13);CHR$(151);CHR$(53);CHR$(32);CHR$(32);CHR$(32);CHR$(53);
CHR$(32);CHR$(32);CHR$(32);CHR$(53);CHR$(32);CHR$(32);CHR$(32);CHR$(32);CHR$
(32);CHR$(32);CHR$(32);CHR$(32);CHR$(106)
4070 PRINT TAB(8,14);CHR$(151);CHR$(53);CHR$(32);CHR$(32);CHR$(207);CHR$(32);CHR$(53);
CHR$(32);CHR$(201);CHR$(32);CHR$(53);CHR$(32);CHR$(32);CHR$(32);CHR$(32);CHR$
(32);CHR$(32);CHR$(32);CHR$(32);CHR$(234)
4080 PRINT TAB(8,15);CHR$(151);CHR$(53);CHR$(32);CHR$(32);CHR$(32);CHR$(53);
CHR$(32);CHR$(32);CHR$(32);CHR$(53);CHR$(32);CHR$(32);CHR$(32);CHR$(32);CHR$
(32);CHR$(32);CHR$(32);CHR$(32);CHR$(106)
4090 PRINT TAB(8,16);CHR$(151);CHR$(53);CHR$(32);CHR$(201);CHR$(32);CHR$
(53);CHR$(32);CHR$(207);CHR$(32);CHR$(53);CHR$(32);CHR$(32);CHR$(32);CHR$(32);
CHR$(32);CHR$(32);CHR$(32);CHR$(32);CHR$(234)
4100 PRINT TAB(8,17);CHR$(151);CHR$(53);CHR$(32);CHR$(32);CHR$(32);CHR$(53);
CHR$(32);CHR$(32);CHR$(32);CHR$(53);CHR$(32);CHR$(32);CHR$(32);CHR$(32);CHR$
(32);CHR$(32);CHR$(32);CHR$(32);CHR$(106)
4110 PRINT TAB(8,18);CHR$(151);CHR$(53);CHR$(32);CHR$(201);CHR$(32);CHR$
(53);CHR$(32);CHR$(201);CHR$(32);CHR$(53);CHR$(32);CHR$(32);CHR$(32);CHR$(32);
CHR$(32);CHR$(32);CHR$(32);CHR$(32);CHR$(234)
4120 PRINT TAB(8,19);CHR$(151);CHR$(117);CHR$(240);CHR$(240);CHR$(240);CHR$
(117);CHR$(240);CHR$(240);CHR$(240);CHR$(117);CHR$(240);CHR$(240);CHR$(240);
CHR$(240);CHR$(240);CHR$(240);CHR$(240);CHR$(250)
4200 RETURN
5000 REM APPEND THE INPUTS
5010 REM ONE INPUT
5020 PROCline(4,I$)
5030 RETURN
5100 REM TWO INPUTS
```

```
5110 PROCline(3,"B")
5120 PROCline(5,"A")
5130 RETURN
6000 DEFPROCline(K,G$)
6010 PRINT TAB(0,K);G$;"( )";CHR$(151);CHR$(44);CHR$(44);CHR$(44);CHR$(44);
CHR$(44);CHR$(44);CHR$(44)
6020 ENDPROC
```

Program 2   LOGIC TUTOR

```
  1 MODE 7
 10 REM BOOLEAN FUNCTIONS
 20 PRT=&FE60:REM USER PORT
 25 DDR=&FE62:REM DATA DIRECTION REGISTER
 30 DIM I%(4):REM NUMBER OF INPUTS PER GATE
 35 DIM T$(4,4):REM FUNCTION VARIABLES (INPUTS,OUTPUTS)
 40 DIM A%(4):REM INPUT DATA FROM USER PORT
 50 DIM VI%(4):REM VALUES FOR INPUT DATA
 60 DIM F%(4):REM MENU VALUE OF FUNCTION
 70 N=0:M=0:REM INPUT AND OUTPUT REFERENCE NUMBERS
 80 SR=&7C00:REM SCREEN VALUE
 90 ?DDR=240:REM BITS 0 TO 3 ARE INPUTS, BITS 4 TO 7 ARE OUTPUTS
100 FOR M=1 TO 4:F%(M)=0:NEXT M
110 CLS
120 PRINT TAB(12,0);"BOOLEAN FUNCTIONS"
121 PRINT TAB(0,2);"SELECT DESIRED FUNCTION BY ENTERING ONE"
122 PRINT TAB(0,4);"OF THE FOLLOWING NUMBERS."
123 PRINT TAB(6,6);"1      AND"
124 PRINT TAB(6,8);"2      OR"
125 PRINT TAB(6,10);"3      NOT"
126 PRINT TAB(6,12);"4      EXCLUSIVE-OR"
127 PRINT TAB(6,14);"5      EQUIVALENCE"
128 PRINT TAB(6,16);"6      NAND"
129 PRINT TAB(6,18);"7      NOR"
130 PRINT TAB(0,20);"THEN PRESS RETURN."
140 INPUT S$
145 S%=VAL(S$)
150 IF S%<1 OR S%>7 THEN 140
151 CLS:PRINT TAB(0,5);"YOUR SELECTION IS"
152 IF S%=1 THEN PRINT TAB(20,5);"AND"
153 IF S%=2 THEN PRINT TAB(20,5);"OR"
154 IF S%=3 THEN PRINT TAB(20,5);"NOT"
155 IF S%=4 THEN PRINT TAB(20,5);"EXCLUSIVE-OR"
156 IF S%=5 THEN PRINT TAB(20,5);"EQUIVALENCE"
157 IF S%=6 THEN PRINT TAB(20,5);"NAND"
158 IF S%=7 THEN PRINT TAB(20,5);"NOR"
160 PRINT TAB(0,8);"WHICH OUTPUT FOR THIS FUNCTION ?"
170 PRINT TAB(0,10);"ENTER ONE OF W, X, Y OR Z "
180 PRINT TAB(0,12);"AND THEN PRESS RETURN."
190 INPUT O$
200 IF O$<>"W" AND O$<>"X" AND O$<>"Y" AND O$<>"Z" THEN 190
210 IF O$="W" THEN M=4
220 IF O$="X" THEN M=3
230 IF O$="Y" THEN M=2
240 IF O$="Z" THEN M=1
245 F%(M)=S%
246 IF S%=4 OR S%=5 THEN 280
250 IF S%<>3 THEN 290
```

```
260 CLS:PRINT TAB(0,2);"THE 'NOT' FUNCTION HAS ONE INPUT."
270 I%(M)=1:GOTO 340
280 CLS:PRINT TAB(0,2);"THIS FUNCTION HAS TWO INPUTS."
285 I%(M)=2:GOTO 350
290 PRINT TAB(0,15);"HOW MANY INPUTS ?"
300 PRINT TAB(0,18);"ENTER 1, 2, 3 OR 4 AND THEN PRESS RETURN"
310 INPUT I$
320 I%(M)=VAL(I$)
330 IF I%(M)<1 OR I%(M)>4 THEN 310
340 IF I%(M)=1 THEN PRINT:PRINT;"WHICH INPUT ?":GOTO 360
345 CLS
350 PRINT TAB(0,4);"WHICH INPUTS ?"
360 PRINT:PRINT"ENTER A, B, C OR D FOR EACH REQUEST."
365 IF I%(M)=1 THEN 400
370PRINT:PRINT"IT IS POSSIBLE TO USE ONE INPUT MORE"
380PRINT:PRINT"THAN ONCE, PROVIDED YOU HAVE ASKED"
390PRINT:PRINT"FOR ENOUGH INPUTS."
400 FOR N=1 TO 4:T$(N,M)="":NEXT N
410 FOR N=1 TO I%(M)
420 INPUT I$
430 IF I$<>"A" AND I$<>"B" AND I$<>"C" AND I$<>"D" THEN 420
440 T$(N,M)=I$
450 NEXT N
460 REM ***********************
470 REM DISPLAY FUNCTIONS AND TERMINALS
480 REM ***********************
490 CLS
500 FOR M=1 TO 4
501 C=(M-1)*6
505 IF F%(M)=0 THEN 610
510 GOSUB 1000:REM DISPLAY FUNCTION
530 ON F%(M) GOSUB 1100,1200,1300,1400,1500,1600,1700
540 PRINT TAB(13,C+2);P$
550 PRINT TAB(31,C+2);"( )";CHR$(91-M)
590 REM DISPLAY INPUTS
600 ON I%(M) GOSUB 5000,5100,5200,5300
610 NEXT M
620 PRINT TAB(0,24);"PRESS 'F' FOR MORE FUNCTIONS,'E' TO END";
630 A$=INKEY$(0)
640 IF A$="F" THEN 110
650 IF A$="E" THEN END
660 REM GET DATA
670 FOR N=1 TO 4
680 A%(N)=0
690 IF ?PRT AND 2^(N-1) THEN A%(N)=1
700 NEXT N
710 REM
720
730 REM CHANGE INPUT VALUES ON SCREEN
740 FOR PN=0 TO 22
750 SC=SR+PN*40
760 J=?SC-64
770 IF J<1 OR J>4 THEN 790
780 ?(SC+2)=(A%(J)+48)
790 NEXT PN
800 REM CALCULATE OUTPUT DATA
810 FOR M=1 TO 4
820 IF F%(M)=0 THEN 980
```

```
 830 FOR N=1 TO I%(M)
 840 IF T$(N,M)="A" THEN VI%(N)=A%(1)
 850 IF T$(N,M)="B" THEN VI%(N)=A%(2)
 860 IF T$(N,M)="C" THEN VI%(N)=A%(3)
 870 IF T$(N,M)="D" THEN VI%(N)=A%(4)
 900 NEXT N
 910 ON F%(M) GOSUB 3100,3200,3300,3400,3500,3600,3700
 920 REM SEND OUTPUT TO USER PORT
 930 H=(2^(8-M))
 940 ?PRT=(?PRT AND (255-H))
 950 K%=H*VO%
 960 ?PRT=(?PRT OR K%)
 970 IF ?(31615+240*M)<>32 THEN ?(31616+240*M)=(48+VO%)
 980 NEXT M
 990 GOTO 630
1000 REM BOX DISPLAY
1010 PRINT TAB(11,C);CHR$(151);CHR$(55);CHR$(96);CHR$(96);CHR$(96);CHR$(96);
CHR$(96);CHR$(96);CHR$(107);CHR$(135)
1020 PRINT TAB(11,C+1);CHR$(151);CHR$(53);"        ";CHR$(106);CHR$(135)
1030 PRINT TAB(11,C+2);CHR$(151);CHR$(53);"        ";CHR$(106);CHR$(44);CHR$
(44);CHR$(44);CHR$(44);CHR$(44);CHR$(44);CHR$(44);CHR$(44);CHR$(44);;
CHR$(135)
1040PRINT TAB(11,C+3);CHR$(151);CHR$(53);"        ";CHR$(106);CHR$(135)
1050PRINT TAB(11,C+4);CHR$(151);CHR$(117);CHR$(112);CHR$(112);CHR$(112);CHR$
(112);CHR$(112);CHR$(112);CHR$(122);CHR$(135)
1060 RETURN
1100 P$="  AND":RETURN
1200 P$="   OR":RETURN
1300 P$="  NOT":RETURN
1400 P$="EX OR":RETURN
1500 P$="EQUIV":RETURN
1600 P$=" NAND":RETURN
1700 P$="  NOR":RETURN
3000 REM DETERMINE OUTPUTS FOR EACH FUNCTION
3100 REM AND FUNCTION
3110 VO%=1
3120 FOR N=1 TO I%(M)
3130 VO%=VO% AND VI%(N)
3140 NEXT N
3150 RETURN
3200 REM OR FUNCTION
3210 VO%=0
3220 FOR N=1 TO I%(M)
3230 VO%=VO% OR VI%(N)
3240 NEXT N
3250 RETURN
3300 REM NOT FUNCTION
3310 VO%=0
3320 IF VI%(1)=0 THEN VO%=1
3330 RETURN
3400 REM EXCLUSIVE-OR FUNCTION
3410 VO%=1
3420 IF VI%(1)=VI%(2) THEN VO%=0
3430 RETURN
3500 REM EQUIVALENCE FUNCTION
3510 VO%=0
3520 IF VI%(1)=VI%(2) THEN VO%=1
3530 RETURN
```

```
3600 REM NAND FUNCTION
3610 VO%=1
3620 FOR N=1 TO I%(M)
3630 VO%=VO% AND VI%(N)
3640 NEXT N
3650 IF VO%=0 THEN VO%=1:RETURN
3660 IF VO%=1 THEN VO%=0:RETURN
3700 REM NOR FUNCTION
3710 VO%=0
3720 FOR N=1 TO I%(M)
3730 VO%=VO% OR VI%(N)
3740 NEXT N
3750 IF VO%=0 THEN VO%=1:RETURN
3760 IF VO%=1 THEN VO%=0:RETURN
5000 REM APPEND THE INPUTS
5010 REM ONE INPUT
5020 PROCline(2,T$(1,M))
5030 RETURN
5100 REM TWO INPUTS
5110 PROCline(1,T$(1,M))
5120 PROCline(3,T$(2,M))
5130 RETURN
5200 REM THREE INPUTS
5210 PROCline(0,T$(1,M))
5220 PROCline(2,T$(2,M))
5230 PROCline(4,T$(3,M))
5240 RETURN
5300 REM FOUR INPUTS
5310 PROCline(0,T$(1,M))
5320 PROCline(1,T$(2,M))
5330 PROCline(3,T$(3,M))
5340 PROCline(4,T$(4,M))
5350 RETURN
6000 DEFPROCline(K,G$)
6010 PRINT TAB(0,K+C);G$;"( )";CHR$(151);CHR$(44);CHR$(44);CHR$(44);CHR$
(44);CHR$(44);CHR$(44);CHR$(44)
6020 ENDPROC
```

Program 3   LOGIC MAKER

```
  1 MODE 7
 10 REM BOOLEAN FUNCTIONS
 20 PRT=&FE60:REM USER PORT
 25 DDR=&FE62:REM DATA DIRECTION REGISTER
 30 ?DDR=240:REM BITS 0 TO 3 AS INPUTS, 4 TO 7 AS OUTPUTS
 40 DD=31994:DC=32114:DB=32234:DA=32354
 50 DZ=32012:DY=32132:DX=32252:DW=32372
 60 REM DECLARE OUTPUTS
 70 Z=0:Y=0:X=0:W=0
100CLS
110 PRINT TAB(10,0);"BOOLEAN FUNCTIONS"
120 PRINT TAB(0,3);"You may enter any desired function"
130 PRINT TAB(0,5);"by quitting this program and changing"
140 PRINT TAB(0,7);"lines 5010 to 5100 of this program."
150 PRINT TAB(0,9);"If you do not change the function,"
160 PRINT TAB(0,11);"then it is automatically chosen to be"
170 PRINT TAB(0,13);"A  AND  B, which appears at output Z."
180 PRINT TAB(0,21);"Press 'C' to observe the function."
```

```
200 PRINT TAB(0,23);"Press 'E' to quit the program.";
210 A$=GET$
220 IF A$<>"E" AND A$<>"C" THEN 210
230 IF A$="E" THEN 400
240 REM DISPLAY FUNCTIONS
250 CLS
260 PRINT TAB(8,3);"INPUTS          OUTPUTS"
270 PRINT TAB(8,6);"D( )            Z( )"
280 PRINT TAB(8,9);"C( )            Y( )"
290 PRINT TAB(8,12);"B( )             X( )"
300 PRINT TAB(8,15);"A( )             W( )"
320 PRINT TAB(0,23);"Press 'E' to quit the program.";
330 IF A$<>"E" THEN 500
400 IF A$="E" THEN CLS:PRINT TAB(0,8);"Type LIST 5000,5100  then press
RETURN"
410 PRINT TAB(0,10);"Enter any desired functions"
420 PRINT TAB(0,12);"as proper BASIC statements, "
430 PRINT TAB(0,14);"and then restart the program with RUN."
440 STOP
500 REM GET INPUTS FROM USER PORT
505 A=0:B=0:C=0:D=0
510 IF (?PRT AND 1) THEN A=1
520 IF (?PRT AND 2) THEN B=1
530 IF (?PRT AND 4) THEN C=1
540 IF (?PRT AND 8) THEN D=1
560 REM DISPLAY INPUTS
570 ?DD=D+48
580 ?DC=C+48
590 ?DB=B+48
600 ?DA=A+48
610 REM CALCULATE FUNCTION
620 GOSUB 5000
700 REM CHANGE OUTPUTS
710 IF (Z AND 1) THEN ?PRT=(?PRT OR 128):?DZ=49
720 IF (NOT Z AND 1) THEN ?PRT=(?PRT AND 127):?DZ=48
730 IF (Y AND 1) THEN ?PRT=(?PRT OR 64):?DY=49
740 IF (NOT Y AND 1) THEN ?PRT=(?PRT AND 191):?DY=48
750 IF (X AND 1) THEN ?PRT=(?PRT OR 32):?DX=49
760 IF (NOT X AND 1) THEN ?PRT=(?PRT AND 223):?DX=48
770 IF (W AND 1) THEN ?PRT=(?PRT OR 16):?DW=49
780 IF (NOT W AND 1) THEN ?PRT=(?PRT AND 239):?DW=48
790 A$=INKEY$(0)
800 GOTO 330
5000 REM BOOLEAN FUNCTIONS
5010  Z= A AND B
6000 RETURN
```

ZX 81 program listings

These programs require the graphics characters. These are indicated in the listings as the corresponding letter or number keys. When entering these letters or numbers remember that each is actually a graphics character and should be preceded by entering the graphics mode (SHIFT and 9). To distinguish these letters and numbers, when they refer to graphics characters, they are enclosed in square brackets []. These brackets should not be typed. For example:

[7] means an upper half-line graphics character

[Q] means a lower-right corner

[A] means a solid line

and

[66666666] means a row of bottom half-line graphics characters.

Program 1 LOGIC GATES

```
 10  REM LOGIC GATES
 20  REM DEFINE INPUTS AND OUTPUTS
 30  LET O = 22500
 40  LET I = 22500
100  CLS
120  PRINT AT 0,7;"LOGIC GATES"
130  PRINT
140  PRINT "WHICH FUNCTION ?"
150  PRINT
160  PRINT "CHOOSE BY PRESSING ONE"
170  PRINT
180  PRINT "OF THESE NUMBERS."
190  PRINT
200  PRINT "1. A AND B"
210  PRINT
220  PRINT "2. A OR B"
230  PRINT
234  PRINT "3. NOT A"
236  PRINT
240  PRINT "4. A EXCLUSIVE-OR B"
250  PRINT
260  PRINT "5. A EQUIVALENCE B"
270  PRINT
280  PRINT "6. NOT (A AND B)"
290  PRINT
300  PRINT "7. NOT (A OR B)"
320  LET L = (CODE INKEY$)−28
330  IF L<1 OR L>7 THEN GOTO 320
```

```
333   IF L = 3 THEN GOTO 600
340   REM DRAW LOGIC GATE
350   GOSUB 1000
360   REM COLLECT INPUT STATES
370   GOSUB 3000
380   REM COMPUTE OUTPUT
390   GOSUB (L*100 + 2000)
400   REM DISPLAY LOGIC STATES
402   POKE O,Z
405   PRINT AT P,17;Z
410   PRINT AT P,0;"[AAAAA]"
420   PRINT AT P,23;"[AAAAA]"
430   LET R = P
440   GOSUB 3000
450   IF R<>P THEN GOTO 500
460   IF INKEY$ = "" THEN GOTO 440
470   REM KEYPRESS
480   GOTO 100 500 REM CHANGE DISPLAY
510   PRINT AT R,17;" "
530   PRINT AT R,0;"      "
540   PRINT AT R,23;"      "
550   GOTO 380
600   REM NOT
610   CLS
615   PRINT "PRESS ANY KEY TO CHANGE THE GATE"
620   PRINT AT 2,6;"[6666666666]"
630   PRINT AT 3,6;"[5          8]"
640   PRINT AT 4,1;"A [AAA5]    NOT [8AAAAA] OUTPUT"
650   PRINT AT 5,6;"[5          8]"
660   PRINT AT 6,6;"[7777777777]"
800   PRINT AT 9,5;"[E777E77777777R]"
810   PRINT AT 10,5;"[5] A [5] OUTPUT [8]"
820   PRINT AT 11,5;"[W666W66666666Q]"
830   PRINT AT 12,5;"[5    5         8]"
840   PRINT AT 13,5;"[5] 0 [5        8]"
850   PRINT AT 14,5;"[5    5         8]"
860   PRINT AT 15,5;"[5] 1 [5        8]"
870   PRINT AT 16,5;"[5    5         8]"
880   PRINT AT 17,5;"[W666W66666666Q]"
890   GOSUB 4000
900   POKE O,Z
960   PRINT P,13;Z
961   PRINT AT P,0;"[AAAAA]"
962   PRINT AT P,19;"[AAAAA]"
```

```
963   LET R = P
964   GOSUB 4000
965   IF R<>P THEN GOTO 980
966   IF INKEY$ = "" THEN GOTO 964
970   GOTO 100
980   REM CHANGE DISPLAY
981   PRINT AT R,13;" "
982   PRINT AT R,0;" "
984   PRINT AT R,19;" "
990   GOTO 900
1000  REM DRAW LOGIC GATE
1010  CLS
1015  PRINT "PRESS ANY KEY TO CHANGE THE GATE"
1020  PRINT AT 1,10;"[6666666666]"
1040  PRINT AT 2,10;"[5          8]"
1050  PRINT AT 3,5;"B [7775        8]"
1060  PRINT AT 4,11;"[5        8AAAAA] OUTPUT"
1070  PRINT AT 5,5;"A [6665      8]"
1080  PRINT AT 6,10;"[5          8]"
1090  PRINT AT 7,10;"[7777777777]"
1100  IF L = 1 THEN LET L$ = " AND "
1110  IF L = 2 THEN LET L$ = " OR "
1120  IF L = 3 THEN LET L$ = " NOT "
1130  IF L = 4 THEN LET L$ = " EX-OR"
1140  IF L = 5 THEN LET L$ = " EQUIV"
1150  IF L = 6 THEN LET L$ = " NAND "
1160  IF L = 7 THEN LET L$ = " NOR "
1180  PRINT AT 4,12;L$
1200  PRINT AT 9,5;"[E777E777E77777777R]"
1210  PRINT AT 10,5;"[5] A [5] B [5] OUTPUT [8]"
1220  PRINT AT 11,5;"[W666W666W66666666Q]"
1230  PRINT AT 12,5;"[5    5    5          8]"
1240  PRINT AT 13,5;"[5] 0 [5] 0 [5        8]"
1250  PRINT AT 14,5;"[5    5    5    8]"
1260  PRINT AT 15,5;"[5] 0 [5] 1 [5        8]"
1270  PRINT AT 16,5;"[5    5    5    8]"
1280  PRINT AT 17,5;"[5] 1 [5] 0 [5        8]"
1290  PRINT AT 18,5;"[5    5    5    8]"
1300  PRINT AT 19,5;"[5] 1 [5] 1 [5        8]"
1310  PRINT AT 20,5;"[5    5    5    8]"
1320  PRINT AT 21,5;"[W666W666W66666666Q]"
1330  RETURN
2000  REM COMPUTE OUTPUT
2100  REM AND
```

```
2110   LET Z = A AND B
2150   RETURN
2200   REM OR
2210   LET Z = A OR B
2250   RETURN
2300   REM NOT
2310   LET Z = NOT A
2350   RETURN
2400   REM EXCLUSIVE-OR
2410   LET Z = (NOT A AND B) OR (NOT B AND A)
2450   RETURN
2500   REM EQUIVALENCE
2510   LET Z = (NOT A AND NOT B) OR (A AND B)
2550   RETURN
2600   REM NAND
2610   LET Z = NOT (A AND B)
2660   RETURN
2700   REM NOR
2710   LET vo = NOT (A OR B)
2760   RETURN
3000   REM COLLECT INPUTS
3010   LET Q = PEEK I–252
3020   LET B = INT (Q/2)
3030   LET A = Q–2*B
3040   LET P = 13 + 2*B + 4*A
3050   RETURN
4000   REM COMPUTE OUTPUT
4010   LET Q = PEEK I–252
4020   LET B = INT (Q/2)
4030   LET A = Q–2*B
4040   LET Z = NOT A
4050   LET P = 13 + 2*A
4060   RETURN
```

Program 2 LOGIC TUTOR

Comments have been added in lower case. There is insufficient room in the ZX 81 memory for these as rem statements, so they should not be entered.

```
10   DIM T$(4,4) function variables (input,output)
20   DIM A(4) output data from Interspec
30   DIM V(4) values of input data
35   DIM I(4) number of inputs for gate
40   DIM F(4) menu value of function
50   LET N = 0 input reference number
```

```
 60   LET M = 0 output reference number
 70   DIM R$(4)
 80   FOR M = 1 TO 4
 90   LET F(M) = 0
 99   NEXT M
100   CLS
105   PRINT AT 0,7;"BOOLEAN FUNCTIONS"
110   PRINT AT 2,0;"SELECT FUNCTION BY PRESSING"
120   PRINT AT 4,0;"ONE OF THESE NUMBERS."
121   FOR I = 1 TO 7
122   LET L = I*10 + 1090
123   GOSUB L
124   PRINT AT 4 + 2*I,5;I
125   PRINT AT 4 + 2*I,12;P$
126   NEXT I
130   PRINT AT 20,0;"THEN PRESS THE NEWLINE KEY."
140   INPUT S
150   IF S>7 OR S<1 THEN GOTO 140
151   CLS
152   PRINT AT 2,0;"YOUR SELECTION IS ";
153   LET L = 10*S + 1090
154   GOSUB L
155   PRINT P$
160   PRINT AT 5,0;"WHICH OUTPUT FOR THIS FUNCTION ?"
170   PRINT AT 7,0;"ENTER ONE OF W, X, Y OR Z"
180   PRINT AT 9,0;"AND THEN PRESS THE NEWLINE KEY."
190   INPUT O$
200   IF O$<>"W" AND O$<>"X" AND O$<>"Y" AND O$<>"Z"
      THEN GO TO 190
210   IF O$ = "W" THEN LET M = 4
220   IF O$ = "X" THEN LET M = 3
230   IF O$ = "Y" THEN LET M = 2
240   IF O$ = "Z" THEN LET M = 1
244   LET R$(M) = O$
245   LET F(M) = S
246   IF S = 4 OR S = 5 THEN GO TO 280
250   IF S<>3 THEN GO TO 290
260   CLS
265   PRINT AT 2,0;"THE NOT FUNCTION HAS ONE INPUT."
270   LET I(M) = 1
275   LET Q$ = "WHICH INPUT ?"
276   GOTO 350
280   CLS
285   PRINT AT 2,0;"THIS FUNCTION HAS TWO INPUTS."
```

```
286   LET I(M) = 2
287   GO TO 340
290   CLS
297   PRINT AT 2,0;"HOW MANY INPUTS ?"
300   PRINT AT 4,0;"ENTER 1, 2, 3 or 4"
305   PRINT AT 6,0;"AND THEN PRESS THE NEWLINE KEY."
310   INPUT E
320   IF E>4 OR E<1 THEN GOTO 310
330   LET I(M) = E
340   LET Q$ = "WHICH INPUTS ?"
350   PRINT AT 12,0;Q$
360   PRINT AT 14,0;"ENTER A, B, C OR D FOR EACH."
370   PRINT
400   FOR N = 1 TO 4
404   LET T$(N,M) = " "
408   NEXT N
410   FOR N = 1 TO I(M)
420   INPUT I$
430   IF I$<>"A" AND I$<>"B" AND I$<>"C" AND I$<>"D"
      THEN GO TO 420
440   LET T$(N,M) = I$
450   PRINT T$(N,M);" ";
460   NEXT N
490   CLS display functions and terminals
500   FOR M = 1 TO 4
510   IF F(M) = 0 THEN GO TO 610
520   LET R = (M−1)*5
530   LET L = F(M)*10 + 1090
540   GO SUB L
550   PRINT AT R,0;"OUTPUT ";R$(M);" IS THE ";P$
560   PRINT AT R + 2,0;"COMBINATION OF ";
570   FOR N = 1 TO I(M)
580   PRINT T$(N,M);", ";
590   NEXT N
610   NEXT M
620   PRINT AT 21,0;"PRESS F FOR MORE OR E TO END."
630   LET A$ = INKEY$
640   IF A$ = "F" THEN GO TO 100
650   IF A$ = "E" THEN STOP
660   REM get input data
670   FOR N = 1 TO 4
674   LET A(N) = 0
676   NEXT N
681   LET Q = PEEK 22500−240
```

```
682   LET A(4) = INT (Q/8)
683   LET Q = Q–8*A(4)
684   LET A(3) = INT (Q/4)
685   LET Q = Q–4*A(3)
686   LET A(2) = INT (Q/2)
687   LET Q = Q–2*A(2)
688   LET A(1) = Q
700   REM change input values on screen
740   FOR R = 1 TO 21
745   LET W = R–1
800   REM calculate output data
805   LET T = 0
810   FOR M = 1 TO 4
820   IF F(M) = 0 THEN GO TO 960
850   FOR N = 1 TO I(M)
860   IF T$(N,M) = "A" THEN LET V(N) = A(1)
870   IF T$(N,M) = "B" THEN LET V(N) = A(2)
880   IF T$(N,M) = "C" THEN LET V(N) = A(3)
890   IF T$(N,M) = "D" THEN LET V(N) = A(4)
900   NEXT N
910   LET L = F(M)*100 + 2000
915   GOSUB L
920   REM send output to logic board
950   LET T = T + VO*2**(4–m)
960   NEXT M 970 POKE 22500,T
990   GO TO 630
1100  LET P$ = "AND"
1105  RETURN
1110  LET P$ = "OR"
1115  RETURN
1120  LET P$ = "NOT"
1125  RETURN
1130  LET P$ = "EXCLUSIVE-OR"
1135  RETURN
1140  LET P$ = "EQUIVALENCE"
1145  RETURN
1150  LET P$ = "NAND"
1155  RETURN
1160  LET P$ = "NOR"
1165  RETURN
2000  REM compute output values
2100  REM AND
2110  LET VO = 1
2120  FOR N = 1 TO I(M)
```

```
2130   LET VO = VO AND V(N)
2140   NEXT N
2150   RETURN
2200   REM OR
2210   LET VO = 0
2220   FOR N = 1 TO I(M)
2230   LET VO = VO OR V(N)
2240   NEXT N
2250   RETURN
2300   REM NOT
2310   LET VO = NOT V(1)
2350   RETURN
2400   REM EXCLUSIVE-OR
2410   LET VO = 1
2420   IF V(1) = V(2) THEN LET VO = 0
2450   RETURN
2500   REM EQUIVALENCE
2510   LET VO = 0
2520   IF V(1) = V(2) THEN LET VO = 1
2550   RETURN
2600   REM NAND
2610   LET VO = 1
2620   FOR N = 1 TO I(M)
2630   LET VO = VO AND V(N)
2640   NEXT N
2650   LET VO = NOT VO
2660   RETURN
2700   REM NOR
2710   LET VO = 0
2720   FOR N = 1 TO I(M)
2730   LET VO = VO OR V(N)
2740   NEXT N
2750   LET VO = NOT VO
2760   RETURN
```

Program 3 LOGIC MAKER

```
 10   LET I = 22500
 20   LET O = 22500
100   CLS
105   PRINT AT 0,7;"LOGIC MAKER"
160   PRINT AT 5,0;"THIS PROGRAM LETS YOU SET UP"
170   PRINT AT 7,0;"THE OUTPUTS TO BE ANY LOGICAL"
180   PRINT AT 9,0;"COMBINATION OF THE INPUTS."
```

```
190   PRINT AT 12,0;"INITIALLY THE FOLLOWING"
200   PRINT AT 14,0;"COMBINATIONS HAVE BEEN CHOSEN."
210   PRINT AT 16,0;"OUTPUT Z IS A OR B"
220   PRINT AT 18,0;"OUTPUT W IS A AND B"
230   PRINT AT 21,0;"PRESS C TO CONTINUE."
240   IF INKEY$<>"C" THEN GOTO 240
250   CLS
260   PRINT AT 0,8;"THE LOGIC BOARD"
270   PRINT AT 5,7;"[E77777777777777R]"
280   PRINT AT 6,7;"[5              8]"
290   PRINT AT 7,7;"[5]D( )     Z( ) [8]"
300   PRINT AT 8,7;"[5              8]"
310   PRINT AT 9,7;"[5              8]"
320   PRINT AT 10,7;"[5]C( )     Y( ) [8]"
330   PRINT AT 11,7;"[5             8]"
340   PRINT AT 12,7;"[5             8]"
350   PRINT AT 13,7;"[5]B( )     X( ) [8]"
360   PRINT AT 14,7;"[5             8]"
370   PRINT AT 15,7;"[5             8]"
380   PRINT AT 16,7;"[5]A( )     W( ) [8]"
390   PRINT AT 8,7;"[W666666666666666Q]"
400   PRINT AT 20,0;"PRESS KEY B TO CHANGE LOGIC."
500   IF INKEY$ = "B" THEN GOTO 4000
600   REM GET INPUT DATA
610   LET Q = PEEK I-240
620   LET D = INT (Q/8)
630   LET Q = Q-8*D
640   LET C = INT (Q/4)
650   LET Q = Q-4*C
660   LET B = INT (Q/2)
670   LET Q = Q-2*B
680   LET A = Q
700   REM CHANGE INPUT VALUES ON SCREEN
720   PRINT AT 7,10;D
740   PRINT AT 10,10;C
760   PRINT AT 13,10;B
780   PRINT AT 16,10;A
790   GO SUB 5000
800   REM CALCULATE OUTPUT DATA
810   LET S = 8*Z + 4*Y + 2*X + W
820   POKE O,S
830   PRINT AT 7,19;Z
840   PRINT AT 10,19;Y
850   PRINT AT 13,19;X
```

```
860   PRINT AT 16,19;W
870   GO TO 500
4000  REM CHANGE LOGIC FUNCTIONS
4010  CLS
4020  PRINT AT 2,0;"TYPE <RUN> TO RE-RUN THE PROGRAM"
4030  PRINT
4040  PRINT
4050  LIST 5000
4060  STOP
5000  REM LOGIC FUNCTIONS
5010  LET Z = A OR B
5020  LET Y = 0
5030  LET X = 0
5040  LET W = A AND B
5100  RETURN
```

ZX Spectrum program listings

These programs require user-defined line characters, which appear in the listings as letters of the alphabet. When entering these characters remember that each is actually a graphics character and should be preceded by entering the graphics mode (CAPS-SHIFT and 9). When the program is run, each letter is then replaced by its corresponding graphics character as defined by lines 3000 to 3330. To distinguish these graphics characters, they are enclosed in square brackets []. These brackets should not be typed. For example:

[T] is a top-right corner

and

[OOOOOOO] is a continuous line.

Program 1 LOGIC GATES

```
4    PRINT AT 10,10;"Please wait."
5    GO SUB 3000: REM define graphics characters
20   LET a = 0:LET b = 0: REM input data from Interspec
30   LET olda = 5: LET oldb = 5: REM previous input data
40   LET s = 0: REM menu value of function
50   LET p = 11: REM pointer to truth table
60   LET inputs = 95
70   LET outputs = 95
100  CLS
105  PRINT AT 0,7;"LOGIC GATES"
110  PRINT AT 2,0;"Select desired function by "
120  PRINT AT 4,0;"entering one of these numbers."
```

```
121    PRINT AT 6,5;"1        AND"
122    PRINT AT 8,5;"2        OR"
123    PRINT AT 10,5;"3       NOT"
124    PRINT AT 12,5;"4       EXCLUSIVE-OR"
125    PRINT AT 14,5;"5       EQUIVALENCE"
126    PRINT AT 16,5;"6       NAND"
127    PRINT AT 18,5;"7       NOR"
130    PRINT AT 20,0;"Then press the ENTER key."
140    INPUT s$
144    LET s$ = s$(1 TO 1)
145    IF CODE s$>55 OR CODE s$<49 THEN GO TO 140
150    LET s = INT (VAL s$)
200    LET olda = 5: REM reset old values
400    REM display functions and terminals
500    CLS
510    GO SUB 1000: REM display box
520    LET I = s*10 + 1090
530    GO SUB I
540    PRINT AT 4,12;p$
550    PRINT AT 4,23;"( )output"
560    PRINT AT 0,11;"LOGIC GATES"
570    GO SUB 1200: REM draw truth table
590    REM display inputs
600    IF s = 3 THEN GO SUB 5000
610    IF s<>3 THEN GO SUB 5100
620    PRINT AT 21,0;"Press C to change or E to end."
630    LET a$ = INKEY$
640    IF a$ = "c" THEN GO TO 100
650    IF a$ = "e" THEN STOP
660    REM get input data
670    LET a = 0: LET b = 0
681    LET q = (IN inputs)−240
682    IF q>7 THEN LET q = q−8
683    IF q>3 THEN LET q = q−4
684    IF q>1 THEN LET b = 1: LET q = q−2
685    IF q>0 THEN LET a = 1
690    IF olda = a AND oldb = b THEN GO TO 630
700    LET olda = a
710    LET oldb = b
730    REM change input values on screen
740    IF s = 3 THEN PRINT AT 4,4;a: GO TO 800
780    PRINT AT 3,4;b
790    PRINT AT 5,4;a
800    REM display line of truth table
```

```
810   PRINT AT p,2;"        "
820   PRINT AT p,25;"       "
825   PRINT AT p,19;" "
830   LET p = 12 + 2*b + 4*a
840   PRINT AT p,2;"[AAAAA]"
850   PRINT AT p,25;"[AAAAA]"
890   REM calculate output data
900   LET l = s*100 + 2000: GO SUB l
920   REM send output to logic board
940   PRINT AT 4,24;vo
950   PRINT AT p,19;vo
970   OUT outputs,vo
990   GO TO 630
1000  REM display box
1010  PRINT AT 2,11;"[TNNNNNNNNNNNP]"
1020  PRINT AT 3,11;"[P              P]"
1030  PRINT AT 4,11;"[P              LAAAAA]    "
1040  PRINT AT 5,11;"[P              P]"
1050  PRINT AT 6,11;"[UOOOOOOOOOOOP]"
1060  RETURN
1100  LET p$ = " AND ": RETURN
1110  LET p$ = " OR ": RETURN
1120  LET p$ = " NOT ": RETURN
1130  LET p$ = "EX-OR ": RETURN
1140  LET p$ = "EQUIV.": RETURN
1150  LET p$ = " NAND ": RETURN
1160  LET p$ = " NOR ": RETURN
1200  REM draw truth table
1210  PRINT AT 8,8;"[TNNNTNNNTNNNNNNNP]"
1220  PRINT AT 9,8;"[P] A [P] B [P] output [P]"
1230  PRINT AT 10,8;"[UOOOUOOOUOOOOOOOP]"
1240  PRINT AT 11,8;"[P     P     P     P]"
1250  PRINT AT 12,8;"[P] 0 [P] 0 [P]        [P]"
1260  PRINT AT 13,8;"[P     P     P     P]"
1270  PRINT AT 14,8;"[P] 0 [P] 1 [P]      [P]"
1280  PRINT AT 15,8;"[P     P     P     P]"
1290  PRINT AT 16,8;"[P] 1 [P] 0 [P]      [P]"
1300  PRINT AT 17,8;"[P     P     P     P]"
1310  PRINT AT 18,8;"[P] 1 [P] 1 [P]      [P]"
1320  PRINT AT 10,8;"[UOOOUOOOUOOOOOOOP]"
1350  RETURN
2000  REM determine outputs for each function
2100  REM AND function
2110  LET vo = a AND b
```

```
2150   RETURN
2200   REM OR function
2210   LET vo = a OR b
2250   RETURN
2300   REM NOT function
2310   LET vo = NOT a
2350   RETURN
2400   REM EXCLUSIVE-OR function
2410   LET vo = 1
2420   IF a = b THEN LET vo = 0
2450   RETURN
2500   REM EQUIVALENCE function
2510   LET vo = 0
2520   IF a = b THEN LET vo = 1
2550   RETURN
2600   REM NAND function
2610   LET vo = NOT (a AND b)
2660   RETURN
2700   REM NOR function
2710   LET vo = NOT (a OR b)
2760   RETURN
3000   REM line graphics
3010   FOR i = 0 TO 20
3020   FOR j = 0 TO 7
3030   READ row
3040   PRINT USR CHR$ (i + 144) + j,row
3050   NEXT j
3060   NEXT i
3080   RETURN
3100   DATA 0,0,0,255,255,0;0,0
3110   DATA 16,16,16,255,255,16;16,16
3120   DATA 16,16,16,16,16,16;16,16
3130   DATA 16,16,16,31,31,0;0,0
3140   DATA 16,16,16,240,240,0;0,0
3150   DATA 0,0,0,31,31,16;16,16
3160   DATA 0,0,0,240,240,16;16,16
3170   DATA 16,16,16,255,255,0;0,0
3180   DATA 0,0,0,255,255,16;16,16
3190   DATA 16,16,16,31,31,16;16,16
3200   DATA 16,16,16,240,240,16;16,16
3210   DATA 128,128,128,255,255,128,128,128
3220   DATA 1,1,1,255,255,1,1,1
3240   DATA 255,0,0,0,0,0,0,0
3250   DATA 0,0,0,0,0,0,0,255
```

```
3260    DATA 128,128,128,128,128,128,128,128
3270    DATA 1,1,1,1,1,1,1,1
3280    DATA 255,1,1,1,1,1,1,1
3290    DATA 1,1,1,1,1,1,1,255
3300    DATA 255,128,128,128,128,128,128,128
3310    DATA 128,128,128,128,128,128,128,255
5000    REM append inputs
5010    REM one input
5020    PRINT AT 4,1;"A ( )[AAAAA]"
5030    RETURN
5100    REM two inputs
5110    PRINT AT 3,1;"B ( )[AAAAA]"
5120    PRINT AT 5,1;"A ( )[AAAAA]"
5130    RETURN
```

Program 2 LOGIC TUTOR

```
5      GOSUB 3000: REM define graphics
10     DIM t$(4,4): REM function variables (input,output)
20     DIM a(4): REM output data from Interspec
30     DIM u(4): REM values of input data
35     DIM i(4): REM number of inputs for gate
40     DIM f(4): REM menu value of function
50     LET n = 0:LET m = 0: REM input and output reference numbers
60     LET inputs = 95
70     LET outputs = 95
90     FOR m = 1 TO 4: LET f(m) = 0: NEXT m
100    CLS
105    PRINT AT 0,7;"BOOLEAN FUNCTIONS"
110    PRINT AT 2,0;"Select desired function by "
120    PRINT AT 4,0;"entering one of these numbers."
121    PRINT AT 6,5;"1          AND"
122    PRINT AT 8,5;"2          OR"
123    PRINT AT 10,5;"3          NOT"
124    PRINT AT 12,5;"4          EXCLUSIVE-OR"
125    PRINT AT 14,5;"5          EQUIVALENCE"
126    PRINT AT 16,5;"6          NAND"
127    PRINT AT 18,5;"7          NOR"
130    PRINT AT 20,0;"Then press the ENTER key."
140    INPUT s$
144    LET s$ = s$(1 TO 1)
145    IF CODE s$>55 OR CODE s$<49 THEN GO TO 140
150    LET s = INT (VAL s$)
151    CLS: PRINT AT 2,1;"Your selection is ";
```

```
152  IF s = 1 THEN PRINT "AND"
153  IF s = 2 THEN PRINT "OR"
154  IF s = 3 THEN PRINT "NOT"
155  IF s = 4 THEN PRINT "EXCLUSIVE-OR"
156  IF s = 5 THEN PRINT "EQUIVALENCE"
157  IF s = 6 THEN PRINT "NAND"
158  IF s = 7 THEN PRINT "NOR"
160  PRINT AT 5,0;"Which output for this function ?"
170  PRINT AT 7,0;"Enter one of W, X, Y or Z"
180  PRINT AT 9,0;"and then press the ENTER key."
190  INPUT o$
200  IF o$<>"w" AND o$<>"x" AND o$<>"y" AND o$<>"z"
     THEN GO TO 190
210  IF o$ = "w" THEN LET m = 4
220  IF o$ = "x" THEN LET m = 3
230  IF o$ = "y" THEN LET m = 2
240  IF o$ = "z" THEN LET m = 1
245  LET f(m) = s
246  IF s = 4 OR s = 5 THEN GO TO 280
250  IF s<>3 THEN GO TO 290
260  CLS: PRINT AT 2,0;"The NOT function has one input."
270  LET i(m) = 1: GO TO 340
280  CLS: PRINT AT 2,0;"This function has two inputs."
285  LET i(m) = 2: GO TO 350
290  CLS: PRINT AT 2,0;"How many inputs ?"
300  PRINT AT 4,0;"Enter 1, 2, 3 or 4"
305  PRINT AT 6,0;"and then press the ENTER key."
310  INPUT i$
320  IF CODE i$>52 OR CODE i$<49 THEN GO TO 310
330  LET i(m) = INT VAL i$
340  IF i(m) = 1 THEN PRINT AT 8,0;"Which input ?": GO TO 360
350  PRINT AT 8,0;"Which inputs ?"
360  PRINT AT 10,0;"Enter A, B, C or D for each."
370  PRINT AT 12,0;"You may use one of these inputs"
380  PRINT AT 14,0;"more than once, if you have"
390  PRINT AT 16,0;"asked for enough inputs."
400  FOR n = 1 TO 4: LET t$(n,m) = "": NEXT n
410  FOR n = 1 TO i(m)
420  INPUT i$
430  IF i$<>"a" AND i$<>"b" AND i$<>"c" AND i$<>"d"
     THEN GO TO 420
440  LET t$(n,m) = CHR$ (CODE (i$) − 32)
450  PRINT t$(n,m);"   ";
460  NEXT n
```

```
470   REM display functions and terminals
490   CLS 500 FOR m = 1 TO 4
504   IF f(m) = 0 THEN GO TO 610
505   LET row = (m−1)*5
510   GO SUB 1000: REM display box
520   LET I = f(m)*10 + 1090
530   GO SUB I
540   PRINT AT row + 2,12;p$
550   PRINT AT row + 2,24;"( )";CHR$ (91−m)
590   REM display inputs
600   GO SUB i(m)*100 + 4900
610   NEXT m
620   PRINT AT 21,0;"Press F for more or E to end."
630   LET a$ = INKEY$
640   IF a$ = "f" THEN GO TO 100
650   IF a$ = "e" THEN STOP
660   REM get input data
670   FOR n = 1 TO 4: LET a(n) = 0: NEXT n
681   LET q = (IN inputs)−240
682   IF q>7 THEN LET a(4) = 1: LET q = q−8
683   IF q>3 THEN LET a(3) = 1: LET q = q−4
684   IF q>1 THEN LET a(2) = 1: LET q = q−2
685   IF q>0 THEN LET a(1) = 1
700   REM
730   REM change input values on screen
740   FOR r = 1 TO 21
745   LET row = r−1
760   LET j$ = SCREEN$ (row,1)
770   IF j$ = " " THEN GO TO 790
775   LET j = (CODE j$)−64
780   PRINT AT row,4;CHR$ (a(j) + 48)
790   NEXT r
800   REM calculate output data
805   LET sum = 0
810   FOR m = 1 TO 4
820   IF f(m) = 0 THEN GO TO 960
850   FOR n = 1 TO i(m)
860   IF t$(n,m) = "A" THEN LET u(n) = a(1)
870   IF t$(n,m) = "B" THEN LET u(n) = a(2)
880   IF t$(n,m) = "C" THEN LET u(n) = a(3)
890   IF t$(n,m) = "D" THEN LET u(n) = a(4)
900   NEXT n
910   LET I = f(m)*100 + 2000: GO SUB I
920   REM send output to logic board
```

```
930    LET row = m*5-3
940    PRINT AT row,25;vo
950    LET sum = sum + vo*2**(4-m)
       <NOTE ** represents exponentiation>
960    NEXT m
970    OUT outputs,sum
990    GO TO 630
1000   REM display box
1010   PRINT AT row,11;"[TNNNNNNNNNNP]"
1020   PRINT AT row + 1,11;"[P              P]"
1030   PRINT AT row + 2,11;"[P              P]"
1040   PRINT AT row + 3,11;"[P              P]"
1050   PRINT AT row + 4,11;"[UOOOOOOOOOOP]"
1060   RETURN
1100   LET p$ = " AND ": RETURN
1110   LET p$ = " OR ": RETURN
1120   LET p$ = " NOT ": RETURN
1130   LET p$ = "EX-OR ": RETURN
1140   LET p$ = "EQUIV.": RETURN
1150   LET p$ = " NAND ": RETURN
1160   LET p$ = " NOR ": RETURN
2000   REM determine outputs for each function
2100   REM AND function
2110   LET vo = 1
2120   FOR n = 1 TO i(m)
2130   LET vo = vo AND u(n)
2140   NEXT n
2150   RETURN
2200   REM OR function
2210   LET vo = 0
2220   FOR n = 1 TO i(m)
2230   LET vo = vo OR u(n)
2240   NEXT n
2250   RETURN
2300   REM NOT function
2310   LET vo = NOT u(1)
2350   RETURN
2400   REM EXCLUSIVE-OR function
2410   LET vo = 1
2420   IF u(1) = u(2) THEN LET vo = 0
2450   RETURN
2500   REM EQUIVALENCE function 2510 LET vo = 0
2520   IF u(1) = u(2) THEN LET vo = 1
2550   RETURN
```

```
2600   REM NAND function
2610   LET vo = 1
2620   FOR n = 1 TO i(m)
2630   LET vo = vo AND u(n)
2640   NEXT n
2650   LET vo = NOT vo
2660   RETURN
2700   REM NOR function 2710 LET vo = 0
2720   FOR n = 1 TO i(m)
2730   LET vo = vo OR u(n)
2740   NEXT n 2750 LET vo = NOT vo
2760   RETURN
3000   REM line graphics
3010   FOR i = 0 TO 20
3020   FOR j = 0 TO 7
3030   READ row
3040   PRINT USR CHR$ (i + 144) + j,row
3050   NEXT j
3060   NEXT i
3080   RETURN
3100   DATA 0,0,0,255,255,0;0,0
3110   DATA 16,16,16,255,255,16;16,16
3120   DATA 16,16,16,16,16,16;16,16
3130   DATA 16,16,16,31,31,0;0,0
3140   DATA 16,16,16,240,240,0;0,0
3150   DATA 0,0,0,31,31,16;16,16
3160   DATA 0,0,0,240,240,16;16,16
3170   DATA 16,16,16,255,255,0;0,0
3180   DATA 0,0,0,255,255,16;16,16
3190   DATA 16,16,16,31,31,16;16,16
3200   DATA 16,16,16,240,240,16;16,16
3210   DATA 128,128,128,255,255,128,128,128
3220   DATA 1,1,1,255,255,1,1,1
3240   DATA 255,0,0,0,0,0,0,0
3250   DATA 0,0,0,0,0,0,0,255
3260   DATA 128,128,128,128,128,128,128,128
3270   DATA 1,1,1,1,1,1,1,1
3280   DATA 255,1,1,1,1,1,1,1
3290   DATA 1,1,1,1,1,1,1,255
3300   DATA 255,128,128,128,128,128,128,128
3310   DATA 128,128,128,128,128,128,128,255
5000   REM append inputs
5010   REM one input
5020   PRINT AT row + 2,1;t$(1,m);"( )[AAAAA]"
```

```
5030   RETURN
5100   REM two inputs
5110   PRINT AT row + 1,1;t$(1,m);"( )[AAAAA]"
5120   PRINT AT row + 3,1;t$(2,m);"( )[AAAAA]"
5130   RETURN
5200   REM three inputs
5210   PRINT AT row + 1,1;t$(1,m);"( )[AAAAA]"
5220   PRINT AT row + 2,1;t$(2,m);"( )[AAAAA]"
5230   PRINT AT row + 4,1;t$(3,m);"( )[AAAAA]"
5240   RETURN
5300   REM four inputs
5310   PRINT AT row + 1,1;t$(1,m);"( )[AAAAA]"
5320   PRINT AT row + 2,1;t$(2,m);"( )[AAAAA]"
5330   PRINT AT row + 3,1;t$(3,m);"( )[AAAAA]"
5340   PRINT AT row + 4,1;t$(4,m);"( )[AAAAA]"
5350   RETURN
```

Program 3   LOGIC MAKER

```
 10   GO SUB 3000: REM define graphics characters
 60   LET inputs = 95
 70   LET outputs = 95
100   CLS
105   PRINT AT 0,7;"LOGIC MAKER"
160   PRINT AT 5,0;"This program lets you set up"
170   PRINT AT 7,0;"the outputs to be any logical"
180   PRINT AT 9,0;"combination of the inputs."
190   PRINT AT 12,0;"To begin with the following"
200   PRINT AT 14,0;"combinations have been chosen."
210   PRINT AT 16,0;"Output Z is A OR B"
220   PRINT AT 18,0;"Output W is A AND B."
230   PRINT AT 21,0;"Press the SPACE key to continue." s ";
240   IF INKEY$<>" " THEN GO TO 240
250   CLS
260   PRINT AT 0,8;"LOGIC GATES"
270   PRINT AT 5,7;"[TNNNNNNNNNNNNNNNNNNP]"
280   PRINT AT 6,7;"[T                   P]"
290   PRINT AT 7,7;"[T] D( )       ( )Z [P]"
300   PRINT AT 8,7;"[T                   P]"
310   PRINT AT 9,7;"[T                   P]"
320   PRINT AT 10,7;"[T] C( )       ( )Y [P]"
330   PRINT AT 11,7;"[T                  P]"
340   PRINT AT 12,7;"[T                  P]"
350   PRINT AT 13,7;"[T] B( )       ( )X [P]"
```

```
360    PRINT AT 14,7;"[T                      P]"
370    PRINT AT 15,7;"[T                      P]"
380    PRINT AT 16,7;"[T] A( )          ( )W [P]"
390    PRINT AT 17,7;"[UOOOOOOOOOOOOOOOOOOOOP]"
400    PRINT AT 20,0;"Press key B to change logic."
500    IF INKEY$ = "b" THEN GO TO 4000
660    REM get input data
670    LET A = 0: LET B = 0: LET C = 0: LET D = 0
681    LET q = (IN inputs)−240
682    IF q>7 THEN LET D = 1: LET q = q−8
683    IF q>3 THEN LET C = 1: LET q = q−4
684    IF q>1 THEN LET B = 1: LET q = q−2
685    IF q>0 THEN LET A = 1
700    REM
730    REM change input values on screen
740    PRINT AT 7,10;D
750    PRINT AT 10,10;C
760    PRINT AT 13,10;B
770    PRINT AT 16,10;A
780    GO SUB 5000
800    REM calculate output data
810    LET sum = 8*z + 4*Y + 2*X + W
820    OUT outputs,sum
830    PRINT AT 7,19;Z
840    PRINT AT 10,19;Y
850    PRINT AT 13,19;X
860    PRINT AT 16,19;W
870    GO TO 500
3000   REM line graphics
3010   FOR i = 0 TO 20
3020   FOR j = 0 TO 7
3030   READ row
3040   PRINT USR CHR$ (i + 144) + j,row
3050   NEXT j
3060   NEXT i
3080   RETURN
3100   DATA 0,0,0,255,255,0;0,0
3110   DATA 16,16,16,255,255,16;16,16
3120   DATA 16,16,16,16,16,16;16,16
3130   DATA 16,16,16,31,31,0;0,0
3140   DATA 16,16,16,240,240,0;0,0
3150   DATA 0,0,0,31,31,16;16,16
3160   DATA 0,0,0,240,240,16;16,16
3170   DATA 16,16,16,255,255,0;0,0
```

257

```
3180   DATA 0,0,0,255,255,16;16,16
3190   DATA 16,16,16,31,31,16;16,16
3200   DATA 16,16,16,240,240,16;16,16
3210   DATA 128,128,128,255,255,128,128,128
3220   DATA 1,1,1,255,255,1,1,1
3240   DATA 255,0,0,0,0,0,0,0
3250   DATA 0,0,0,0,0,0,0,255
3260   DATA 128,128,128,128,128,128,128,128
3270   DATA 1,1,1,1,1,1,1,1
3280   DATA 255,1,1,1,1,1,1,1
3290   DATA 1,1,1,1,1,1,1,255
3300   DATA 255,128,128,128,128,128,128,128
3310   DATA 128,128,128,128,128,128,128,255
4000   REM change logic functions
4001   CLS
4005   PRINT AT 0,0;"Change the functions as you wish"
4006   PRINT AT 2,0;"Type RUN to restart the program."
4007   PRINT : PRINT
4020   LIST 5000
4030   STOP
5000   REM LOGIC FUNCTIONS
5010   LET Z = A OR B
5020   LET Y = 0
5030   LET X = 0
5040   LET W = A AND B
5100   RETURN
```

Index